A *Talent for Friendship*

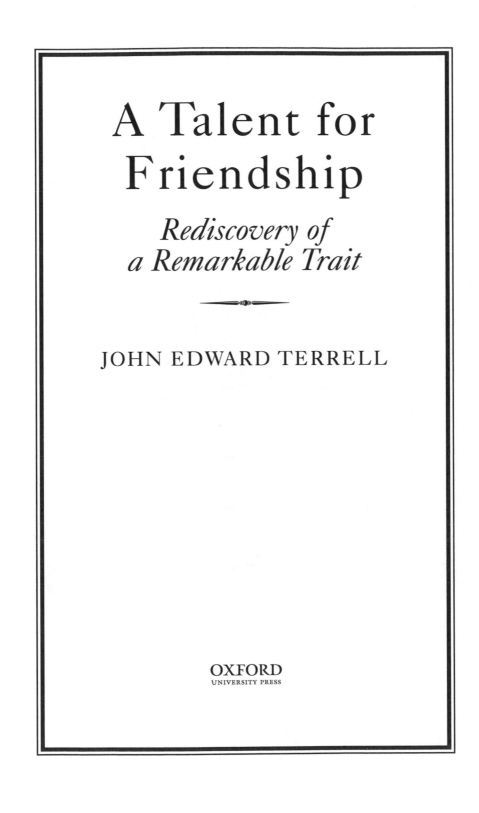

A Talent for Friendship

Rediscovery of
a Remarkable Trait

JOHN EDWARD TERRELL

OXFORD
UNIVERSITY PRESS

OXFORD
UNIVERSITY PRESS

Oxford University Press is a department of the University of Oxford.
It furthers the University's objective of excellence in research,
scholarship, and education by publishing worldwide.

Oxford   New York
Auckland   Cape Town   Dar es Salaam   Hong Kong   Karachi
Kuala Lumpur   Madrid   Melbourne   Mexico City   Nairobi
New Delhi   Shanghai   Taipei   Toronto

With offices in
Argentina   Austria   Brazil   Chile   Czech Republic   France   Greece
Guatemala   Hungary   Italy   Japan   Poland   Portugal   Singapore
South Korea   Switzerland   Thailand   Turkey   Ukraine   Vietnam

Oxford is a registered trademark of Oxford University Press
in the UK and certain other countries.

Published in the United States of America by
Oxford University Press
198 Madison Avenue, New York, NY 10016

Library of Congress Cataloging-in-Publication Data
Terrell, John.
A talent for friendship : rediscovery of a remarkable trait / John Edward Terrell.
pages cm
Includes bibliographical references and index.
ISBN 978–0–19–938645–1 (hardback)
1. Friendship.   I. Title.
BF575.F66T47 2014
302.34—dc23
2014019311

1 3 5 7 9 8 6 4 2
Printed in the United States of America
on acid-free paper

For Nancy, Tom, Jane, John, Jim, Esther, Gabriel, and Roger—Without you, this would not be a book.

Thank you.

Contents

PART THREE: *Selfish Desires*

PART FOUR: *The Social Baseline*

PART FIVE: *Social Being*

PART SIX: *Principles to Live By*

List of Illustrations

Acknowledgments

I THANK THE following students, colleagues, family, and friends for what they have done to help me get this book on the road.

University of Illinois at Chicago: Carolina Bernal, Andra Berzins, Nicole Cyrier, Sandy De Leon, Sara Esparza, Valerie Fegan, John Hicks, Charise Javonillo, Colin LeJeune, Anna Lindquist, Sarah Manandhar, John Monaghan, Jared Oksanen, Jamey O'Neil, Matt Piscitelli, Dani Riebe

Northwestern University: Grace Bialosky, Elyssa Cherney, Liz Coda, Vince FitzPatrick, Mike Gajewsky, Ian Holden, Rita Huen, Teisha Lightbourne, Megan McGee, Anna Rhoad, Melissa Rothman, Lauren Schwartzberg, Linda Song

Places near and far: Melissa Amarello, Tom Anton, Ian Barber, Lane Beckes, Jim Coan, Mark Golitko, Sandy Harcourt, Esmond Harmsworth, Christie Henry, Scott Hunter, Ken Kaye, Janet Dixon Keller, Kevin Kelly, Regina Woodrom Rudrud, Bob Martin, Mac Marshall, John Mitani, Kate Movius, Bruce Patterson, Jim Roscoe, Birgitta Rota, Allen Schechter, Penelope Schoeffel Meleisea, Madeleine Schwartz, Jill Seagard, and John Stowe.

And especially: Nancy Bailey, Tom Clark, Jane Connolly, John Hart, Jim Koeppl, Esther Schechter, Gabriel Terrell, and Roger Zanchetti.

PART ONE

What Makes Us Human?

I
———————

Being Human

WHAT DOES IT mean to be human? This is not only an old and challenging question, but also one that can be dangerous to ask. History shows us that people do not always like the answers others give them, and some may deal with what they find objectionable in ways that are more violent than just using harsh words or hostile stares. Why this should be so is in every way as interesting a question as asking what it means to be human.

Biblical accounts tell us that we are special creatures, although far from angelic. According to the Book of Genesis, our kind of being not only was created in God's own image at the beginning of time, but was also set apart from other earthly life forms to "have dominion over the fish of the sea, and over the fowl of the air, and over the cattle, and over all the earth, and over every creeping thing that creepeth upon the earth" (Genesis 1:26). Most modern biologists, however, are spoilsport enough to point out that every kind of creature—every identifiable biological species—is by definition in its own particular ways both special and observably unique. What is so special, therefore, about our own species, *Homo sapiens*? Does anyone really know?

Biologists today are also insistent that we must bite the bullet and accept the basic scientific fact that as a species we are—like all species—a product of natural circumstances and events, not supernatural ones. Whatever unique talents or special qualities we possess are not simply God-given. Our defining ways—call them our defining *abilities* or *capacities*—to do some things remarkably well (arguing about who should take out the trash, for example), other things perhaps not so well (climbing trees, say), and many things scarcely not at all (such as flying without the assistance of flying machines)—were brought into being over the course of countless generations as the unpredictable yet (in hindsight) logical consequence of utterly down-to-earth natural causes and events. Charles Darwin and other scientists in the 19th century called this natural way of becoming something previously never before seen on earth the "transmutation of species." Most scientists now call it *biological evolution*. I will have more to say about this later on.

Although not all biologists today would leave God entirely out of the story of how we evolved to become human beings, there is broad scientific consensus that we cannot understand what it means to be human without also understanding evolution. It is somewhat ironic, therefore, that anthropologists—who generally see themselves as the ultimate authorities on all things human—are likely to be more conservative than their biological colleagues when it comes to talking about our place in nature.[1] A surprising number of anthropologists even today will tell you that there is nothing terribly natural about human nature. In fact, they are likely to say there is no such thing as human nature at all. Is this true?

The anthropologist Tim Ingold at the University of Aberdeen in Scotland certainly doubts that it is scientifically possible to define a baseline of characteristics that all human beings have in common, despite the commonsense judgment that there must be something that can be called universal human nature. Ingold acknowledges that this may seem an odd conclusion to reach. After all, we know another human being when we see one.

Even so, Ingold is able to come to the brusque conclusion that human nature is an illusion because of how he reads the question *What does it mean to be human?* He takes this concern to be about what all human beings do and have always done everywhere on earth and through all time. Yet he also wisely acknowledges—and here I cannot resist offering a few old clichés—that variation is the spice of life, and there is always an exception to every rule. Hence, as he himself has phrased the assessment, looking for universal and absolute defining attributes of all of humanity is a hopeless task, since whatever characteristics you choose, there are always bound to be those born of man and woman in whom such traits are lacking.[2]

One of the examples he offers to support this dismissive judgment is walking. "Bipedal locomotion is generally regarded as a species attribute of *Homo sapiens*, an integral part of our evolved human nature." Yet not everybody is able to walk upright on two legs; babies must learn how to do so, and not everyone on earth walks in precisely the same way.

But this kind of argument in anthropology counter to the idea of human nature fundamentally rigs the cards against such a possibility.[3] After all, it is basically nonsensical to suggest that what is at stake is whether or not every person on earth marches—and has always marched—to one and the same drummer. Like it or not, as the biological anthropologist Robert Sussman at Washington University in St. Louis has said: "Is there something we can call human nature? Of course there is. Humans generally behave more like each other than they do like chimpanzees or gorillas."[4]

What is key here in what Sussman observes are the words "humans generally behave." The phrase "human nature" does not have to be about what all people must do to merit being called a human being. Rather, asking what is the nature of human nature is about trying to understand *how* and *why* we humans do some things well, some things not so well, and other things not at all.

TAKING THE WORDS "human nature" to mean not *What does everyone everywhere do?* but instead *What are most of us capable of doing?* does not get around the core issue that many people find perhaps most troubling and contentious about asking what it means to be human. Many would read these words as asking *why* we do what we do, not how many of us actually do something that can be looked upon as distinctively—if not necessarily uniquely—human. And the particular worry is often that we may be by nature inherently lazy, intolerant, selfish, aggressive, and habitually violent creatures—in a word, that at birth we are all bullies at heart, so to speak, who need years of training to become kind and socially adept humans.

Some find this a fairly easy worry to pin down. The kindly and much respected evolutionist Edward Wilson at Harvard University has said that when asked whether human beings are innately aggressive he tells people: "This is a favorite question of college seminars and cocktail party conversations, and one that raises emotion in political ideologues of all stripes. The answer to it is yes."[5] Similarly, Wilson's Harvard colleague Steven Pinker, an evolutionary psychologist, has written that the history of our species shows us clearly not only that human beings are ready, willing, and able to kill others of our own kind with alarming frequency, but also that we are brilliant in figuring out clever ways to do so.[6]

Recently Wilson and Pinker have each underscored one of the principal claims behind this way of thinking about ourselves: namely that competition rather than cooperation among groups has been a powerful driving force behind the evolution of our species and our behavior as individuals. As Wilson has now phrased the idea: "Our bloody nature, it can now be argued in the context of modern biology, is ingrained because group-versus-group was a principal driving force that made us what we are.... Each tribe knew with justification that if it was not armed and ready, its very existence was imperiled."[7]

Similarly, Pinker has made the bold assertion that violence has declined down through the ages from a time long ago when the rule of the day was anything but the rule of law, when viciousness, not civility, reigned preeminent. "If the past is a foreign country, it is a shockingly violent one. It is easy to forget how dangerous life used to be, how deeply brutality was once woven into the fabric of daily existence. Cultural memory pacifies the past, leaving us with pale souvenirs whose bloody origins have been bleached away."[8]

Others, however, are not so cynical. As Washington University's Robert Sussman has written: "To say that humans have a propensity for violence says nothing. We also have a propensity for nonviolence. In fact, the norm, or statistically more common behavior, within human groups is cooperation and among human groups is peace. Violence, both within and among societies, is statistically abnormal."[9]

If Sussman is right, then why is asking what it means to be human so often contentious and troubling? There are at least two ways to approach this issue. One is statistical. The other is historical. I touch briefly now on the first one, and then devote the next two chapters to the second approach. We will pick up the first theme again in Chapter 4 when I introduce you to three key players in my own explanation for why, despite our reputation (as a species) for being selfish, violent, brutish, and bloodthirsty, we are so often remarkably talented not just at thinking up new ways to kill others, but also at turning strangers into friends. Each of these three imaginary human characters, whom I like to call Lou, Laurence, and Leslie, has an important and strikingly different personality, or set of characteristics. But before talking about them, let's take first things first.

Recall Sussman's observation just noted about how violence within and among societies is statistically abnormal. I do not know about you, but I think bringing up statistics can be a sure way to dampen any conversation. And it has been my experience that the familiar quip "there are three kinds of lies: lies, damn (or damned) lies, and statistics" commonly attributed to Mark Twain is an oft-used, if defensive, observation likely to be raised whenever calculations and numbers begin to fly fast and furious during heated arguments. In short, offering statistical facts and figures is not an inherently foolproof way to win others over to your point of view.

More to the underlying point here, however, the psychologist and Nobel laureate Daniel Kahneman and his late colleague Amos Tversky have written extensively about statistics, decision making, and how evidently prone we human beings are to make errors that would seem easily avoidable if we looked at things from a solid factual and statistical point of view. As they observed in a well-known paper published in 1973: "In making predictions and judgments under uncertainty, people do not appear to follow the calculus of chance or the statistical theory of prediction. Instead, they rely on a limited number of heuristics which sometimes yield reasonable judgments and sometimes lead to severe and systematic errors."[10]

There is no need to belabor what I want to say. Decades of work in experimental psychology have shown that it may be a common characteristic of the human mind to pay inadequate attention to facts and figures even when they are readily available to us—such as the evident rarity of violence within and among human groups as reported by Robert Sussman—when forming judgments and coming to decisions about what is or is not likely to happen, or what other people are, or are not, likely to do.[11] Is it surprising, therefore, that our gut feelings about human nature may often be so rough-hewn and poorly nailed together that they should not be taken nearly as seriously as many of us seem prepared to do?

Furthermore, it is not hard to see where our personal opinions about human nature come from. After all, each of us is a certifiable human being. Therefore, how can there possibly be any mystery at all about what it means to be human? And aren't the news media always telling us about suicide bombers, rapists, child molesters, and other perpetrators of murder and mayhem not just here and there, but basically everywhere? Who could possibly believe that what Sussman says about our fundamentally pacific ways as a species could or should be taken seriously?

This is not a trifling matter. As an anthropologist myself, I would dearly love to believe that real-time facts and figures have the persuasive power to win over individuals even as evidently cynical and dismissive as Wilson and Pinker to Sussman's fairly rosy appraisal of the basic nature of human nature. But I learned long ago that arguing against the conventional wisdom that human beings are inherently selfish and dangerous is an uphill battle. There are undoubtedly a number of good reasons why this is so, but I believe recent history may have much to do with it—as witnessed by the history of Western philosophy and social thought since the ancient Greeks.

It is time to take a brief look at some of this intellectual, social, and civic history.

2

Baron von Pufendorf

MOST PEOPLE NOWADAYS have probably never heard of Baron von Pufendorf. I certainly hadn't. Yet there I was in 2012 in the great hall of the Pufendorf Institute for Advanced Studies at Lund University in southern Sweden standing near a coffee urn eating a sticky bun and trying my best to look both wise and worldly. Who was Pufendorf? Why was I in Sweden licking my fingers as discretely as possible after lecturing at the Institute about friendship? More to the point, what does Pufendorf have to do with human nature and our remarkable talent for turning strangers into friends?

In the latter half of the 17th century and during the decades of the 18th century running up to the American Revolutionary War of 1775–1783, Samuel von Pufendorf (1632–1694) was held by many to be one of Europe's leading intellectuals.[1] Although his was perhaps not a household name by anyone's measure of popular fame today, he was nonetheless well regarded by those in the know. Even now, scholars take note of his writings on the moral essentials of individual, national, and international human relationships.[2] Although his writings currently may not be as firmly entrenched in high school and college courses as the renowned essays on human nature and civil life by his contemporaries Thomas Hobbes (1588–1679), John Locke (1632–1704), and the later 18th century savant Jean-Jacques Rousseau (1712–1778), Pufendorf argued in ways that many in his day found not only persuasive but also insightful.

This was the era of the Enlightenment in Europe, the Age of Reason, when many educated people dedicated themselves to the advancement of knowledge and the reformation of human society in accord with carefully reasoned principles.[3] In keeping with the philosophical conventions of his time, Pufendorf took as his starting point a question that had been every bit as popular in ancient Greece and Rome as it was in his day: *What had life been like at the beginning of time when our kind of creature was living in a "state of nature" prior to the development of such everyday civil institutions as marriage, property, the sovereign state, and the right of the few to rule over the many?*[4]

Pufendorf reasoned, as did his famous contemporaries and later commentators, that the moral legitimacy and civil effectiveness of all forms of human governance had to be grounded on knowing first of all what kind of creature we are—that is, we need to know what is universally true about everyone on earth, living and dead. In short, we need to know a great deal about *human nature.*[5]

Although the most celebrated philosophical essays on human nature written before the American Revolution may now be those penned by Hobbes, Locke, and Rousseau, Samuel von Pufendorf was eloquent (and notably longwinded) in describing what he judged basic human nature to be all about. Like his contemporaries, he took it for granted that regardless of how good-natured or beastly human beings may naturally be down deep inside, human social life is fashioned to a large degree, and reasonably so, on rational and entirely justifiable *self-interest.*

Also like many in his day, he accepted the biblical claim that when God created us, He willed that we should be an animal superior to all others. In consideration of this awesome but truly divine human burden, therefore, it follows naturally that all of us should try to live our lives, however humble or flamboyant, in a manner and spirit unlike "the life and condition of the brutes." After all, regardless of how animal-like we may seem to be at times, aren't we all much closer to the angels than to livestock, the fish in the sea, the birds of the air, and every creeping thing that creepeth upon the earth?[6]

Additionally, and not surprisingly, Pufendorf kept to the standard and by then antique idea that in our early days as the finest example of God's Creation, it had been both possible and practical for people to live out their lives on earth more or less apart from one another—so much so that it would be reasonable to infer, as Pufendorf observed: "The first men, in order to fill a world still empty, and to seek a roomier habitation for themselves and their flocks, left the paternal homes, separated in different directions, and nearly every male set up a household for himself." It was only later in our history after our forebears had "multiplied remarkably" and had learned through their own bitter, or bittersweet, firsthand experiences "the inconvenience of the isolated life" that "by degrees the nearest neighbors united to form societies, first smaller, then larger, by the voluntary or enforced union of several of the smaller."[7]

Before we go on, let's get one thing straight. There is much more to Samuel von Pufendorf and his philosophy than what I have noted here.[8] However, I need to add only one more point to the list of things I am narrowing in on. Simply put, it is not surprising that a philosopher, however now famous or obscure, writing during the Age of Reason might say that what we needed to do as a species to lift ourselves up by the bootstraps and get ourselves out of our primeval "state of nature" was to reason our way out. As Pufendorf phrased the conventional argument: "since the light of reason has been placed in man, and, by its beams he can guide his actions," it follows that even those existing in the natural state have "the power of doing everything that agrees with sound reason."[9]

Now just how beastly brutish or naturally civilized human beings are likely to be, or become, when ensnared in a state of nature has long been hotly debated in the annals of philosophy and jurisprudence. It is important to note, however, that Pufendorf was well aware that the "state of nature" he was alluding to with such apparent confidence is basically an idealized, imaginary state, a scholarly and rhetorical fiction. As Jean-Jacques Rousseau bluntly acknowledged in the 18th century: "philosophers, who have inquired into the foundations of society, have all felt the necessity of going back to a state of nature; but not one of them has got there."[10] Or as Pufendorf himself admitted: "it is clear that the whole human race has never at one and the same time been in the natural state. For those who were born to our first parents, from whom all mortals draw their origin, as the Holy Scriptures relate, were subject to the paternal authority. Later, however, this natural state did appear among some men."[11]

Why then did Pufendorf and others make up stories about human nature if they didn't really believe in them?[12] The simple answer, at least during the Enlightenment, was that experts then wanted people to accept their premise, or learned argument, that civilized social life is based on a *social contract* drawn up at least figuratively speaking by free, sane, and insightful human beings—a contract that could and should be extended to cover the moral and working relationships that ought to pertain between rulers and the ruled.

Hence the rhetorical fiction of the "state of nature" was chiefly seen as a way to set the stage for philosophizing about the character of civil society—a make-believe counterpoint, a way of talking about the need for civility and social norms by picturing what human life would be like without them.

A benign intellectual ruse, so to speak. But as Pufendorf himself acknowledged, not a very realistic one:

> For if you conceive a man who even in adult age is left alone in this
> world, and without any of the comforts and supports with which the
> ingenuity of men has made life more civilized and less hard, you will
> see an animal, naked, dumb, needy, driving away his hunger as best he
> can by roots and herbs, his thirst by any water he chances upon, the
> severity of the weather by caves, an animal exposed to the wild beasts,
> and alarmed when he meets any of them.... And, to be brief, in the
> natural state each man is protected by his own powers only, in the com-
> munity by those of all. In the former no one has a certain reward of his
> industry; in the latter all have it. In the one there is the rule of passion,
> war, fear, poverty, ugliness, solitude, barbarism, ignorance, savagery;
> in the other the rule of reason, peace, security, riches, beauty, society,
> refinement, knowledge, good will.[13]

3

Ghost Theories

IN HIS AUTOBIOGRAPHICAL 1974 novel *Zen and the Art of Motorcycle Maintenance*, the writer and philosopher Robert M. Pirsig tells us that how we see "the whole blessed world we live in" is run by ghosts—and not just the ghosts of such acclaimed theorists and philosophers as Moses, Christ, Buddha, Thomas Hobbes, René Descartes, and Isaac Newton, but also those of ordinary, now nameless folk. "Your common sense is nothing more than the voices of thousands and thousands of these ghosts from the past. Ghosts and more ghosts. Ghosts trying to find their place among the living."[1]

Although possibly this remarkable novel may not be where he got the idea, the historian Daniel Smail has similarly written that how we see ourselves and the world around us may be haunted by nameless things he calls ghost theories, by which he means not supernatural premonitions but rather "old ideas that continue to structure our thinking without our being fully aware of their controlling presence." An example he offers of such enduring but largely unrecognized attitudes, suppositions, and ideas is the short chronology of the earth's history as framed by the Book of Genesis. History textbooks used in American classrooms between the late 19th century and the 1940s did not abandon the traditional idea that the earth is only about 6,000 years old—a claim derived from sacred religious history—even though geologists, archaeologists, and other scholars had by the mid-19th century discredited this belief. Instead, he reports, American textbooks translated the old biblical chronology in a new secular way: "the Garden of Eden became the irrigated fields of Mesopotamia, and the creation of man was reconfigured as the rise of civilization."[2]

An equally fitting example would be the biblical story of Adam and Eve in the Garden of Eden. We are told in Chapter 2 of Genesis that Adam and Eve were created not as babes in the wood but rather as fully functional adults. We are also told that God planted a garden in Eden and then had Adam till the soil and care for this garden. And seeing that it was not right that Adam should be entirely alone, God created Eve to assist him in these divinely assigned tasks:

> Genesis 2:21 And the LORD God caused a deep sleep to fall upon Adam, and he slept: and he took one of his ribs, and closed up the flesh instead thereof;
>
> 2:22 And the rib, which the LORD God had taken from man, made he a woman, and brought her unto the man.
>
> 2:23 And Adam said, This is now bone of my bones, and flesh of my flesh: she shall be called Woman, because she was taken out of Man.
>
> 2:24 Therefore shall a man leave his father and his mother, and shall cleave unto his wife: and they shall be one flesh.
>
> 2:25 And they were both naked, the man and his wife, and were not ashamed.

Nowadays it is widely although not universally acknowledged that this traditional account is merely an early recorded attempt at grappling rationally with our self-awareness as human beings that there must have been a time before which we did not exist as a species. However, I have taken the liberty of including these actual passages from the King James Version of the Christian Bible not to convert you to this point of view, but rather to give substance to an observation and a conclusion.

Observation: Given this biblical view of human origins, it is not surprising that Enlightenment thinkers would take it as read that human beings living in a state of nature would be able to survive as solitary forest creatures or as close-knit families on their own divorced from any need to associate with other people. After all, hadn't this first couple done so quite handily? This traditional (or "ghost") idea, however, overlooks the modern evolutionist's perspective on human nature—namely, that we are inherently social creatures and the basic unit of human society is *not* the individual (together perhaps with his or her helpmate), but rather the individual and her or his relationships with others (as we will discuss in the chapters ahead).

Conclusion: Both during the Enlightenment as well as today, conventional ideas and assumptions about liberty, freedom, and the sanctity of the individual (and according to some, the role of women in society) can at least in part be traced back to these famous passages in the Genesis account of the earth's primal history.[3] And so, too, can ideas still popular about history as a story of human progress—about change over time since the origin of everything that has transformed the character and complexity of human society (see Chapter 12).

Seen from this perspective, for example, it can be argued that much of the philosophical underpinning of modern libertarianism is in keeping with Genesis as interpreted most notably by the Enlightenment philosopher John Locke. As the philosophers Eric Mack and Gerald Gaus at Tulane University have summed up the libertarian view of society: "Each individual's life, well-being or preference satisfaction is thought of as having supreme importance in and of itself, not merely in so far as it contributes to social life, well-being, or preference satisfaction."[4] As we shall see, this view is largely contrary to what is known about our evolved baseline need to be part of a social, not a solitary, world.

WE ARE STILL being haunted by yet other ghost ideas, too. One of these is the assertion, as well as the fear, that within each of us lurks a beast dying to get out—much like the evil Mr. Hyde in Robert Louis Stevenson's novella *Strange Case of Dr. Jekyll and Mr. Hyde*. Except in our case, the role of Mr. Hyde is played by human nature as imagined during the Enlightenment, for instance, by the philosopher Thomas Hobbes. His grim view of what our lives would be like in a state of nature free of all the trappings of civil society is famously captured by his phrase "a perpetuall warre of every man against his neighbor." Nowadays the words used to describe human nature are more often taken from biology, genetics, and neo-Darwinian evolutionary theory than from the Enlightenment, but the underlying assertion remains the same: we are all apparently selfish, aggressive, violent creatures.

Yet another idea still haunting us is one closely tied to the pessimism of this last one. This is the suspicion, and the fear, that strangers cannot and must not be trusted. Said simply: human nature being what it is, it would be foolish in the extreme to depend on the kindness of strangers. And it is only rational, therefore, to treat strangers as potentially savage and dangerous foes.

These two ghost ideas—together they could be called the "tragic tale of the savage and the beast"—are firmly entrenched in how many of us think about ourselves as people, citizens, and players on the global stage of politics, economics, and international law. We see other people—and ourselves, too—as inherently selfish, self-centered, and self-interested. We despair that even the world's great religions may not be able to save us from our own base designs and desires.[5]

All of these old ghost ideas need to be laid to rest. One way to do so is to ask why and how are we not only able to make friends but also keep the friends we already have. Human beings excel at making friends. Although it is difficult to say how unique we are in this respect as a species, there are first-rate reasons—as we shall see—for saying that being good at making friends even with total strangers is one of the defining characteristics of our species of primate.

It took millions of years to make this happen, but once our prehistoric forerunners had evolved both the *capacity* and the *predisposition* to make friends even with total strangers, they were finally able to open a new door to the world beyond the confines of immediate kin and nearby neighbors. By extending their social world—their social networks—in this exceptional way, our forebears were at last free to cultivate the world. And we have been doing so ever since. Looked at from an evolutionary perspective, Facebook, Twitter, and Snapchat are simply new and admittedly more rapid ways of doing something that our species had mastered eons ago in other, more pedestrian ways.

IT WAS NO accident that I was in Lund, Sweden, at the time I wrote about at the start of Chapter 2. I had been in the Netherlands at a scholarly conference at Leiden University. Learning I would be on his side of the Atlantic, my friend and research colleague Dr. Eric Clark, Professor of Human Geography at Lund University, invited me to come over afterwards to give a lecture or two on whatever topics I felt like talking about. So there I was at the Pufendorf Institute for Advanced Studies talking about "The friendship hypothesis: Evolutionary and anthropological perspectives on human response to culturally diverse and inequitable social fields"—a title not entirely of my own creation that strikes me now, as it did then, as somewhat wordy although pretty much on target.

Janus, the ancient Roman deity of gates, doorways, beginnings, and transitions for whom January was named was often portrayed in antiquity as having two faces, one looking back and the other to the future. Like Janus, the friendship hypothesis at the center of that lecture—and now one of the principal themes of this book—asks us to look back into our evolutionary past to discover what are our biologically inherited strengths and weaknesses as a species. This seems to me to be a perfectly worthy project in its own right, but I have not written this book only to talk about the past. Far from it. I am convinced that if we take this hypothesis seriously, we human beings may be able to tinker with our evolutionary heritage in social rather than biological ways to help us achieve greater control over the future of our species.

The Friendship Hypothesis

PROPOSITION—Our evolved ability, our psychological and biological capacity, to make friends even with strangers is a defining characteristic of our species, an evolved human trait marking us apart from most other species on earth just as surely as the other diagnostic traits that have been singled out as being characteristic of our kind, such as walking upright on two legs, having opposable thumbs and a prominent chin, and possessing the powers of both speech and complex abstract reasoning.

EVOLUTIONARY SIGNIFICANCE—Even when there is no conscious intent that they should do so—and I would argue that there often is not, at least not nowadays—our friendships by their very nature connect us with one another in ways that create astonishingly far-reaching social networks capable of transmitting vitally useful information, mobilizing people to action, and in other ways, too, buffering us, our families, and our communities against the trials and tribulations of life.

HISTORICAL IMPLICATIONS—Even the most sedentary human groups have always had ways of safely initiating, cultivating, and maintaining social ties beyond the immediate horizons and familiar constraints of their daily lives and daily rounds.

☑ Depending in part on the particular circumstances and vagaries of life, people have always found seemingly practical reasons, as well as socially sanctioned excuses, for engaging in more distant social relationships beyond the confines of their hamlet or village community—not the least of which has commonly been the need for suitable marriage partners.

☑ However, the biological and psychological underpinnings of our human need for friendship both near and far are built in goodly part on our basic animal and cognitive responses to what may be labeled somewhat tongue-in-cheek as our five "human senses," or B.R.U.C.E. for short. These five are our sense of...

Belonging to something bigger than just ourselves

Responsibility for the success and happiness of others, not just ourselves

Understanding where other people are coming from even when we may not agree with them

Commitment to something bigger than just our own personal success

Engagement with other people in meaningful and productive ways

4

The Secret Lives of Lou, Laurence, and Leslie

I AM PREPARED to wager that you, too, have personally witnessed on more than one occasion the bizarre phenomenon I want to relate here. One afternoon I was on a major expressway on my way out of Chicago headed toward my farm in southwestern Wisconsin during the afternoon rush hour. It was probably around 4:30 or 5:00. I noticed out of the corner of my eye that a car was rapidly entering the expressway on a ramp to my right. The car showed absolutely no signs of slowing down, or even that the driver was aware of the crowded and dangerous road conditions about to be encountered.

Cars around me started quickly and somewhat erratically responding to the threat by adjusting their speed and trying to move as rapidly as possible out of the way to avoid hitting or being hit by this new arrival on the scene. Yet the driver of this offending car that was the thorn in our collective vehicular side was still giving the rest of us absolutely no indication of being at all mindful of the situation. How on earth could anyone be so negligent, so unawares, so clearly tuned out?

You've probably figured out what the driver of this rogue car was doing instead of paying attention to the roadway and driving conditions. The driver was on a cell phone happily chatting with someone somewhere off in cyberspace as if nobody else on earth was anywhere nearby.

It would be easy to dismiss this behavior by calling it just plain stupid. Easy, but not right. While undoubtedly something bad could have happened if the rest of us hadn't taken remedial steps to adapt to this alarming situation, taking the time and making the effort to psych out not just what people in general are capable of doing, but also what particular individuals—this driver, for instance—are likely to do sooner or later is not a frivolous exercise.

Labeling someone as stupid may be comforting and tension-reducing, but isn't terribly helpful.

Said another way, a vital human survival skill is being good at reading other people's moods, actions, and likely intentions. In this regard, it goes without saying that negotiating life's demands and challenges from the cradle to the grave—or from Chicago to rural Wisconsin on a Friday afternoon—would certainly be a whole lot easier if our primate ancestors had somehow been able to hand down to us as part of our human evolutionary heritage the gift of telepathy to communicate directly with the minds of others. Unfortunately, such a skill does not come naturally to us.

Hence the quandary, the catch-22, of being a human is that although our species may be much smarter on the whole than other kinds of animals on earth, our sort has been struggling to figure out one another from the get-go, or at any rate at least from the time of birth. And although the strategies devised for getting into the minds of others have often been levelheaded, they have sometimes been fairly farfetched.

In the early 19th century, for instance, the science of phrenology was in vogue in some European and US circles.[1] Nowadays often lampooned as a bizarre pseudoscience dedicated to reading the psychological character of a person by paying close attention to the swells, bumps, and valleys felt on the outside of the brain case, the major weakness of this astonishing way of pur- portedly dealing with the problem of mind reading in the absence of genuine clairvoyance was its key premise that our brain has a number of—exactly how many was then much debated—different "organs" of personality, each sup- posedly corresponding to a different type of mental "faculty" such as *combat- iveness, destructiveness, cautiousness, benevolence*, and *hope* (Figure 1).[2]

On similarly controversial but perhaps more credible grounds, the found- ing father of psychoanalysis, Sigmund Freud, famously proposed at the end of the 19th century and well into the 20th that instead of numerous separate organs, the human psyche can be divided like Julius Caesar's ancient Gaul into three parts labeled the *id*, the *ego*, and the *superego*.[3] Although psychoanalysis both then and now has had its forceful critics as well as its devoted defenders, there is no question that Freud and his followers had successfully tapped into a rich vein of both popular and scientific enthusiasm for analyzing and (at least figuratively) dissecting the human brain and its glorious mysteries.

Currently, however, the cutting-edge work being done on this perennially popular topic is by and large in the hands of neuroscience researchers using a variety of sophisticated machine-aided brain imaging techniques—such as *functional magnetic resonance imaging* (fMRI), which measures brain activity

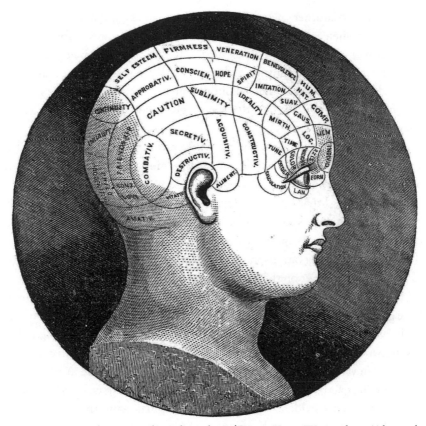

FIGURE 1 Late 19th century phrenology chart. (*Source*: Karen Watson, http://thegraph-icsfairy.com/vintage-clip-art).

by detecting changes in blood flow therein while the owner of the brain under scrutiny is performing simple, carefully controlled tasks at the behest of the scientists running the show, or rather the experiment.[4] Even modern brain imaging, however, is not without its real difficulties and its vocal critics, although as Klaus Fiedler at the Department of Psychology, University of Heidelberg, has observed, when it comes to scientific experimentation of all sorts, voodoo correlations are everywhere, not just in modern neuroscience.[5]

In any case, it is easy to sympathize with the plight of neuroscience researchers today. Being able to see in one way or another what is happening inside our skulls in no way ensures that the researchers will also be able to interpret correctly what they see there—say, when someone recognizes a face as being familiar, and then is able to recall whose face it is (a cognitive skill that for me breaks down almost invariably whenever I have to introduce one of my friends to another guest at a party). And needless to say, the challenge is even greater when a neuroscience researcher is trying to unravel, for instance, what the brain is doing when we are dreaming, acting silly, or being creative.[6] No wonder then that reading journal articles today in neuroscience may bring to mind the old parable about the blind men and the elephant. This field of science is obviously still so new that seemingly nobody yet can see the whole "elephant" for what it is.[7]

Acknowledging, therefore, the old wisdom that truth is hard to come by, and that even with the help of hugely expensive modern machinery our brains may still be largely off-limits when it comes to mind reading, there do seem to be a few things that can be said with confidence about the impact of the brain on what it means to be human and on the role of friendship in helping us all make things work out for us as a species. To mix clichés and metaphors shamelessly, five observations in particular are worth going out on a limb for so that they can be put on the table for consideration.

First, the brain is not made out of the biological equivalent of separate little gray-matter Lego blocks or mobile applications, each having its own specially evolved—or "pre-wired"—purpose and function. Instead, the brain is a vast network of interconnected ("wired") cells that work together in countless ways and in varying combinations to get us through life.[8] Case in point: The entire brain is active when people are engaged in creative tasks. There is no good neuroscience evidence to back up the popular claim that creativity in located somewhere in the right side of the brain.[9]

Second, what our brain is actually capable of doing for us critically depends to an extraordinary degree on what our brain learns how to do after—and undoubtedly also before—birth. Much of what it means to be human, in other words, depends on what we learn as infants, children, and adults by interacting not just with the physical world around us, but also with other people around us, and specifically from what they teach us intentionally or unawares about how to think and how to do things (see Chapter 21).[10] The formal name for this latter kind of knowledge acquisition is *social learning*, to distinguish it from generic *stimulus–response learning* that can happen even when other people are not present or involved. Such as learning as a child behind your mother's back that it is not a good idea to stick a paperclip into the wrong (hot-wired) slot of an electrical outlet.

Third, thinking isn't free. The brain is an immensely costly biological operation to run, second only to the heart in its metabolic demands for oxygen and energy (specifically, glucose or blood sugar). Consequently, how our brain works as an elaborate natural machine is a trade-off, or balance, between doing something cheaply (in terms of energy costs) and doing something well.[11] Our brain isn't perfect, and it should be no surprise, therefore, that as much as some of us may try, nobody is perfect either in what he or she can do, will do, and has done.

Fourth, as big as it is, our brain also has real physical constraints—it must fit effectively and well within our skull, for example. And as clever as we have shown ourselves to be as a species in coming up with ways to work around our inherent biological limitations (for instance, by inventing mobile phones and airplanes), we have not yet devised any way to link one human brain with another physically in the ways we can now do for computers using Ethernet cables, Wi-Fi, and Bluetooth. The best inventions we have been able to come up with so far in this regard are art, language, writing, mathematics, and computer systems. As wonderful as these creations are, they are all notoriously error-prone and often clunky in how they link us together mentally, if not spiritually. Hence, as the late and justifiably renowned psychologist George A. Miller famously observed back in what became an equally renowned and brilliantly written journal article in 1956: "the span of absolute judgment and the span of immediate memory impose severe limitations on the amount of information that we are able to receive, process, and remember."[12]

What limitations did he have in mind? It is generally accepted that what Miller in 1956 called "immediate memory"—and is now more often called "working" and "short-term" memory[13]—refers to the amount of information that we can actively keep in our conscious mind and work with at any one time. Famously, this is said to be the "magical number" 7 plus or minus 2 items. In Miller's own words: "Everybody knows that there is a finite span of immediate memory and that for a lot of different kinds of test materials this span is about seven items in length."[14]

Fifth, acknowledging that our on-board biological computer called the brain has genuine size and performance limitations makes it easier to see why we make mistakes, love metaphors that get a point across without having to go into a lot of detail, try to come up with other kinds of shortcuts and simplifying routines, may too quickly jump to conclusions that would fall apart if we gave the problem more time and effort, and the list goes on and on when it comes to itemizing our known human performance foibles and failings.

BY NOW YOU have probably recalled from your memory store one human performance failure vividly illustrating how far off the mark—or the road— our brainy cranial computers can take us. Yes, I am referring to that late afternoon driver on a mobile phone that time when I was leaving Chicago for home in Wisconsin. Among the several possible explanations for such unwise behavior one strikes me as the most probable. Rather than sheer stupidity or intentional neglect, the individual involved was simply someone who was happy to be connected with whoever was at the other end of the wireless line, and who had forgotten that none of us should overestimate how much our brain can handle consciously at any one given time. Only seven things plus or minus two items, say.

Conventional wisdom would probably insist that this driver was simply too preoccupied, which is probably true, but this also is not an altogether helpful way of labeling what happened or could have happened back then. More to the point, the driver was clearly not driving blind. However much the fact that the rest of us got out of the way may have saved the day from becoming a disaster, this errant individual did manage successfully somehow (perhaps more unconsciously than consciously) to complete the task of joining our forward moving fray.

Then if the word "preoccupied" does not really cut the cake, what would be a better way to describe what happened? Although there is no need to go into detail about how the human brain copes with the complexities of life despite the limitations of its capacity for immediate or short-term conscious memory storage, enough is now known about information processing within that secret vault on top of our shoulders to conclude that we are always highly selective about what we deem worthy of moving into working memory where we can then ponder and perhaps act on the information delivered there for conscious deliberation.[15]

Although much remains mysterious about the biological and chemical realities behind information processing of this sort, researchers nowadays find it useful to talk about thinking as something that we are capable of doing in two closely related but differing ways.[16] The first way of thinking, commonly labeled *System 1* or *Type 1* but more conventionally called *habit* and *intuition*, can be done quickly without calling for a lot of effort, and happens more or less unconsciously. The second kind of thinking, labeled *System 2* or *Type 2* but popularly called *conscious awareness* and *reasoning*, is harder to do (psychologists like to describe it as "effortful"), takes longer to accomplish, and is usually something we are more or less consciously aware of doing. Since nobody is yet entirely sure how the brain actually works when we are thinking in these two contrasted ways, the better part of wisdom suggests they shouldn't be called "systems," but rather something less definite—say, "ways" or "types"—but we don't have to resolve this particular neuroscience issue here and now, so let's stick to the conventional System 1 or 2/Type 1 or 2 and leave the resolution of this concern to others.

In keeping with this simple dual distinction, Jonathan Evans at the Center for Thinking and Language at the University of Plymouth in the United Kingdom has suggested that System 2/Type 2 processes should be seen as "those that require access to a single, capacity-limited central working memory resource, while Type 1 processes do not require such access. This implies that the core features of Type 2 processes are that they are slow, sequential, and capacity limited."[17]

As others would also do, Evans has emphasized that the ease, speed, and efficiency of System 1/Type 1 thinking comes at a cost. The quick and easy and basically unconscious work called for can be a false friend. Why? Because doing something rapidly and intuitively may feel right even when it is actually the wrong thing to do,[18] like driving as if blind onto a crowded expressway late on a Friday afternoon.

MAYBE ALL THIS "system" talk makes sense to psychologists, but if you are like me, calling something "System 1" or "Type 1" and so forth can be confusing, and to be honest, perhaps more than a little boring. At any rate, when I am trying to think about thinking from their informed psychological point of view, I have found it helpful and more memorable to change their stodgy labels. I have given the name "Lou" to System 1/Type 1 thinking and "Laurence" to System 2/Type 2 (please see Table 1).

Why Lou? Because how this type of thinking is usually described by experts reminds me of Lou Costello in the old comedy duo "Abbott & Costello" widely popular in the 1940s and early 1950s. To my mind, Lou (a.k.a. System 1/Type 1) is the go-to guy who gets things done quickly but not necessarily altogether well.

But then why the name Laurence for System 2/Type 2 rather than William or Bud in honor of William "Bud" Abbott? Although Abbott as portrayed on radio, television, and the silver screen would certainly seem to qualify as a suitable human icon for the second way of thinking, as a child I never liked Abbott's abusive treatment of poor old Lou. And in my mind, System 2/Type 2 as a style of thinking is far more cerebral, reflective, and cultivated than the character played by Bud Abbott. It is more like Sir Laurence Olivier, for example, and hence the label Laurence.

But who is this character named Leslie also included in my list of actors in search of a play or at rate for something to think about? Let me explain first my choice of this name, and then I will get to the point of introducing this character to the plot I am spinning.

Table 1 Three Actors in Search of a Play

Lou (also known as **System 1** or **Type 1**)—thinking that is unconscious, automatic, quick, perhaps emotional, and easy to do—in short, information processing in the brain done mostly without conscious awareness; a type of thinking that may be evolutionarily old and is probably also within the mental capabilities of other animal species; the realm of our habitual selves

Laurence (called **System 2** or **Type 2**)—thinking that is conscious, slow, takes effort, and is purposeful—usually said to be involved in "higher order" cognitive processes such as logical reasoning and decision making; may or may not be unique to our species; the realm of intentional environmental niche construction

Leslie—thinking that is contemplative, abstract, may be counterfactual, and is largely detached from an individual's immediate realities; may or may not be unique to our species; the realm of cognitive niche construction

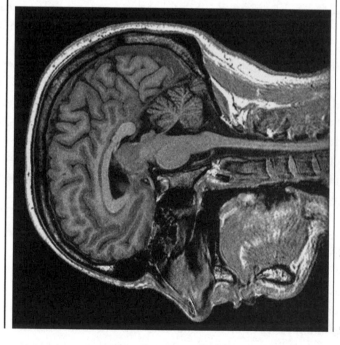

I selected the label Lou in part because this name can be gender-neutral, and after all, we are talking about how all of us think, not just individuals of the male sex. And while I suppose I could have paid no attention whatsoever to my inner voice and opted for a name other than Laurence, I liked the rhythm of saying "Lou and Laurence" together. Similarly, I settled on Leslie because both men and women can have this name, and I like the resonance of the first vowel in *Le*-slie with the initial vowels in *Lou* and *La*-urence. ("Lou, Laurence, and Leslie" sounds rather melodic, does it not?) Truth be told, probably another reason I went for Leslie as a label was my personal admiration for the refined, sensitive, and debonair British stage and film actor Leslie Howard in the old movies *The Scarlet Pimpernel* (1934) and *Gone with the Wind* (1939).

This is probably more detail than you feel you need about why I have named my characters Lou, Laurence, and Leslie. Surely what is more relevant is who is Leslie? Or rather, what type of thinking is she or he supposed to represent?

As described in the psychological literature, System 1/Type 1 and System 2/Type 2 stand for differing ways in which we human beings deal with what is (or may soon be) happening around us "in the real world" that could affect our well-being, comfort, happiness, and perhaps even our survival. As usually described, in other words, these two styles of thinking are *reflexive, reactive,* or *adaptive.* They are differing ways of responding to and making decisions about information coming in from "outside" us. Scientific articles and books about these ways of thinking, therefore, usually focus the reader's attention on rationality, social awareness, problem solving, decision making, errors of judgment, and the like. All of these are good and relevant things to think about. But this is not the be-all and end-all of human thought, or of what it means to act like a human being. Let me explain.

TALKING AND WRITING about the characters I call Lou and Laurence have become so standard and usual in experimental psychology and neuroscience today that there is even a name for it—*dual process theory.*[19] The same cannot be said for Leslie, who is often not even in the picture when these other two characters are on the scene. Since we are talking about something as basic to our species as human psychology in all its richness, I find this neglect surprising.

I think it could be argued, however, that even the ancient Romans had a name for Leslie. They called him *genius*—the guiding spirit or soul of a person giving that individual his or her unique talents. As Thomas Bulfinch wrote in his famous 19th century *Mythology*: "The Romans believed that every man had his Genius, and every woman her Juno: that is, a spirit who had given them being, and was regarded as their protector through life. On their birthdays men made offerings to their Genius, women to their Juno."[20] But unlike the ancient Romans, I see Leslie as just a name for a way of thinking, not a lofty personal motivating spirit acquired at birth. In other words, there can be no Leslie without a Lou and a Laurence.[21]

But does this mean Leslie should be labeled properly as System 3/Type 3 thinking in keeping with the formal designations that psychologists have bestowed on Lou and Laurence? Probably not. Daniel Kahneman, who has done much to advance dual process theory, has been careful to underscore that these two "systems" are largely metaphorical ways of talking about how our brains process information:

> System 1 and System 2 are so central to the story I tell … that I must make it absolutely clear that they are fictitious characters. Systems 1 and 2 are not systems in the standard sense of entities with interacting aspects or parts. And there is no one part of the brain that either of the systems would call home.… [Yet these two] characters are useful because of some quirks of our minds, yours and mine. A sentence is understood more easily if it describes what an agent (System 2) does than if it describes what something is, what properties it has. In other words, "System 2" is a better subject for a sentence than "mental arithmetic."[22]

With this understanding (or qualification) in mind, what then are some of the characteristics of this neglected way of thinking that I am calling Leslie? The greatest difference between Leslie, on one hand, and both Lou and Laurence, on the other, is that unlike the latter duo, Leslie isn't committed to dealing with what is happening in the world around him or her. Leslie, in other words, is our brain when we are detached from our surroundings and thinking thoughts great or small that are not necessarily "of the moment" or even "of this world."[23] Case in point: I definitely think the driver's Leslie was in charge when that rogue automobile joined the traffic on the expressway going out of Chicago.

Experts writing about human psychology today fully recognize that our minds are not always trying to deal with real problems in the real world. After all, we all know that all of us have fantasies, possess powers of often wild imagination, and engage in day-dreaming. According to some estimates, as astonishing as it might sound, each of us in fact is likely to spend as much as half our waking moments engaged in thinking that is "stimulus independent"—that is, decoupled from our surroundings,[24] In other words, Leslie-type thinking.

What really astonishes me, however, is that experts writing about our human ability to detach or decouple in this fashion from everyday reality are likely to call this human talent "mind wandering."[25] True, we all know that our minds are capable of wandering off topic—say, during a mind-numbing committee meeting—even when we know at some level of awareness (after all, even when Leslie is in command our Lou and Laurence aren't actually asleep) that we really ought to be paying proper attention to what someone else is saying or showing, or what is all too concretely happening around us.[26] But surely mind wandering is not all there is to Leslie's way of thinking.[27] For instance, when we are engaged in such thinking we can use the time available while detached from reality to think about what *could* be or *should* be, not just about this or that with chaotic, wandering abandon.[28] In other words, when Leslie is at work, our minds can be creative and imaginative, not just willy-nilly. Said more simply, Leslie is not some poor lost soul wandering haplessly in the desert.[29]

By the same token, however, Leslie is not just our mind being intent on creatively solving problems by thinking intensely about them first, although such useful real-world work may indeed sometimes get done willfully or not. But what I think we should see as Leslie thinking cannot be summed up either as just willy-nilly mind wandering or alternatively as soberly purposeful problem solving.[30] Here's why.

Ecologists and other environmental scientists have suggested that how we humans are able to remake the world around us when we put our minds and backs to the effort should be called "niche construction."[31] In ecology and the biological sciences generally, the word "niche" means "way of life," and every species is said to have its particular place, or niche, in the economy of life. Human beings are just one of a number of species that excel at making and remaking their way of life, their place in the grand scheme of things, their ecological niche. In other words, human beings excel at niche construction.

Similarly, I would argue that even when it might look for all the world like we are off somewhere in Lalaland daydreaming, our Leslie minds may actually be hard at work engaged in a kind of niche construction that is possibly but not necessarily unique to our species. By detaching from the realities of the moment and turning our mind to our inner thoughts, we can ponder what I like to call "coulds & shoulds" of life. We can devote our mind to a kind of imaginary niche construction that does not even have to be "of this world" at all. We can see seemingly impossible things in our mind's eye. We can engage in "what if" fantasies of remarkable, perhaps sometimes sexually charged, and even quite unrealistic complexity. We can invent imaginary worlds, invent new things, rewrite the story of our life to our heart's content—all in the mind rather than in the real world. And if we need an elegant term for all this wonderful mental gymnastics, I suggest we call it not mind wandering, but rather and more appropriately instead "cognitive niche construction." Personally, however, I like calling this simply exploring the world between my ears.

THERE IS MORE to be said about cognitive niche construction (see Chapter 21). For now, what needs to be on the table is why I have introduced you to Lou, Laurence, and Leslie now rather than later. The ancient Romans accepted that every person's personal *genius* could be a force for the good or for evil. Similarly, Leslie—the remarkable gift that evolution has given us that makes it possible for our kind of animal to be imaginative, creative, and even out-of-this-world at least in our own heads—can also be our greatest human handicap.

According to the psychologists Matthew Killingsworth and Daniel Gilbert at Harvard University, "a human mind is a wandering mind, and a wandering mind is an unhappy mind. The ability to think about what is not happening is a cognitive achievement that comes at an emotional cost."[32] This may be true, although again, there is no reason to think of Leslie as just a poor and sad lost soul. Yet more fundamentally, the ease with which the human mind can detach itself from reality and contemplate instead both possible and even impossible coulds & shoulds may lead not just to unhappiness but also to madness. Even more challenging, our evolved capacity to engage in cognitive niche construction can lead not only to personal unhappiness but also to human discord, family arguments, feuds, international disagreements, and sometimes violence and death.

Do I sound far too melodramatic? Let me explain briefly why I have mentioned this idea now, although I return to this topic again in the chapters to follow.

In Chapter 3, I proposed an evolutionary hypothesis about what it means to be human—the *friendship hypothesis*. In a nutshell, this hypothesis states that we are social animals with an evolved and compelling need for companionship—even with strangers. I have been arguing as well that our species has evolved the ability to engage in what I have called Leslie thinking. By whatever rubric one chooses, what I have been talking about is our evolved ability to detach mentally from the world around us and even imagine things and events that are impossible, not just improbable.

Critically, however, I have also noted somewhat unhappily that our primate ancestors were unable to bestow upon us an evolved ability to get into the minds of others—sadly, we are not telepathic. And thus far in human history we have not proved to be clever enough to invent a way for one human brain to be effectively and directly "plugged into," "hard-wired," or "wirelessly connected" with others.

As Hamlet says, there's the rub. Or more concretely, there is the paradox at the heart of human evolution, one that I think we should call the "Leslie effect." As individuals, we have the evolved biological and cognitive capacity to imagine all sorts of things that *could* be and perhaps *should* be. As social animals, we may want and may actually feel strongly compelled to share our personal imaginings—our personal coulds & shoulds—with others. We may even want them to accept and adopt as their own our private vision of the world and what it could or should be like.[33] But if mind wandering can lead to unhappiness, Leslie thinking can lead to frustration and sometimes anger, or worse.[34] What if we cannot get others to go along with our coulds & shoulds? Should we even trust them when they say they do? What recourse do we have?

The challenge that our species faces in the 21st century is not the ghost idea that we are a species biologically predisposed by evolution, or our ancient sins, toward violence and mayhem. Enlightenment scholars were wrong. We are not cursed or condemned by the sins or misdeeds of our ancestors. The challenge we must somehow overcome if we are to survive much longer as a species is how to handle the Leslie effect.

In a word or two, or rather two verbs: as a species, we are not struggling against the odds to *control* our bestial inner selves or wild savages lurking out there in the darkness just beyond the security of our campfires; instead, as a species, we are struggling to *create* reliable ways to cultivate trust and communication betwixt our ingenious but otherwise isolated human brains.

This dilemma, this challenge to the welfare and survival of our species, is not new. I have written this book to talk about this challenge, and about what we can do about it if we set our minds to it—and not just our Lou and Laurence minds, but also our Leslie mind with its evolved capabilities for empathy, creativity, inventiveness, and introspection.

The Leslie Effect

PROPOSITION—The evolution of the human brain has made it possible not only for us to remake the world physically to suit our survival needs (our ability to do so is nowadays sometimes called environmental "niche construction"), but also for us as individuals to escape into our own thoughts—and freely imagine there not only how things *could* be, but also *should* be (in this book, I am calling this uncommon evolved capacity our fondness for "cognitive niche construction").

EVOLUTIONARY SIGNIFICANCE—As history shows, as individuals and communities we may try to persuade others—sometimes forcefully—to go along with how we individually and collectively "see" things *could* and *should* be as we see them in our mind's eye.

HISTORICAL IMPLICATIONS—Both as individuals and as communities, we must deal with our species' thorny evolutionary legacy:

- ☑ As individuals, we are markedly social animals who absolutely *must* have others in our lives for our biological and psychological survival.

- ☑ Yet we also have the cognitive freedom to *detach* mentally from the realities of life, and we may then turn around and insist on imposing our personal vision of what could and should be on others who may not understand or be willing to accept our personal imaginings.

- ☑ Therefore, our dilemma as a species is not that we are inherently violent and selfish creatures by nature, but rather that it is so difficult for us to agree and act on the principles by which we should translate the "virtual worlds" seen in our heads into the experienced realities of our daily lives.

PART TWO

The Archaeology of Friendship

5

Suddenly All Was Chaos

IT WAS EARLY in the evening. The sun had just set. There had been a strong but localized earthquake of around magnitude 7.0 shortly before, at 6:49 PM. Many of those who had fled their shaking homes were still out on the beach. There were now sizable cracks in the ground here and there. The sea itself had retreated far down the beach, exposing areas of the near-shore sea bottom. There was an unpleasant odor variously described afterwards as like kerosene, gasoline, oil, or hydrogen sulfide. Then suddenly all was chaos. Estimates of the death toll have varied, but it is believed that between 2,000 and 2,500 people suddenly vanished from the face of the earth as three great waves—the largest ultimately nearly 50 feet high—struck the coast, one after another.

The villages of Malol and Sissano at the farthest ends of the lagoon suffered heavy damage. The villages of Arop and Warapu on the narrow strip of beach sand between these two were completely destroyed. No houses were left standing. Many trees were snapped off or totally uprooted. Some people were impaled alive on broken mangrove stumps. Many of the victims were children, swept like dry leaves out into the great lagoon behind the beach. According to one later report, an infant was deposited, miraculously alive, on the floating roof of a house.

Some of the survivors described the sound of the deafening waves as like a jet plane landing. Others said the roar was more like that made by a large helicopter. The crashing waves carried with them masses of sea life—sharks, fish, and even sea turtles—and left this bizarre catch behind on the beach and in the lagoon.

A half an hour or so later, a strange yellow glow in the sky made it possible for survivors to search awhile for family members. Then there was nothing but the blackness of night. Those who survived, and who had been lucky enough to find one another, clung to each other for comfort and hope. Somehow the survivors made it through the night with broken limbs and battered bodies lost in the awful silence where once flourishing villages had stood.

Possibly as many as 10,000 or more people on the north coast of New Guinea were left homeless.[1]

THE U.S. GEOLOGICAL Survey (USGS) has a webpage that regularly lists and maps earthquakes around the world.[2] The USGS estimates that there are several million detectable earthquakes every year. Based on information collected since 1900, there are likely to be 15 major earthquakes (7.0–7.9) and one great earthquake (8.0 or above) in any given year. Revealingly, 90 percent of the world's earthquakes happen around the edge of the Pacific Plate, a seismic belt popularly known as the Pacific Ring of Fire.

Although the idea was controversial when I was going to college, it is now a well-accepted geological fact that the earth's lithosphere, the rock-hard outer layer or crust of our planet, has become shattered into a number of large, irregularly shaped jigsaw-puzzle pieces called tectonic plates (somewhat cryptically, since the word "tectonic" derives from the Greek word *tekton* meaning "builder" or "carpenter"). Over the long span of geological time, these great pieces of earth have been moving around and rubbing against one another. Where they do so, earthquakes and volcanic eruptions are common.

New Guinea's rugged northern coast runs along the edge of one such plate. Australia, New Guinea, and New Zealand are in effect all passengers on an immense Indo-Australian Plate that is moving at a rate of about 2 3/4 inches (about 70 mm) each year in a northeasterly direction, and is colliding against the mighty Pacific Plate with a lateral shear of about 4 1/3 inches (about 110 mm) per year. There is ample geomorphological evidence all along this coastline showing that rapid geological uplift and subsidence have been common events there.

All told, earthquakes, volcanic eruptions, and their associated after-effects (such as ocean tsunamis and landslides) are potentially catastrophic events that occur locally on this coastline roughly every 50 ± 25 years. Furthermore, the El Niño climate cycle may bring severe local drought followed by high rainfall, flooding, and landslides, leading at times to equally catastrophic landscape change.[3]

The most devastating waves of the 1998 New Guinea tsunami were confined to about 24 miles (40 km) of coastline centered on Sissano Lagoon 20 miles (32 km) west of the town of Aitape in West Sepik Province. Earlier villagers in this region had experienced tsunami waves that were sizable enough to be memorable—notably in 1907 and 1935. In addition, official records indicate that during the previous years before 1998, there had been at least nine major earthquakes of magnitude 7.4 or greater near the epicenter of the 1998 earthquake. Having access to this information, one later analysis of the 1998 disaster concluded that this region should have been seen as a high tsunami risk area, and hence this recent event should have come as no surprise. Such an observation strikes me as a fine example of blaming the victim.

What made the three waves of this 1998 tragedy so unexpectedly massive was how they had got their start. At the time of the disaster, not even earth scientists fully realized how dangerous tsunamis can be when they are caused by submarine mass failure (SMF)—by underwater landslides or slumps— rather than by earthquakes. For this reason, the cause of the 1998 tsunami remained controversial for years.

Soon after the event, however, scientists who came out to New Guinea to see for themselves what had happened began to suspect that the earthquake that day hadn't actually caused the three waves that followed 20 or so minutes later. Speculation early on was that an SMF had probably been the main culprit. The earthquake itself simply had not been strong enough to cause such huge and destructive waves.

Years of research since 1998 have led to the conclusion that the quake may have triggered but not actually caused a sizable underwater chunk of New Guinea to slump, or collapse, into the sea about 15½ miles (25 km) off the Sepik coastline. This conclusion is not altogether surprising, as this shoreline runs along the sharp, steep edge of the Australian Plate. It has been estimated that the size of the piece that gave way was about 2.6 miles long (4.2 km), 2.8 miles wide (4.5 km), and almost a half mile thick (750 meters). This repositioned continental fragment had a total volume of 1.5 cubic miles (6.4 km³)— a sizable piece of underwater real estate to break off and quickly sink deeper into the ocean.[4]

SOON AFTER THE tsunami, my research colleague Rob Welsch and I were asked by the Papua New Guinea (PNG) government to return to this coast to help assess the damage. Two months later, Rob was able to do so. One of our friends there, the former headmaster of a local school, related to him how he and his family had been about to sit down to dinner in the village of Warapu when the earthquake happened. Later, on seeing the first huge wave coming at them, they tried to flee. But then the first wave hit, and the next thing our friend knew, he was deep under water.

When he was able to get to the surface of the lagoon and breathe, he could not find any of his family. In horror, he concluded they were all dead. Although badly hurt, and after spending a grim night floating in the black darkness among loose debris in the lagoon, come morning, he finally made it safely ashore. To his astonishment and joy, he discovered that his wife and children were alive and safe, if not exactly 100 percent well.[5]

THIS WAS NOT the first time that disaster had struck this part of the world. People living on this coastline of New Guinea have been coping for untold millennia with two contrary and unavoidable realities of life. By far the best local places to live are the biologically complex lagoons found at widely scattered intervals behind the beaches here and there on the coast. These inviting lagoons provide thousands of people locally with abundant land, swamp, and lagoon resources—including fish, shellfish, mangrove swamp foods and raw materials, sago swamp palms, and forest products. Yet this same sandy strip running along where the land meets the sea is also just about the worst possible place to be when natural disasters strike—as happened when the 1998 tsunami hit.

This tsunami was every bit as devastating—although on a smaller geographic scale—as the later Indian Ocean tsunamis on the day after Christmas 2004 that are estimated to have killed more than 230,000 people. Or the tsunami in 2011 off the coast of Japan following the most powerful earthquake ever recorded there that killed almost 20,000 people and led to a major nuclear power plant disaster at Fukushima, Japan.

There are those today who would have us believe that human social life is based on something called *reciprocal altruism*. Simply put, it is said that human beings have an ingrained tendency to do something for other people when they are reasonably sure that the favor, whatever it is, will be returned—if not in kind, at least in some other way having equal value.[6]

It may be that most human beings do have what might be called an innate sense of fairness that first begins to become apparent in their dealings with others quite early in childhood.[7] Acknowledging this is a far cry from saying that all of us are always concerned about whether we are getting truly equal return on the time, energy, and resources we "spend" not on ourselves but on others. Available evidence suggests to the contrary that most of us are generally and simply predisposed to be kind and helpful to others. As two investigators observed not long ago (rather cryptically perhaps): "Individuals appear to have authentically prosocial preferences that drive cooperation in ways not consistent with rationalist explanations."[8]

The primatologist Joan B. Silk has observed that there is good evidence that although people value reciprocity in their relationships with their friends, they may actually avoid keeping a careful accounting of benefits given and received, and many may even become offended if friends reciprocate immediately and directly. "Thus, the dynamic of friendship," she observes, "does not fit the logic of models of reciprocity and presents a puzzle for evolutionary analysis."[9]

But is figuring out why it might be wise to have friends regardless of the expense, so to speak, really puzzling? The tsunami catastrophes in 1998, 2004, and 2011 point in the direction of at least one good reason it might be short-sighted to be too calculating and cold-hearted about attending to the costs and benefits of maintaining good ongoing relationships with others. Who could possibly have predicted how much people would need others in the wake of these terrible events? Devastating earthquakes and tsunami may not happen all that often in any of our lives, but aren't they just extreme illustrations of the greater truth that human beings survive by having other people in their lives? After all, in the game or battle called life, nobody really knows what might happen next. From this down-to-earth perspective, friendship is not just a kind of spiritual bling, a costly luxury item—and certainly not a benefit that can be effectively reduced to simple bean counting.[10]

EVEN NOWADAYS IN the golden age of Google and Wikipedia there are those who are still inclined to believe that there is at least one remote place left where old-fashioned savagery, skullduggery, deceitful treachery, and perhaps cannibalism, too, still hold sway despite whatever refined roles friendship, reciprocity, and civic discourse may play in most other places around the world. I am referring, of course, to the place we have just been talking about—the massive and rugged island of New Guinea in the southwest Pacific, the second largest island on earth. Under the banner headline "Cannibal Isle for Prince Charles," for instance, the journalist Deborah Sherwood in the racy popular British tabloid *Daily Star* on September 3, 2012 exclaimed to her readers that Charles and his wife Camilla were going to be braving 1,000 cannibals on their Diamond Jubilee tour around the world in a month's time. "They will visit the remote South Pacific island of Papua New Guinea where cannibals make soup from genitals and eat human brains raw. Some travelers fear to even set foot on the island because they are so scared."[11]

Not a banner moment for British journalism. What I have found on New Guinea's northern coastline since 1990 that has led me to see to the contrary that the custom there of inheriting friendships with families in other communities near and far—despite the astonishing linguistic diversity of this part of the world—has contributed directly to a remarkable story of social and cultural stability in one of the world's most environmentally challenging places. As improbable as it may sound, we have even been able to use the tools and techniques of modern archaeology to piece together some of the revealing ancient history of human friendship in this admittedly remote corner of the world.

6

A Wimpy Idea

IT WAS 1990. I was in Papua New Guinea. It was then and there that I began to question how most of us conventionally think about friendship. Some may not share this view, but wouldn't most of us agree that although friendships are nice to have, we can do without them? Aren't moms and dads, brothers and sisters, aunts and uncles, and other kin, too, much more important than friends, with or without the benefits that modern friendship sometimes bestows? Possibly, but in April and May that year something began to seem not quite right to me about this traditional view of friendships as nice but not necessary.[1]

What happened then that started changing my mind about the role of friendship in human evolution and history? I can pinpoint the day, if not the time. I was in a small hotel in Port Moresby, the capital city and main port of entry on this huge island's south coast (Figure 2). My research colleague Rob Welsch and I had just returned from the north side of the island where I had suddenly, and quite dramatically, come down with a bad case of malaria.

According to the World Health Organization, an average of 1.5 to 1.8 million suspected cases of malaria are seen at health care facilities annually in Papua New Guinea. This disease is the leading cause of all outpatient hospital visits, and the fourth leading cause of hospital admissions. Malaria is now endemic in every one of the country's nineteen provinces, including those that until fairly recently were malaria free. Together with pneumonia, malaria accounts for one-third of all recorded deaths.[2]

Although I was finally getting over the attack, I was still feeling weak and exhausted. If you have never had malaria, count yourself lucky. The symptoms of the disease can include headache, fever, fatigue, nausea, and vomiting. But it is the chills and sweating that really knock you down. The modest word

FIGURE 2   Map of the southwest Pacific Islands. (*Artist*: Jill Seagard.)

"chills" doesn't even begin to describe the shaking you experience. Yes, it's dramatic, just like in the movies.

After checking into our hotel, Rob had gone off to visit a friend of ours in town who was also, like the two of us, an anthropologist. Since I was finally getting better, I didn't feel too abandoned. Rob was anxious to tell our friend about what we had found up there on the remote north coast near the small town of Aitape—a place that had figured prominently in the deadly confrontations of World War II in the Pacific.

Rob returned to our hotel after the visit visibly angry and crestfallen. We both had thought for sure that when Rob related to him what we had learned about how friendships between families in different, and often distant, communities on the coast are passed down from one generation to the next, our professional colleague, too, would at once see how important this fact is. Knowing this helps explain, for example, why people in northern New Guinea share so much in common although people in different villages there often speak different, sometimes even radically different, languages. Hence Rob had been dismayed when on hearing what Rob had to report about these inherited friendships, our friend and fellow anthropologist had simply retorted: "Friendship? That's a pretty wimpy concept."

It is possible that this terse remark had not been intended as an insult. Nonetheless, it did hit home. When Rob told me later what had been said, I was shocked. Why would anyone with a PhD in Anthropology from one of America's finest universities be so quick to dismiss friendship as wimpy?

MY HIGH SCHOOL physics teacher liked to say that the obvious is seldom seen. I have come to see friendship as a fine example supporting his favorite maxim. Most of us seem to take our friendships so much for granted that we don't see them as a big deal. I am convinced this is a mistake.

Recall, for example, how Baron von Pufendorf and his contemporaries in the 17th and 18th centuries had described what they saw as the "natural state of man" before we had started going down the supposedly long road toward civility, cultivation, and exalted nobility. They had held several elementary ideas to be more or less self-evident, just as many today still similarly see them as reasonable and undoubtedly correct. One is the premise that if we are to gain from living together socially with others of our kind without giving into their unreasonable demands and possible abuses we have got to understand human nature. As Rousseau put it: "how shall we know the source of inequality between men, if we do not begin by knowing mankind?"

As a counterpoint to this idea, it was also said that we need to acknowledge and do our best to live up to an equally self-evident truth, one long credited by many to the Creator himself. This is the notion that we are *not* animals, and therefore we need to do our best to not behave like brutes. Far from it—we are something special, perhaps even God's favored creation. In short, we are different from other creatures in important, even divine, ways. We have souls, for example. They do not. Or so it was often assumed.

Third, it was also taken more or less as self-evident that it is natural and entirely rational for each of us to be self-interested. True, the Enlightenment thinker Thomas Hobbes took the idea of looking out for No. 1 to an extreme when he claimed that "it is manifest that during the time men live without a common power to keep them all in awe, they are in that condition which is called war; and such a war as is of every man against every man."[3] Others, however—Samuel von Pufendorf, for instance—had a less jaundiced view of human nature. For Pufendorf, self-interest is understandable and entirely justifiable up to a point, so long as self-interest does not become downright selfishness, true greed, treachery, or any of the other possible and assorted human sins.[4]

A fourth characteristic of Enlightenment thinking about human nature is the presumption that back when the descendants of Adam and Eve were all still living in a state of nature, people had no real need for friends because everyone then had been able to live out their lives in solitude in small family groups, or perhaps even as solitary forest dwellers. Recall Pufendorf's claim that this had been a time when "nearly every male set up a household for himself." Even Rousseau—who supposedly had a benevolently positive view of our primeval human story, but who really did not stand out from the rest in this regard[5]—found it "impossible to conceive why, in a state of nature, one man should stand more in need of the assistance of another, than a monkey or a wolf of the assistance of another of its kind."[6]

THE ENLIGHTENMENT AS a period in Western history, art, and culture is conventionally said to have been fostered by the scientific and philosophical advances of mid-17th-century scholars and to have lasted until the upheavals of the French Revolution during the final years of the 18th century. Although nowadays the word "savage" is generally used to label someone or something as wild, furious, seething, out of control, brutal, cruel, ferocious, and so on, it is worth keeping in mind that during the Enlightenment, Thomas Hobbes's claim that "savages" living in a state of nature are (or were) inherently cruel, bloodthirsty, and violent was an extreme interpretation of life at the beginning of social history. As we have now briefly discussed, savagery was commonly seen then more as a state of being—a way of life—than as an emotional predisposition.[7] The hallmark of savagery was not so much its barbaric ways as its political fragmentation and social isolation. As described, for example, in the entry under *savages* in Denis Diderot's famous 18th century French encyclopedia: "There is this difference between *savage* and barbaric peoples, that the first form small scattered nations which prefer never to unite with others, in place of which the barbarians often unify, & this occurs when one chief submits to another." Significantly, as this same entry then further states: "Natural liberty is the sole object of the policy of the *savages*; with that liberty, only nature and the climate exercise dominance over them."[8]

In other words, although nowadays the term "savagery" brings to mind acts of violence and treachery, during the Enlightenment this same word could embody and call to mind such noble ideals as liberty, freedom, and independence—ideas enshrined at the end of the Enlightenment in the famous words "life, liberty, and the pursuit of happiness" displayed for all to see in the opening lines of the American Declaration of Independence.[9]

IN 1990 WHEN Rob Welsch and I visited the Sepik coast for the first time (Figure 3), the Enlightenment had been over for two centuries, for better or

FIGURE 3 Fish weir at Sissano Lagoon, Sepik coast, 1990. (*Photograph*: author.)

for worse. Although the ageless question *What is human nature?* had certainly not lost any of its tinder-like knack for sparking rancorous debate, few at the close of the 20th century were still writing about the state of nature before human beings had entered into a more cultivated state of society— although there were (and there still are today) archaeologists, primatologists, and even social anthropologists who seemed to be channeling Thomas Hobbes or Jean-Jacques Rousseau in their writings about ancient or modern hunter-gatherers.[10]

Even so, it dumbfounded Rob and me that our friend and fellow anthropologist would dismiss friendship as a wimpy concept. Surely he knew that in the popular press, travel brochures, cable television documentaries, and even some learned science and social science journals the state of nature envisioned by Rousseau, Hobbes, and others was not only alive and well, but was called New Guinea? Surely he knew that for many outsiders a place like New Guinea continued to be seen as a place where savage violence, treachery, cannibalism, and warfare continued to hold sway. How could any anthropologist not see that inheriting friends generation after generation in places near and far on the Sepik coast was a fact of life that flew directly in the face of centuries of foreign prejudice, ignorance, and belief?

Wimpy? I don't think so.

7

In the Footsteps of A. B. Lewis

ROB WELSCH AND I had not gone out to New Guinea in 1990 thinking we would end up studying anything even remotely like friendship. Instead we wanted to see firsthand whether it would be worthwhile to mount a museum expedition to this part of the world. This was the first time for both of us on the island's north coast. However, we had each done anthropological field work before in Papua New Guinea (PNG), the modern nation-state that includes the eastern half of New Guinea Island as well as many other neighboring islands, large and small. Rob had lived among the Ningerum of western central PNG in the late 1970s as part of his PhD training in medical anthropology at the University of Washington. I had done my field work on Bougainville Island in the North Solomons Province in 1969–1970 for a PhD degree in Anthropology from Harvard University.

Why were we thinking of doing new field work in northern PNG? I had been the curator of Oceanic Archaeology and Ethnology at the Field Museum of Natural History in Chicago since September 1971. Rob had started working at the Museum in the mid-1980s as a research associate in the Department of Anthropology. We went out to PNG in the spring of 1990 because of what is at the Museum.

In the years since we first began working together in the late 1980s, Rob Welsch has become one of the world's leading experts on what has been called the "museum period" in anthropology. He argues that a better label would be the "expedition period." In any case, you can find no better example of what either label means than the Field Museum.[1]

"The Field," as it is affectionately known, was established in 1893 near the end of the World's Columbian Exposition, also called the Chicago World's Fair, to take responsibility for the scientific collections from around the world on exhibit at the fair. These collections had been assembled for display there as a tangible, visible way of taking the pulse of the world 400 years after the arrival of Christopher Columbus in the New World in 1492.

By the time of the fair, there was great demand in Europe and the United States for curios and other types of "native handicrafts" made in places still seen both by Europeans and Americans as far-off, exotic, and agreeably dangerous, as well. Why there was such intense demand back then is now debated, but undoubtedly one of the reasons was that "rude things" were viewed by many as confirming and bearing mute witness to the "Progress of Civilization"—which was a coded way of asserting the ambitious claim that Europeans and Americans, unlike other people on earth, had succeeded brilliantly in lifting themselves up by their own bootstraps far above the level of the "primitive savage."

Frederick Ward Putnam of Harvard, the chief scientist in charge of the anthropology displays at the Chicago fair, made this popular Euro-American boast abundantly clear in what he wrote for an official guidebook to the 1893 Exposition: "The first rude attempts in human art and industry are here illustrated, and form a striking contrast to the splendors of modern civilization so lavishly displayed on every side [i.e., to be seen elsewhere at the Fair in the buildings and kiosks dedicated to introducing visitors to the fair to such modern-day marvels as electricity and neon lights, the hamburger, Juicy Fruit gum, and the Ferris Wheel]."[2]

Whatever the full mix of their motivations, museums around the world at the close of the 19th century were competing intensely with one another to find for their galleries collectable mementos testifying in demonstrable ways both to times long past through the acquisition of archaeological specimens, and also to the antique ways of wild savages seen as being stuck in the past, although living in the present. The competition between museums was so tough that at times there were even threats of lawsuits when the issue of exactly which museum deserved to collect precisely what was under dispute.[3]

From the "savage's" point of view, this strong foreign demand for their handicrafts was a godsend. People around the world who were seen by foreigners as being uncivilized began churning out "artifacts" and "specimens" to satisfy the foreign call for them. As a result, to put the matter delicately, knowing just where and how you could still collect the "real thing," rather than only such tawdry "new things," added genuine zest to the competitive quest for locating and getting museum-worthy collectables.

Then came World War I. After the war, foreign demand for rare and exotic items made by savage hands never returned to the prewar level of intensity and public interest. The museum period in Anthropology was over. Needless to say, anthropologists still went out to foreign places, but now they did so more to see firsthand and record what was going on "among natives in their villages" than to carry back stuff to be put in museum storerooms and shown off in glass-fronted display cases full of little labels and strange foreign names.

GIVEN WHAT I HAVE just related about late 19th and early 20th century museum history, it is hardly astonishing that the fledgling Columbian Museum of Chicago, which changed its name in 1894 to the Field Columbian Museum, and then in 1905 to the Field Museum of Natural History, participated vigorously in the rush to find good things to bring home. After all, the poet Carl Sandburg did not call Chicago "The City of Big Shoulders" for nothing.

One of the Field Museum's most notable and active collectors at the start of the 20th century was George A. Dorsey (1868–1931), who was the first person in the United States to receive a PhD in Anthropology—from my

FIGURE 4 The canoe that brought Lewis to Sapi village on Tumleo Island in 1909—looking back toward the New Guinea mainland. (© The Field Museum, CSA31730; *photograph*: Albert B. Lewis. Reprinted with permission.)

alma mater Harvard University. Dorsey served as Curator of Anthropology at the Field between 1897 and 1914. Much of his collecting was done in North America and Mexico, but in 1908 he left Chicago on an eight-month trip around the world collecting stuff in places as far-flung as Egypt, India, Japan, the Philippines, Java, and the South Seas.

Dorsey spent two months during this lengthy jaunt touring islands in the southwest Pacific, including New Guinea and the Solomons. When he got back to Chicago, he convinced the Museum's Administration and Board of Trustees that wonderful and rare things were still to be had out there in the Pacific for relatively little money. By all accounts, Dorsey had great powers of persuasion. The following year he was able to send the Museum's newest curator, Albert Buell Lewis (1867–1940), back to Oceania to do some serious collecting.

Lewis left Chicago in the spring of 1909, and did not return until the spring of 1913. He was definitely a serious collector. While away, he purchased 14,385 items and had them shipped back to Chicago. He also took nearly 2,000 large glass-plate photographs to illustrate afterwards what life and times were like then in the Great South Sea (Figure 4).

Given the sheer volume of his shipments home, it is easy to see why scholars working with what is today called the "Lewis Collection" sometimes go away from Chicago after visiting the Museum a bit discouraged, to say the least. What Lewis had been able to learn firsthand about what he was collecting was often quite limited. Hence the information available today in the Museum's catalog records and computerized database on any given item in this Collection may be so minimal that it can be challenging, if not impossible, to fathom what the item in question was supposed to be used for, how it had been made, its social meanings, and perhaps, too, its spiritual and religious significance.

IN THE MID-1980S, Rob and I began wondering whether doing field work in New Guinea "in the footsteps" of A. B. Lewis might be a good way to learn more about the many thousands of things made there that Lewis had shipped back to Chicago before World War I. We also wanted to see if any of the customs and traditions Lewis had seen and photographed had somehow managed to survive the passage of time and the impact of World War II on this island's widely scattered communities.

We were especially interested in exploring the Sepik coast for two reasons. First, many of the items in Lewis's vast collection had come from places on this coast. Second, his field notes about these particular items include details not only about where on the coast he had purchased what he had obtained there, but also about where the sellers had themselves obtained the items in question. Both kinds of information seemed to us to be invaluable, since knowing where things not only had been made but also locally traded between places might help us reconstruct past social and economic relationships between communities there at the turn of the 20th century. (Remember, this was before our first trip to the Sepik coast in 1990, so we did not yet know that a much better way of talking about such relationships there is to call them inherited friendships.)

However, many of our professional colleagues outside the Field Museum were not at all convinced by our reasons for wanting to do new anthropological field research on the Sepik coast. In fact, they were often blunt in telling us that it would be utterly pointless to go to this part of the world to explore the research prospects there. Surely, they said, little if anything Lewis had seen and recorded could possibly have survived all that had happened in northern New Guinea since Lewis's turn-of-the-century investigations.

WHEN ROB AND I were finally able to visit the Sepik coast briefly in 1990 on research funding from the Walgreen Foundation, Rob was keen to hire a small boat to take us over as soon as possible from the small mainland town of Aitape where we were staying to Tumleo Island, one of the several beautiful small coral islands just off the Aitape coast. Lewis had first stepped ashore on Tumleo—locally famed for its handmade pottery—on Thursday, September 16, 1909.

We landed at Sapi, a village on the south side of the island facing Aitape a few kilometers away. This is the beach where Lewis, too, must have landed. When we climbed out of the outboard boat that had brought us over from the mainland, nobody was around except for a few small children, an elderly woman plaiting a palm-leaf basket, and an elderly man—who was sitting on a log on the beach painting a small dugout canoe with black paint from a can.

Here was someone who clearly looked like the sort of local person we needed to talk to, someone plainly knowledgeable about how folks there made things (the canoe was a promising sign), and someone who also looked old enough that he might be able to tell us what he had heard from his parents or grandparents about what life on Tumleo had been like back decades earlier in Lewis's day.

We introduced ourselves, and soon Rob was sharing cigarettes with him. He told us his name was Leo Naway. Finally Rob got around to explaining to him in greater detail why we had come over from Aitape. Ever the dutiful assistant, I got out one of our big blue ring-binders filled with pictures of objects from Tumleo Island in the Lewis Collection at the Museum that we had brought with us from Chicago.

Mr. Naway was obviously charmed by our photographs. I pride myself on being able to read body language, but in this instance, the task was not difficult. Rob began to probe gently to discover what Mr. Naway might be able to tell us about the diverse objects shown in our pictures. This was not an easy job. By then, the three of us were surrounded by smiling and giggling children, all of whom were trying to get a peek at what the strangers had brought with them.

Naway patiently answered our questions, but finally he evidently decided that it was time to respond to our inquiries in a different way. He had just come upon our pictures of ceramic cooking pots made on Tumleo many decades earlier. Back in Lewis's day, women were the potters on the island (as they are still). Mr. Naway may have felt it would be easier to talk about such things if a woman joined our impromptu conversation.

He called out to his daughter-in-law Helen. When she appeared and had been introduced, he asked her to go into her house and bring out something for the two American visitors to see. She went in, and soon returned with

FIGURE 5 Rob Welsch and Helen Naway at Sapi Village on Tumleo Island, 1990. (*Photograph*: author.)

two clay cooking pots (Figure 5). These pots had been made on Tumleo by her mother only shortly before our arrival. Both were nearly identical to the pre–World War I clay pots from Tumleo at the Museum.

WE HAD THE same déjà vu experience everywhere that we went on this coast during the next few days in 1990. When we started showing people our photographs, they would disappear into their homes. Again and again, they would bring out newly made items for us to see. Again and again, they were able to match what was in our museum photographs item for item. Given more time on the coast, it was plain that anyone could easily put together a contemporary collection nearly identical to Lewis's old collection in Chicago, item for item. This is precisely what we did during our longer return trips to this coast later in the 1990s.

To be sure, some of the things still being made on this coast displayed clear signs of change since Lewis's visits there in 1909 and 1910.[4] For example, people were now commonly using colorful imported nylon twine to make fishing nets rather than locally collected plant fibers. And although baskets and fish traps were still being constructed out of native plant materials, women were sometimes adding colorful pieces of plastic and nylon to give them added charm. Similarly, some people now had modern cars and outboard motors, and everybody loved to go over to Aitape to shop when they could. But setting aside such obvious signs of the "outside world," what we first saw was proof that local crafts and traditions were most definitely not dead on this coast. What we were witnessing was showing us firsthand a degree of continuity between the past and the present that astounded us, especially given what our research colleagues back home in the United States had been telling us would undoubtedly be the case.

8

Confronting the Obvious

EVEN IF IT is true that the obvious is seldom seen, presented with the obvious staying power of local crafts, customs, and traditions on the Sepik coast, it would be hard to ignore an equally obvious question. Why? Or more to the point, *how*? How on earth had it been possible for people on this coast to remain so true to their own ways despite all that the 20th century had thrown at them?

With research funding from the National Science Foundation and the National Endowment for the Humanities, Rob Welsch and I were able to return to New Guinea in the mid-1990s. Between March 1993 and February 1994, for instance, we carried out an extensive dual anthropological and archaeological program of investigations to document how social, political, and economic ties among communities both near and far along the Sepik coastline are framed and supported by widely shared ideas, conventions, and expectations about how people ought to behave toward one another as friends.

The ethnographic objects at the Field Museum directly of interest to us as museum curators—for example, locally made cooking pots, bows and arrows, woven baskets, and the like—were bought by A. B. Lewis and others many decades ago at villages along the 440 miles (710 km) of coastline between the international border with Indonesia in the west and the modern town of Madang in the east. Too big an area to tackle as anthropologists. The main focus of our own research in the 1990s, therefore, was chiefly the small town of Aitape and nearby offshore islands located in the 125 miles (200 km) of coastline between Serra (Serai) Village west of Aitape and the modern town of Wewak to the east.

Except for the harbors at Madang and Wewak in Papua New Guinea, and Jayapura (formerly Hollandia) and Sarmi to the west in Indonesia—each of which is today a center of commerce of some local importance—most of this long and rather straight shoreline is steep, swampy, or in other ways uninviting, is sparsely inhabited, and has relatively little to offer the commercial markets of the world other than inland forest timber.

We established our field headquarters on Ali Island just off the coast at Aitape and immediately to the east of Tumleo. Working with Wilfred Oltomo from the Papua New Guinea National Museum and Art Gallery in Port Moresby, we visited more than 80 villages in some 42 communities. We made extensive collections of locally made contemporary items for the Field Museum and the National Museum in nearly all of these communities, with important collections from about 30 of them.

People who don't work in museums may not always appreciate that what is key about museum collections is not just what's in them—however rare, unusual, beautiful, or revealing—but also what is known and recorded about what's in them. From this perspective, what we were hearing about the things we were collecting from people locally and how such things were often given away to friends near and far was at times amazing.

New Guinea is famous for the diversity of its languages, popularly said to number about 1,000. Linguists report, for example, that more than 60 different languages belonging to perhaps 24 major language groupings are spoken along the coastline between Jayapura and Madang. The explanation for so many languages almost invariably favored by most people who have never been to New Guinea is that people there must live unbelievably isolated lives—perhaps because of the ruggedness of the mountains and treacherous disease-infested swamps, or alternatively due to human barriers of long standing such as warfare and rampant witchcraft (Figure 6).

We were astonished, therefore, to learn from one man on Tumleo Island that he had inherited friendships with other families in 15 different communities spread out over a geographic distance of 155 miles (250 km) where 10 languages different from his own mother tongue are spoken. Similarly, at the village of Ulau on the mainland just east of Aitape, another person told us about his friendships in 15 communities over a distance of 75 miles (120 km) where 8 languages other than his own are in use. Yet another man we talked with on Tarawai (Tendanye) Island just off the Sepik coast east of Aitape had friends in 33 communities over a distance of 168 miles (270 km), where at least 18 languages other than his own Boiken language are spoken. Almost as astonishing, at Kep yet farther east and nearer to the mouth of the Sepik

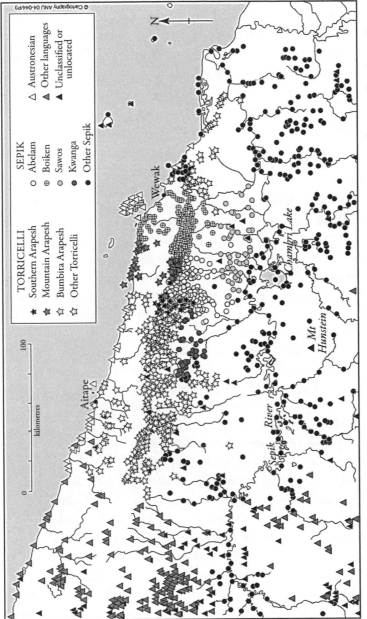

FIGURE 6 Geographic distribution of language families in the Sepik region of northern New Guinea. (*Source:* Allen, Bryant J. 2005. The place of agricultural intensification in Sepik foothills prehistory, figure 3. In *Papuan pasts: Cultural, linguistic and biological histories of Papuan-speaking peoples*, Andrew Pawley, Robert Attenborough, Jack Golson, and Robin Hide, eds. pp. 585–623. Pacific Linguistics No. 572. Canberra: Australian National University. Reproduced with permission.)

River, another person interviewed had friendships in 28 communities spread out over 86 miles (140 km) where 10 different languages other than his are spoken.

These statistics are impressive, and add weight to the idea that inheriting friendships in different places on this coast, far from being wimpy, takes a great deal of work, at least when it comes to being understood! What is equally impressive is that although a great many different languages are spoken on this coast, and each local community, therefore, may have its own word for "friend," everybody shares basically the same ideas—the same values—about what makes someone a good friend, and about how friends should behave toward one another.[1]

In this regard, it is important to stress that inherited friendships on this coast have little to do with the sorts of commercial activities generally called trade or barter. Instead, when friends give one another such things, what's involved are seen as gifts, not purchases. No bargaining or haggling is involved—and definitely no discussion of the value, quality, or price of anything. This would be ill mannered. There is also a strong ethic of generosity— not in the competitive sense of wanting to give someone much more than he or she can possibly give you in return as a way of shaming the person publicly and thereby proving your superiority. Rather, the aim is to avoid being labeled publicly as tightfisted or ungrateful.

What seems particularly important is that people in this part of the world gain a great deal of personal satisfaction from being out and about visiting friends, joking with them, feeling so warmly connected with people in other places, and getting to know their children who will inherit these friendships—just as their own children will do on their parents' death.

This having been said, I should add that what these traditional family friendships mean to different people on this coast does vary from person to person depending, in part, on individual and family needs, as well as on how interested the individuals involved are in keeping old friendships alive and cultivating new ones. For example, families on Ali, Tumleo, and the other small offshore islands near Aitape need to get sago (one of this locality's most important starch foods) and building materials from their friends on the mainland. People living in mainland communities, on the other hand, generally are able to be much more self-sufficient. They may value their inherited friendships on the islands and elsewhere along the coast less out of a sense of need and more as a ready-built social network ensuring hospitality, safe passage, and good times during travels away from home.

PEOPLE ON THE Sepik coast have told us also that in earlier times before Europeans came to try to impose foreign rule there, inherited friends could also be counted on to help you defend your family and community against marauders. Furthermore, your friends could be counted on to help you seek revenge against offenders. We were told, however, that open reprisals were rare events in the past, perhaps because it was well known by one and all both near and far that attacks on one community would inevitably lead to retaliations not only by anyone who happened to survive, but also by their friends—drawn from here, there, and elsewhere.

Stepping back from these particular details, what became clear during our field work in 1993–1994 was that these friendships form a vast network of intersecting social relationships that in its entirety encompasses thousands of people in scores of places along the coast, on the offshore islands, and into the hinterland behind the coast, as well. No one actually knows, or for that matter really needs to know, the full extent of this social realm, this encompassing social network. The important fact is that this network not only works, but it does so *not* because everybody involved speaks the same language, has exactly the same customs and traditions, looks on marriage or politics the same way, and so on, but rather because everyone involved shares the same basic underlying values, ideals, and expectations about how friends should behave toward one another—to put it in a word—as friends.

9

The Archaeology of Friendship

IN LIGHT OF what I have just reported to you about inherited friendships on the Sepik coast, do you agree with me that this part of the world almost sounds too good to be true? "How long have these friendships been going on?" was certainly a thought that occurred to Rob Welsch and me often while we were working there intensely in the 1990s. We knew that many anthropologists believed that people in New Guinea started traveling between places near and far only after the arrival of Europeans had put a halt to their alleged penchant for intervillage warfare. Under this scenario, therefore, perhaps the exchange of objects between what 20th century anthropologists were calling "trading partners" rather than inherited friends was a substitute for war, an alternative way of resolving conflicts between communities.[1] Yet even before we had learned what we now know, we were pretty sure that people on the Sepik coast simply must have been handing down their friendships to their children long before Europeans began showing up on this coast in the late 19th century with a gleam in their eye hoping to tap into whatever riches New Guinea might have to offer them.

Germany assumed colonial rule over northeastern New Guinea in 1884 under the banner of "The Protectorate of the New Guinea Company." By the turn of the century, the name had been changed. This part of the island was being called the "Imperial Colony of German New Guinea." Whatever the label, the Germans were there to make money. Bringing "the white man's peace" to their new possession ultimately became an expedient thing to do, but altruism was not a priority item on the agenda at the start of their colonial experience in the South Seas. What is more, their "rule" over their new imperial colony was for the most part the political equivalent of "only skin deep." These foreign intruders largely stuck to the coast and offshore islands, and left the huge interior of New Guinea to fend for itself. As the historian Stewart Firth has written: "The overwhelming majority of New Guinea's people, perhaps five in every six, never saw a single German in the thirty years of German rule, even though some of these no doubt came into possession of a material artifact of German origin such as a piece of hoop iron or a nail."[2]

AN IMPERIAL GOVERNMENT station was not established at Aitape until 1906 (the concrete remains of the old German-era jail can still be seen on Kiap Point overlooking the town below). Even with this solid German foothold in place, according to Firth, the "Aitape district was an object lesson in the limits of German power."[3] As the official annual report for 1907–1908 described the realities of the situation, it was proving extraordinarily difficult for this outpost "to gain any influence or to achieve recognition of its authority."

Rob and I were fairly confident, therefore, that even if they had been much more effective than they evidently were at imposing law and order German-style, the 25 years between the beginning of German rule in 1884 and A. B. Lewis's arrival on the coast in 1909 could not possibly have been time enough for the institution of inheriting friendship to become so well entrenched there. Our firsthand observations about this local social institution led to the inescapable conclusion that people all along this coast had been linked with one another in various ways for a very long time. But for how long? How many decades, centuries, or millennia?

Hyman Marx, a jovial and wonderfully opinionated curator in the Department of Zoology at the Field Museum many years ago loved to tell anyone who would listen about the advice on how to succeed in science that he had been given many years before by another curatorial humorist at the Museum: "Never go anywhere for the first time." Doing the first science in a previously unstudied part of the world may sound romantic and adventurous, but there is an obvious downside. Pioneering in science often means not having a clue what on earth you will find.

IN 1996 ROB and I returned to Aitape on the Sepik coast with several colleagues from Australia and the PNG National Museum in Port Moresby to do the first archaeological excavations ever in this part of the world. We wanted to see if we could pin down at least some of the local history of inherited friendships on this coast. True, this was not strictly speaking our "first time" at Aitape. However, this was the first time anyone had tried to dig there archaeologically. Although we were hopeful, we were totally unsure what, if anything, we would come across. We were not even sure that there was much of anything archaeological waiting for us to dig up.

The town of Aitape is only 3 degrees south of the equator. The tropical heat, humidity, and heavy rains that are a normal part of life in this part of the world are highly destructive of anything organic, such as houses, house posts, wood carvings, outrigger canoes, woven baskets, elaborate dance paraphernalia, and the like. Scratch items like these from the menu of things for an archaeologist to find on this coast, and there is not all that much left except for things, say, made out of stone or pottery such as stone axes and cooking pots. Although we did not return to Chicago late in 1996 empty-handed, what we brought back home to study more closely in the A. B. Lewis Memorial Laboratory just across from my office at the Museum would not look like much to most people. It was mostly just small bits and pieces of old pots and stone tools. And some bones, too.

Yet it was enough solid evidence, nonetheless, to be able to say with some confidence—now after years of laboratory study involving in some instances laser-based analytical techniques that were for the most part totally unheard of back in 1996—that the practice of inheriting friends in places often far from home has probably been on the Sepik coast for far longer than Rob or I ever dared imagine in the 1990s.

PIECING TOGETHER THE evidence for suggesting this as a conclusion has been much like what homicide detectives do on a regular basis, not at a crime scene, but back in their forensic laboratories. And during our laboratory investigations, we made some discoveries along the way that were totally unexpected—discoveries that not only confirm the wisdom of the old saying "expect the unexpected," but also strengthen the case for thinking that inheriting friends on the Sepik coast is a social convention that must be thousands of years old.

But I am getting ahead of my story. As Ivan Shatov says in Fyodor Dostoyevsky's 1872 novel *The Possessed* (also called *Demons* or *The Devils*): "To cook your hare you must first catch it." First, therefore, what are some of the bits and pieces we brought back to Chicago?

Between the middle of September and the end of October 1996, we had completed 14 archaeological excavations ranging in area from 50 cm² to 300 cm² (20–118 in.) on the crests of the low foothills on the southeastern side of Aitape. Apparently due to the shallowness of the soil and the chemical destructiveness of tropical weather, only two of these mainland excavations yielded well-preserved pottery sherds—archaeologists generally prefer using this term for broken pieces of pottery, although many other people call them "shards"—as well as worked pieces of stone, shells (mostly from brackish and lagoon species), and bones (both human and animal). In addition, three 100 cm² excavations 10 meters apart that reached a maximum depth of approximately 168 cm (66 in.) below the present land surface were done on Tumleo Island, which is 4 km (2.5 m.) off the Aitape coast.

When all of the things we dug up in 1996 were tallied at our field headquarters at Aitape before returning to Chicago, we were pleased to see that we had gathered a great deal of substantial "material evidence." Laboratory analyses of these archaeological finds literally took years to complete. But we now know, for instance, that the two new pots Helen Naway showed Rob and me on Tumleo in 1990—you may recall that they had been made by her mother shortly before our visit that year—were material witness to a pottery-making tradition on this island that was at least 1,500 to 2,000 years old (Figure 7). Moreover, analyses at the Museum by my research colleague Mark Golitko of the clays used by ancient potters on Tumleo during the last two millennia hint that even the recipes used by different potters on this island when blending

FIGURE 7 Pottery-making on Tumleo Island, Sepik coast, 1909. (© The Field Museum, CSA31729; *photograph*: Albert B. Lewis. Reproduced with permission.)

together clays of different sorts to create a mixture suitable for making good strong and reliable pots have evidently been handed down there from mother to daughter for centuries, possibly even for millennia.

There is other archaeological evidence, too, pointing to the historical longevity of the art of pottery-making on Tumleo Island. We have found that the designs used by potters to decorate their nearly finished pots before firing them have had the same underlying design logic to them for countless years. Although the design motifs used have changed over the past 2,000 or so years, the changes have not been chaotic or random. Far from it, the designs have evolved in a surprisingly orderly fashion—again confirming that modern pottery-making on Tumleo is the living expression of an enduring artistic tradition now thousands of years old.[4]

I think these findings are telling us something important about how life has been lived on this coast over the course of these many centuries. Like inherited friendships, pottery-making, too, is a family matter, a family tradition. Hence the survival of the potter's craft on Tumleo Island, the handing down of recipes for blending clays together, and the continuous use of historically related decorative motifs, when considered together, suggest that life on this coast has also been remarkably stable—a likelihood that is seemingly not at all in keeping with what most people would expect of an allegedly savage and dangerous place like New Guinea.

MOST ARCHAEOLOGISTS LOVE potsherds, but most archaeologists are willing to concede that it is a good idea to have other evidence, too, when you are trying to figure out what happened in the past. Fortunately in 1996 we also dug up and temporarily brought back temporarily to Chicago for analysis hundreds and hundreds of flakes of obsidian—a natural glass of volcanic origin—that had been carried to Aitape and the nearby offshore islands in ancient times from geological sources on far-off islands to the east and northeast of New Guinea where this natural glass has been mined for many millennia. When flaked, obsidian has extremely sharp edges, a trait that makes it perfect for shaving; for smoothing down woodcarvings like masks, bowls, or drums; for skin scarification; and for other purposes.

Thanks to recent analytical advances, we now know that people on the Sepik coast have been sufficiently well connected with people elsewhere that they have been able to get chunks of this useful and exotic natural material for many centuries from several different volcanic sources on islands to east and northeast of New Guinea. In the Museum's Elemental Analysis Facility, Golitko has used two new analytical techniques—portable X-ray fluorescence (pXRF) and laser ablation–inductively coupled plasma–mass spectrometry (LA-ICP-MS)—to determine the chemical composition of more than 1,600 pieces of this glass collected during our archaeological survey work in 1993–1994 and our excavations in 1996.[5]

Measuring the chemical composition of pieces of obsidian is valuable information because different volcanic sources are known to have different chemical profiles, or "signatures." By comparing the signatures of archaeological pieces of this glass (archaeologists like to call such pieces "specimens") found on the Sepik coast with the signatures of different known volcanic sources in the New Guinea region it becomes possible to pinpoint with remarkable accuracy exactly where the obsidian specimens originally came from.

Mark's analyses have established that communities on the Sepik coast and the nearby islands have had social and economic ties not only with people elsewhere on New Guinea Island, but also on other more distant islands, too, for at least the last 2,000 years—and quite possibly since the mid-Holocene around 6,000 to 7,000 years ago. Given what we now know about inherited friendship on this coast today and in the recent past, it seems likely, too, that obsidian glass probably reached the Aitape area through such social connections rather than by people, say, from Aitape or Tumleo themselves sailing directly all the way to where this glass can be mined.[6]

THERE IS OTHER evidence, too, for the enduring importance of inherited social ties between families living in different communities on this coast. Because no one had carried out excavations in the Aitape area prior our 1996 archaeological expedition, once back in the laboratory at the Field Museum my research colleague Dr. Esther Schechter and I not only had to start studying the pottery sherds brought to Chicago for analysis from a position of complete ignorance, but we also needed to proceed cautiously. We literally had to piece together the history of pottery-making as a local craft or industry on the Sepik coast potsherd by potsherd.

One design found on some of the sherds we were analyzing seemed bewildering. It was not a rare pottery design, but it looked basically just like a bunch of oddly gouged-out lines.

Then one day Micah Urban, a research volunteer working with us in the Lewis Laboratory, came across two small potsherds that he was able to glue together. The design that showed up on these two reunited sherds was totally unexpected. It did not take much imagination to see that the motif incised and impressed on them was almost certainly meant to be a stylized face—rather than just a random and chaotic bunch of little lines and impressions.

Micah's reassembled sherds were chronologically older than the oddly grooved sherds that had been so perplexing Esther and me. But once Micah showed us his discovery, we could see that some of the grooved designs we were struggling to interpret might also be elements, or design attributes, of motifs possibly also representing faces of some kind.

Esther and I went back to work and took another look at our enigmatic grooved sherds. Sure enough, we quickly saw that if you have Micah's design motif in your mind's eye, what we had been looking at was now—in effect—looking back at us. Those oddly grooved lines were not so odd after all. They often came together to form stylized pairs of "eyes." After we knew what to look for, we found numerous other examples of these mysterious eyes. We were still, however, not at all sure what to make of them.

At this point I need to add another element to the story. We had earlier noted an incised diamond-shaped design often found on sherds from pots made in the Aitape area during the last 500 years or so that we described as "eye-like"—although, to be honest, we were far from confident that this design was actually supposed to be seen as "eyes."

We had already seen, too, that potters in this part of New Guinea had often combined these diamond-shaped incised "eyes" with herringbone-like designs to create more complicated composite design patterns. With remarkable originality, we had begun calling this more intricate design the "eye & herringbone" motif.

However, Esther and I had been taking it for granted that short of climbing into a time machine and going back a few hundred years into the past to ask local potters to tell us what this eye & herringbone design was supposed to mean, there was absolutely no possible way for both of us to decipher correctly this particular motif's true symbolic intent, or meaning.

But we were forgetting the wisdom of the cliché "expect the unexpected."

ON ANOTHER DAY after Micah's discovery—I do not now recall precisely when this was—Esther and I were trying to figure out what had been the original shape of a certain kind of pot that had a rim, or "lip," that was distinctly triangular in cross section.

Now if a potsherd is big enough, it is often possible to arrive at a good idea of how big the original pot was, as well as its shape, by measuring a sherd's surface curvature. Said another way, if you put most potsherds on a table, you are able to rock them back and forth a little bit if they came from a pot that was round and had a rounded bottom—which is often the case since cooking pots with round rather than flat bottoms can be put directly on an open fire without smothering the flames.

On the occasion I am telling you about, Esther and I were in despair. Try as we did, we simply could not figure out what pots with such a distinctive triangular rim had once looked like. Finally I put one such sherd on the lab table in front of us, and started poking at it—exclaiming to Esther as I did so how frustrating it was not to be able to figure out the shape and size of the actual pot that had, so to speak, given it birth.

But then suddenly we both stared in amazement at this innocent little potsherd. *It wasn't rocking*. As a matter of fact, this little sherd was clearly as flat as a pancake. We soon realized that it was not a *potsherd* at all. It was really a *platter sherd*—a piece from a large, flat ceramic plate or platter (see a large plate or turkey platter in your mind's eye, and you've got it).

THIS FINDING WAS puzzling since there are absolutely no ceramic plates or platters in the collections from New Guinea at the Field Museum. In fact, I know of nowhere in the South Pacific where flat pottery dishes are made and used today in any traditional island setting, although I am quite certain that platters are now brought out on the fourth Thursday in November each year for serving the family celebratory dinner in the State of Hawai'i, and perhaps also in American Samoa.

You can understand, therefore, why Esther and I were mildly stunned to discover that we were dealing in some instances with platter sherds, not potsherds.

Little victories can be sweet, and as the saying goes, "whatever rocks your boat." Or doesn't rock your sherd. We were both thrilled. Who would have ever imagined such a find from the Sepik coast? It was the real thing— a prehistoric New Guinea platter sherd!

We were about to break for lunch, but I said to Esther that maybe we should take a moment and go into the collections storeroom of the Department of Anthropology to take a quick look at some of the wooden serving platters from the Sepik coast that I knew we had in storage there, since this part of New Guinea is famous for its carved and often quite beautiful wooden platters and bowls. Maybe these modern wooden vessels would help put our archaeological platter sherds in historical perspective.

After we had consulted the department's computerized collections database for the specific storeroom locations of the Museum's wooden platters, we went to Central Anthropology Storage to look for them.

FIGURE 8 Detail showing the "eye & herringbone" design on a shallow wooden bowl from Sissano, Sepik coast. (FMNH no. 144977, Voogdt and others Collection, 1913; © The Field Museum, 114370; *photograph*: John Weinstein. Reproduced with permission.)

Wouldn't you know that the first "specimen" we came across turned out to be a wooden platter that Rob and I had collected on the Sepik coast in 1993? I turned this wooden platter over, and I was both astonished and more than a little amused to find I had completely forgotten the design that had been carved around the rim on the underside. It was a design Esther and I knew well, since it was a common one on late prehistoric pottery made in the Aitape area. Yes, you have probably guessed it already. It was the design we were calling the eye & herringbone motif (Figure 8).[7]

Things were finally beginning to add up, although I am not going to try to tell you that Esther and I had reached the point where we were sure that what we were finding was the equivalent of 2 + 2 = 4. Looking back now, I can see that we had only begun then to assemble the needed clues.

10

The Sign of the Sea Turtle

ARCHAEOLOGISTS ARE NOW fairly certain that the art and craft of pottery-making arrived in the South Pacific around 3,250 to 3,500 years ago—probably brought in by a potter, or potters, arriving there from somewhere in island Southeast Asia. The technology involved then spread from island to island in the western Pacific at least as far east as Fiji, Tonga, and Samoa.¹

The first local Pacific potters left most of the pots they made undecorated, presumably because they intended them only for everyday use in cooking and food storage. However, they did occasionally put quite ornate designs on some of their creations—usually pots having unconventional shapes. Experts today refer to these fancy pots and dishes as "decorated Lapita ware"—a label derived from the name of an archaeological site in New Caledonia where this widespread pottery style was first definitively identified. New Caledonia is an archipelago in the Pacific to the south and east of New Guinea.

Archaeologists have had difficulty figuring out the meaning or meanings of the designs that the so-called Lapita people put on these unusual and fairly rare pottery vessels. Occasionally, however, some of the designs look like they are supposed to be seen as highly stylized drawings of faces of some kind. Nobody today can recall exactly who first had the bright idea, but several decades ago someone decided that these Lapita "face designs" are so human-like that they must be anthropomorphic. The idea then soon became popular in archaeological circles that these "faces" were probably intended by Lapita potters to be representations of their ancestors.

It is not clear why this symbolic interpretation became so quickly accepted by archaeologists and other experts working in Oceania. Many kinds of animals, real or imagined, have two eyes and other facial features that could be mistaken as human-like, especially when drawn on a clay pot in a very stylized fashion—as is true of these ornately decorated Lapita pots and dishes.

ALTHOUGH RARE AMONG the potsherds Esther and I were studying, once Micah had shown us the way, we began to suspect that some of the decorated potsherds we were examining might also have faces of some sort on them, not just enigmatic "eyes." If so, perhaps such faces might be evidence that pottery-making on Tumleo and elsewhere on the Sepik coast could be traced historically back over the centuries to the art and craft of Lapita pottery-making 3,000 or more years ago. Therefore, once Esther and I realized that at least some of the wooden platters and shallow bowls from the Sepik coast in the collections at the Field Museum have what we were calling the eye & herringbone design motif carved on them much like the designs we were finding on late prehistoric pottery in the Aitape area, we extended the scope of our museum studies to include all of the wooden bowls and platters from the South Pacific in the Museum's ethnographic collections. We wanted to see if there was more to eyes & herringbones than meets the eye, so to speak.

Although it took us a while to do so—we had to track down and examine more than 1,000 objects in the Museum's collections—eventually we were able to establish that the eye & herringbone motif is statistically the most common design or pattern carved on wooden platters and bowls in the Field's holdings brought back to Chicago from the Sepik coast by A. B. Lewis and others. Perhaps as revealing, it soon also became obvious that the eye & herringbone design was apparently *never* carved on wooden vessels made elsewhere in the Pacific a century or so ago. We began to have greater confidence, therefore, that we were on the trail of something good.

Then one day we finally hit pay dirt. We discovered that sometimes the patterns carved on Sepik bowls and platters are surprisingly lifelike. Specifically, we came across carved designs that were clearly intended by their artisans to be seen as representations of turtles (Figure 9).

Turtles? Why turtles? Via the Internet, I asked some of my research colleagues in the Pacific to help Esther and me track down whether—and if so, how—turtles might somehow fit into the historical puzzle we were piecing together. One of the individuals responding to my call for help was someone I did not then know—Regina Woodrom Luna, a marine biologist in Hawaiʻi working on a PhD in anthropology so that she could do a more effective job of alerting Pacific Islanders to the importance of protecting the world's sea turtles from extinction.

0 ⸺⸺ 5 cm

FIGURE 9 Wooden bowl or platter from Tandanye (Tarawai) Island, Sepik coast, 1908, 5 cm scale. (FMNH no. 148556, George A. Dorsey Collection, 1908; © The Field Museum, A114374d; *photograph*: John Weinstein. Reproduced with permission.)

Regina asked me to send her, if possible, pictures of some of the designs we were trying to figure out. I quickly did so as a reply email attachment. Just as quickly, she got back to me. Identifying the design I had sent her was a no-brainer for anyone who knows her sea turtles.

In its most complete form, what Esther and I had been calling the eye & herringbone motif was almost an exact portrayal of the track left on a sandy beach when a female sea turtle comes ashore to lay her eggs. Regina said she could even make a reasonable stab at guessing the species of sea turtle represented by this particular design (Figure 10).

There are five main sea turtle species in the Pacific: hawksbill (*Eretmochelys imbricata*), olive ridley (*Lepidochelys olivacea*), loggerhead (*Caretta caretta*), green (*Chelonia mydas*), and leatherback (*Dermochelys coriacea*). The walking gait of the first three species is symmetrical—diagonally opposite limbs move together. The gait of the latter two species, however, is a "powerstroke"—all the limbs extend and then retract simultaneously.

Although the tracks of the green and leatherback are similar from the point of view of locomotion, the designs we were finding on prehistoric pottery—and on historic and modern wooden bowls and platters—most

FIGURE 10 *Top left*: Green sea turtle on her way to a nesting site. (Photograph courtesy of Regina Woodrom Luna.). *Top right*: Track of a Green sea turtle, *Chelonia mydas*, at Atol das Rocas. *Bottom left*: Track rotated to emphasize similarity with design motif occurring on Wain Ware and modern wooden bowls and platters made on the Sepik coast (similarity first noted by Regina Woodrom Luna). (Photograph courtesy of Paula Baldassin. *Source*: http://www.seaturtle.org). *Bottom right*: Wain sherd. (*Artist*: Eric Wert.)

closely resemble tracks left by green sea turtles. This identification makes sense, too. Green and hawksbill turtles are evidently the two species traditionally most important to Pacific Islanders. And note that I just wrote *hawksbill*, not leatherback. And here's the punch line: hawksbills have a symmetrical gait, not a "powerstroke."

But again, why sea turtles? Evidently for a variety of reasons.

REGINA ARGUES THAT throughout the Pacific sea turtles have long been held to be sacred, even seen as the embodiment of gods. In the Marquesas, for example, the sea turtle could be used instead of a human sacrifice as a gift to the victor to end a war. Far from being surprised by such reverence, she has found during rescue work with sea turtles that even present-day residents and visitors to Hawai'i may cry, become filled with joy, scream, fight, and almost come to blows over the health of these magnificent animals. And not one person has been able to explain to her why they love turtles. In her words, "they just do." She adds, even so, that one of their characteristic traits in particular is undeniably remarkable.

As a sea turtle biologist, I have participated in necropsies of freshly deceased turtles. Therefore, I know the sea turtle's ability to live on land and in the sea or to breath air is not the most amazing thing about them. What stands out to anyone who has ever seen one killed is their ability to continue to make life-like movements long after they are dead. Even after severing their spinal column, removing their brain and all internal organs; leaving nothing but the shell with flippers and tail attached and a bit of fluids, that sea turtle is still 'swimming' over an hour later when you pick up the carcass to properly dispose of it.[2]

It is almost like icing on a cake to be able to report to you that turtles are also very much part of the Pacific archaeological record, particularly at places where Lapita potsherds are found. As Melinda Allen at the University of Auckland has summarized the situation, turtle bones in great numbers are invariably recovered from the oldest archaeological sites on islands in the central and eastern Pacific, parts of Oceania that were not colonized by human beings until about 3,000 years ago or even later—that is, until people making Lapita pots and their later descendants reached these more distant islands and archipelagoes. "So repetitive is the pattern that Pacific archaeologists now consider an abundance of turtle bone part of a suite of diagnostic signatures that identify human arrival in a pristine environment."[3]

Therefore, while neither Esther nor I would have ever dreamed that analyzing potsherds from the Sepik coast would set us on the trail or track of sea turtles in Pacific lore and religion, such was evidently the right way to resolve the puzzle we were piecing together. We are now fairly sure, in fact, that at least some—maybe most—of the "faces" sometimes put on Lapita pots and flat-bottomed dishes by their makers are *not* intended to be seen as human-like. Instead, they are probably the faces (as well as the eyes and beach tracks) of sea turtles.[4]

II

Drawing Conclusions

LIKE CRIME SCENE investigators, archaeologists must deal with what people do after the fact. Archaeologists sometimes find it frustrating that they cannot actually watch something like inherited friendships in action in the past right before their eyes—as Rob Welsch and I were able to do firsthand in the 1990s. But therein, too, is both the challenge and fun of doing archaeology.

It would be my guess that most crime scene investigators may see their job in the same way. The levels of uncertainty and frustration may not always be balanced by an exhilarating sense of challenge and excitement, but the rewards of doing this kind of after-the-fact research and educated guesswork are real enough. People wouldn't devote their lives to such work if it were only for the money, believe me.

Since in both forensic and archaeological investigations you cannot observe what people are doing, you have to determine instead what may be the most reasonable way of explaining what you actually do see before your eyes, namely just the surviving traces and residues of what happened. And as Dr. John Watson heard often (rather annoyingly so, I suspect) from his pal Mr. Sherlock Holmes, there is usually more than one likely way to explain how things have ended up looking the way they do after the fact, or after the crime.

The technical term for this kind of uncertainty is *equifinality*, a word that basically means that it is possible to get to more or less the same final resolve, or outcome, by different ways and means. Writing history would be much easier than it is if it were always possible to explain things in the very same way every time regardless of the time and place or prior events. But such is not the case. This is one of the chief reasons why historians are bemused by scientists who think every observable effect has one and only one cause. How naïve!

Given that this is a book about human nature and the role of friendship in human evolution, and not a book about history, archaeology, or science, I have not put out on the table for your inspection all of the material evidence we have gathered since 1990 concerning the anthropology and archaeology of inherited friendship as a social institution on the Sepik coast of New Guinea, only the following:

1. Contrary to what most people (including Rob and me prior to our first visit in 1990) assumed would be the case on this coast at the end of the 20th century, the local ways and traditional means observed and photographed by our predecessor A. B. Lewis before World War I were most definitely alive and well in the closing years of the last century despite all that the 20th century had thrown at these small communities beside the sea.

2. Despite the fact that people on this coast fled into the hills when northern New Guinea became a major battle line during World War II, after peace returned, they came home and picked up the pieces of their lives almost as if the war had never happened—so much so, that by the time Rob and I got there in the 1990s, we were able to duplicate the collections Lewis and others had made there more than three generations earlier.

3. As one result of the archaeological excavations we did in 1996, we now know that the art of pottery-making has evidently been an unbroken craft tradition on Tumleo Island—this area's major pottery-making center—for something like 2,000 years, and possibly for longer than this (although here I have not tried to give you the reasons we now have for suspecting this may be true).

4. Using sophisticated new laboratory techniques, Mark Golitko has been able to show also that different potters on Tumleo evidently have been, for hundreds and possibly thousands of years, faithful to their own distinctive family recipes for blending together clays from different natural sources to create mixtures suitable for making pots.

5. Mark has been able to establish that people on Tumleo and elsewhere on the Sepik coast have been obtaining obsidian glass from natural volcanic sources on islands to the east and northeast of New Guinea for 1,500 to 2,000 years, and possibly for 6,000 to 7,000 years, if not longer.

6. Esther Schechter and I have similarly been able to show through our own laboratory analyses that the designs that Sepik potters have been putting on their pots before firing them have been variations on a single stylistic design and symbolic tradition, a tradition we have now tentatively traced

all the way back to the beginning of pottery-making in the Pacific—specifically, to a style of ancient pottery in the southwestern Pacific called Lapita.

7. Using both our newly gained archaeological information, and data we have gleaned from the historic Sepik coast collections at the Field Museum, Esther and I have been able to challenge the long-accepted idea that the "face" designs sometimes put on Lapita pots 3,000 or more years ago are meant to be seen as anthropomorphic. Instead, the faces on Lapita vessels from thousands of years ago and certain seemingly stylized designs on historic and modern carved wooden bowls and platters made on the Sepik coast may be alternative ways of alluding to the same basic symbolic theme—sea turtles, and presumably also the spiritual as well as the more down-to-earth significance of such creatures in Pacific Islands life and lore.

These several lines of evidence are only circumstantial when it comes to deducing anything at all about the role of friendship in human history on the Sepik coast. This does not necessarily mean, however, that when taken together, this evidence is irrelevant, although it may not be possible to do what Sherlock Holmes always insisted should be done when making forensic deductions based on observed facts.

In *The Sign of the Four* (published in 1890), Sir Arthur Conan Doyle has his good detective explaining his procedure to Watson not once but twice in two differing ways. The first time around (1890, chapter 1): "Eliminate all other factors, and the one which remains must be the truth." Then again later (chapter 6): "How often have I said to you that when you have eliminated the impossible, whatever remains, however improbable, must be the truth?"

No archaeologist would be foolish or brave enough to try to sound as confident as Mr. Holmes about his or her forensic abilities and alertness to all relevant and observable facts. All archaeologists, even so, try to take a stab in the direction of living up to such an admirable example of how the best detective work should be done.

In this spirit, therefore, permit me put on an imaginary deerstalker cap so that we can get stuck into a case that Dr. Watson would have probably written down for consideration by Arthur Conan Doyle as *The Sign of the Sea Turtle*.

ON THE LABORATORY table in front of us are a variety of strange clues ranging in exotic detail all the way from the nesting imprints of turtle flippers on sandy beaches to allegedly anthropomorphic faces on ancient potsherds.

Lurking in what Holmes would call our "little brain attics" are two competing propositions, or hypotheses, about the significance, or insignificance, of our human capacity to make friends even with strangers. Our task is to decide which of these two alternative theories leads us to the most probable interpretation of the wholly unexpected tenacity of cultural traditions and social practices on the Sepik coast of the far-off island of New Guinea.

The first theory—let's call it the "Friendship Is Wimpy Hypothesis," or Hypothesis 1, for short—is the conventional wisdom that people are by nature so fundamentally aggressive and distrustful of one another that only an emotion as powerful as familial love can effectively control our animal urges and desires. Even then, considering the current high rates of domestic violence, child abuse, date rape, and the like, even love may not be powerful enough to be a decisive force for good in the world. Therefore, in view of how allegedly violent most of us are down deep inside, feelings as diffuse as friendship simply do not have a snowball's chance to influence human history or evolution. It would be basically absurd to suggest such a wimpy idea.

The alternative proposition, needless to say, is the one I call the Friendship Hypothesis. At the core of this idea—Hypothesis 2—is the claim not only that being good at making friends is a defining trait, or characteristic, of the species *Homo sapiens*, but also that our evolved capacity to do so is critical to our survival as a species. Why? Because even when there is no conscious intent for them to do so, *friendships by their very nature connect people with one another in ways that create amazingly far-reaching social networks capable of transmitting vitally useful information, mobilizing people to action, and in other ways, too, buffering individuals, families, and communities against the trials and tribulations of life.*[1]

Now let's get down to work. Given these two divergent hypotheses, which one best fits what is now known about the anthropology and archaeology of the Sepik coast?

IT IS A commonplace in science to say that it isn't a good idea to make explanations more complicated than they need to be. As Holmes says in *A Study in Scarlet* (1887): "Before turning to those moral and mental aspects of the matter which present the greatest difficulties, let the inquirer begin by mastering more elementary problems." In keeping with this dictum, let us consider the Sepik coast from the point of view of elementary if *A* and *B,* then *C* logic.

Given [*A*] how environmentally demanding, and at times downright deadly, this coast can be as a place to live and raise a family, and [*B*] how communities beside the coastal lagoons or on the small offshore islands are strategically all but indefensible against hostile attacks by outsiders (they are well exposed to marauding attacks by anyone intent on doing them harm, or worse), then I suggest that in keeping with Hypothesis 1, a reasonable inference would be [C] human history on this coast has been an often chaotic tale of social and demographic instability coupled with rapid and abrupt historical changes resulting from such natural catastrophes as earthquakes, droughts, and tsunamis, or from social disruptions such as open warfare, outside invasions, forced relocations, and the like. I would also suggest that such a depressing portrait of the past on this coast is one that would strike absolutely nobody anywhere else in the world as at all remarkable or unexpected. After all, we are talking about the dangerous and savage place called New Guinea are we not?

In support of this particular if *A* and *B*, then *C* proposition, it is not hard to find expert testimony favoring this negative (and conventional) set of expectations about the most likely tone and texture of our history as a species in this part of the world. For instance, the historian Stewart Firth—who has written in depth about the history of German New Guinea before World War I—has said without qualification that coastal villages in the Aitape district "banded together in large communities for protection against marauders from the hills."[2]

Perhaps, but let's not forget about equifinality. What Firth has perhaps overlooked is that it may very well be the resource productivity of the rich lagoons in this part of the Sepik coast that makes these large communities possible in the first place. Undoubtedly there may be safety and strength in numbers, but suggesting, as Firth does, that the large size of these coastal villages shows us that people living in them allegedly banded together at some unknown time in the past to protect themselves from outside evil-doers ignores an alternative and entirely mundane environmental and economic explanation. These villages were and are today large because these lagoons— as well as the waters around the nearby offshore islands—are and were then the most environmentally productive "bread baskets" of this part of New Guinea. It may be true that "you are what you eat." But my wager is that the villages on these lagoons and islands are as large as they are because it is also true that "you are *where* you can eat."

Now let's consider the alternative Hypothesis 2. Both [A] and [B] as already stated still apply. But given this alternative proposition, what might we reasonably expect [C]—the human history of this coast—to have been like? I would be among the first to agree that there is still much to be learned about the prehistory of the Sepik region. As archaeologists, we have barely begun to scratch its surface. Yet I think enough is now known to suggest that, as echoed in the seven points I noted earlier, [C] has been a story of long-term human endurance, cultural continuity from start to today, and boiling it down to a single word, historical and cultural *stability*.

How to account for this evident stability, of course, remains an open question. Yet I am now even more certain than I was back in 1990 that one of the main reasons for the evident stability of how people on this coast as well as on the offshore islands have been able to live out their lives is how well they have succeeded in cultivating the art of building and maintaining friendships—or in today's manner of speaking, *social networks*—with people and families in places other than their own home town.

But why should you or anybody else care about what has been happening over the course of hundreds and maybe thousands of years in a faraway and remote place like the Sepik coast? What are the odds, in fact, that how people have been living their lives on this coast amounts to little more than an odd exception to the old Enlightenment rule made most forcefully by Thomas Hobbes that—in keeping with Hypothesis 1—people are basically a nasty and aggressive product of evolution, or Creation, and that friendship is simply too wimpy a social phenomenon to make any real difference to how history has played out elsewhere in the world?[3]

PART THREE

Selfish Desires

12

Houston, We've Had a Problem

IN 1990 WHEN Rob Welsch and I were visiting Tumleo Island off the Sepik coast for the first time, I pointed out to him an outrigger canoe on the beach at Sapi that looked incredibly like the canoe pictured in one of the old Lewis photographs from 1909. "But you know what's missing here, don't you?" I said to Rob. "This canoe doesn't have a bundle of sago on it." In Lewis's photo, someone had placed large bags of this favorite local food on the canoe that Lewis then immortalized in grainy glass-plate photographic black-and-white (Figure 11).

After touring the island, we returned in the late afternoon to the same beach at Sapi. The canoe in question was still there. But during our absence, somebody had contributed a new element to the picturesque beach scene. A large bundle of sago had been left there, although this time around—unlike back in 1909—the bundle had been set down next to the canoe, not on it.

The sense of déjà vu was overpowering. I quipped at once to Welsch: "*Now* I know why we had to come here! Lewis didn't have color film. But we do!"

On another day at another village—this time at Warapu on the mainland—Rob and I were walking down the beach which was all but deserted. Far off ahead of us were two young boys. I noticed that the boys were leaving small footprints in the sand. I turned to Welsch and said: "You know, Rob, we have a problem."

"What?" Rob asked.

"Well, you know we call our project 'In the Footsteps of A. B. Lewis.'"

"Yes, what of it?"

"Well, look at that."

"Yes?"

"The problem is we don't know his shoe size."

FIGURE 11 Sago in canoe, Tumleo Island, 1909. (© The Field Museum, CSA31737; *photograph*: Albert B. Lewis. Reproduced with permission.).

Without doubt what we were witnessing during our first visit to this beautiful coast in 1990 presented us with a problem, but not one as prosaic as whether we could learn the actual shoe size of a long-deceased Field Museum curator. Nor was the problem life-threatening, although what comes to mind now is the famous statement made on April 14, 1970, when the astronaut John L. "Jack" Swigert reported back to the earth during the *Apollo 13* mission to the moon that an oxygen tank on board their spacecraft had exploded: "Okay, Houston, we've had a problem here."

Admittedly our problem was one of an utterly different character. A problem that was somewhat like an onion. After peeling back the topmost layer, we found another more profound issue below it that was also badly in need of resolution. And below that one, yet another deeper down.

THE EXPERTS WHO had reviewed our first research proposal to the National Science Foundation (NSF) had been unequivocal in saying that it would be pointless to waste American taxpayer dollars to fund our proposed field research on this coast in the footsteps of A. B. Lewis. Reading their comments even now a quarter of a century later casts a gloom over the bright and sunny room I am sitting in. Below this superficial problem, however, lay a deeper concern. Although these reviews might constitute a very small statistical sample, it was obvious to us that they were telling us something fundamentally disturbing about the field of anthropology. It was plainly the general opinion that this part of New Guinea was the sort of place where absolutely nothing "native" could possibly have survived what the 20th century had visited upon its citizens. What had once been there was over and done with. End of story.

I am convinced, however, this is not all there is to the story, or rather the problem, we were facing. There is yet another deeper underlying layer to it all. In believing so confidently that what had once been on this coast was no more, what these grant reviewers were saying to the NSF was entirely in keeping with both popular and scholarly opinion about a place like New Guinea— or for that matter, any other reportedly "primitive" or "savage" place in the world. Such places simply and surely cannot stand up for themselves in the face of colonialism and what is now popularly called globalization. And Rob and I were finding this deep-seated opinion about a place we were coming to love profoundly shocking.

These days, most educated people avoid the words *primitive* and *savage* like the plague. After all, aren't we all equal in the eyes of God and/or the Eyes of the Law, or something? Yet as recently as 50 years ago, it was commonplace even for knowledgeable people to talk about, for instance, "primitive art." Nowadays, the same subject matter is called "Art of Africa, Oceania, and the Americas." Same meaning, different words. It is still being thought of as the art of all those other less important, less successful, and ultimately doomed people. Globalization will see to that.

Although this deeper problem Rob and I were confronting has historical roots going back long, long before the 19th century, there is no doubt that the expansion of European colonialism during that century had honed and solidified the world view it reflected.[1] Consider, as a case in point, what the renowned 19th century English philosopher and sociologist Herbert Spencer had to say about it all.

DURING THE AGE of Enlightenment in the 17th and 18th centuries, as we have previously seen (Chapters 2 and 3), our history viewed as the story of God's finest Creation was envisioned as a tale about how it had been both logical and necessary for rational beings—namely us—to surrender some of their natural rights, individual freedoms, and independence in order to secure peace, political stability, and human happiness. However, the Industrial

Revolution that began in the later 18th century and ultimately transformed social life and economic realities throughout much of the globe in the 19th century—together with the American and French revolutions at the end of the previous century—radically reworked how both learned and ordinary folk envisioned the history of our species. By the 19th century, faith in God had been replaced for many by an abiding faith instead in Progress with a capital "P." And as the historian Robert Nisbet once observed, Herbert Spencer was the supreme embodiment in the late 19th century of the Idea of Progress.[2]

The name Herbert Spencer (1820–1903) is rarely heard today. Yet Spencer was indisputably one of the most influential British thinkers of the Victorian era. Many people then considered him to be both a great man and a towering intellect—a sterling exemplar of the scientific spirit of his times.[3]

Like his contemporary Charles Darwin, Spencer had a theory of evolution, but one in many respects far more encompassing than Darwin's own. His views on the subject were also more compatible than Darwin's with how many then thought about history and its milestones. Frankly, Spencer's convictions are still far more compatible than Darwin's with how many today picture change and evolution, and here I am not just thinking of religious fundamentalists who hold firm to the idea that the Heavens and the Earth were created during one memorable week in 4004 B.C.[4]

Chief in Spencer's philosophy were ideas about progress, which he took to be not only about gradual change over time marked by descent with modification—the kind of change that Darwin, too, put his faith in—but also about change with a definite purpose or direction in mind, namely, leading onward and upward. Do not be fooled here, however, by the word *progress*. In Spencer's day, this term meant much more than just advancement, improvement, or things in general getting better and better. For Spencer and others, progress and evolution were synonymous, and alike referred to a process by which—or so he thought—organisms, human societies, and things in general, too, change over time from being simple to being complex, from being homogeneous (uniform) to being heterogeneous (differentiated), and from all things being more or less alike, independent, and self-sufficient to everything being varied, orderly, and mutually dependent on one another. "This law of organic progress," he wrote, "is the law of all progress."[5]

This claim can also be taken another step, although not necessarily in the right direction. If progress means evolving from the simple to the complex, then when it comes to ourselves, where can we find human beings alive today or in the past whose ways and means fall toward the allegedly simple end of the spectrum of human progress? You guessed it. New Guinea, of course! As well as all those other exotic places in the South Pacific. And yes, Africa and the Americas. Today we call this 19th century world view Euro-American racism and colonialism.

Add to all this another fact. It was Spencer, not Charles Darwin, who coined the well-known phrase "survival of the fittest." Not surprisingly perhaps, Spencer also believed that primitive people are less fit than any Englishman is because they are naturally violent and child-like in handling— or not even dealing with—their emotions. Yet true to his faith in progress (and perhaps in Thomas Hobbes), he thought that the ancient and violent ways of primitive people combined with their emotional simplicity of being had actually spurred us on our way as a species down or rather up the road of Progress toward Civilization. In his own words:

> Shudder as we must at the cannibalism which all over the world in early days was a sequence of war—shrink as we may from the thought of those immolations of prisoners which have, tens of thousands of times, followed battles between wild tribes—read as we do with horror of the pyramids of heads and the whitening bones of slain peoples left by barbarian invaders—hate, as we ought, the militant spirit which is even now among ourselves prompting base treacheries and brutal aggressions; we must not let our feelings blind us to the proofs that inter-social conflicts have furthered the development of social structures.[6]

This is good stuff, isn't it? Violence begets progress. Who could ask for more?

SPENCER WAS A true child of the 19th century, but what about the century that followed? Did the 20th century mind also share the same Victorian vision of our kind evolving over the course of time from a simple, bloodthirsty, and overly emotional state of being toward a more complex, tolerant, and refined level of social existence?

Yes and no. Consider the case of Franz Boas (1858–1942). During the first half of the 20th century, no other person was more closely identified with the study of our own species and our cultural, linguistic, and biological diversity as a species than this famous German-American anthropologist. Indeed, it was Boas more than anyone else who gave American anthropology in the 20th century both its sense of mission and its sense of academic identity.

Yet in his 1928 popular book *Anthropology and Modern Life,* Boas gave all of us a colorful but by no means then an unconventional depiction of wild, unfriendly savages in ancient or distant places. In this well-received volume, he asserts that "in primitive human society every tribe forms a closed society." He then goes on to explain (here I have condensed what he wrote somewhat to keep it short):

> In the early days of mankind our earth was thinly settled. Small groups of human beings were scattered here and there; the members of each horde were one in speech, one in customs, one in superstitious beliefs.... They were held together by strong bands of habit. The gain of one member of the horde was the gain of the whole group....
>
> Beyond the limits of the hunting grounds lived other groups, different in speech, different in customs, perhaps even different in appearance, whose very existence was a source of danger.... They acted in a different manner; their reasoning and feeling were unintelligible; they had no part in the interests of the horde. Thus they stood opposed to it as beings of another kind, with whom there could be no community of interest....
>
> Thus the most primitive form of society presents to us the picture of continuous strife.... Always on the alert to protect himself and his kindred, man considered it an act of high merit to kill the stranger.
>
> The tendency to form closed societies is not by any means confined to primitive tribes. It exists to a marked extent in our own civilization. Until quite recent times, and in many cases even now, the old nobility formed a closed society. The patricians and the plebeians, Greeks and barbarians, the gangs of our streets, Mohammedans and infidels,—and our own modern nations are in this sense closed societies that cannot exist without antagonisms.[7]

It is fascinating, isn't it? These words sound almost as though they could have been written by Samuel von Pufendorf in the 17th century.

VIEWS COMPATIBLE WITH those of Spencer in the Victorian Era and Boas in the 20th century are alive and well today in the 21st century.[8] As I noted earlier, for instance, the historian Daniel Smail has argued that the narrative of Western Civilization as it is presently understood by historians has not fully escaped from the chronological grip of sacred history as promulgated by early modern European historians and their predecessors in the Judeo-Christian tradition, a view of history that located the origins of humankind in the Garden of Eden in 4004 B.C.[9] He may be right, but it is not just the shallowness of this biblical view of history that may still be getting in the way of seeing the story of our species in all its depth and richness.

We are also still in the grip of the old biblical idea of salvation in all its many connotations of deliverance, redemption, rescue, and even atonement. Nowadays, however, I would argue that the theological implications of such words are avoided by phrasing the idea instead as the "search for origins" not just in the limited sense of the beginnings of things, but also as the search for the actual time and place where what had once been true about all human beings—the Enlightenment's "state of nature"—had at long last been transformed and pushed upward in the direction of what we would later become.

Undeniably this ghost idea, which I think might be labeled the "Salvation of the Savage," continues to guide much of the science of archaeology. Many today, for instance, would agree with what the archaeologist Douglas Price has concluded: something remarkable in human history *did* indeed happen in the ancient Near East—not the biblical Creation, but instead what has often been called the Rise of Civilization.[10]

You have probably heard before what I am referring to, but if not, here is this popular idea in a nutshell. Around 10,000 or so years ago, it is said, people in the Near East finally stopped behaving like hunters and gatherers and invented something new instead called agriculture. And the rest, as the saying goes, is history, or as Price has stated the case: "The transition from hunting and gathering to agriculture is arguably the most important event in human prehistory, representing a shift from foraging to farming, from food collection to food production, from wild to domestic, that sets the stage for most of the significant subsequent developments in human society."[11]

Herbert Spencer would have said all this differently perhaps, and so might other archaeologists and anthropologists today.[12] Even so, it is not farfetched to suggest that the point of view voiced by Price is almost biblical in character. As Smail has observed, even the chronology of the "transition to agriculture" is roughly compatible with biblical history.[13]

However, regardless how true or false you take this archaeological point of view to be, what should not be overlooked is that this way of thinking about our human past *requires* the idea of the savage (however defined) to make sense. After all, transitions need things to transform. Maybe we don't call hunter-gatherers "savages" any more, but isn't this still what they are or were in the eyes of many?

In 1537 Pope Paul III (1468–1549) settled a dispute then raging in Europe that adds weight to this evident connection between European ideas about savages and biblical ways of interpreting the world and its inhabitants. He issued an official and binding decree forbidding the enslavement of the inhabitants of the New World, unknown to the Bible and Europe before Columbus's voyages, on the grounds that they were rational human beings having souls capable of being saved by conversion to Christianity. Sadly, as history shows us, this papal pronouncement had almost no positive effect on the actual lives and fates of those whose humanity it so condescendingly confirmed.[14]

WHILE ROB WELSCH and I were walking behind those two small boys far off in the distance on that quiet and lovely beach at Warapu in 1990, I think we both had similar worries in mind. Yes, no doubt about it. We definitely now had more than enough firsthand information about what life was really like on this coast at the end of the 20th century to ask again for federal funding to return for a much longer time to get to know this beautiful part of New Guinea better as both anthropologists and museum curators. And as I have already related, we were successful. But it was also obvious to both of us that sooner or later we were going to have to address the deeper underlying reasons we likely had not received federal funding the first time around.

The problem we were dealing with wasn't just that most of the reviewers of our original grant proposal had been wrong about what life was like then on the Sepik coast. We now also knew that we had to take a much closer look at the role of friendship not just there but also in human social life generally and our species' evolutionary history.

Nobody even today would contest that people in this remote part of the modern world lacked the material wealth in 1990 of people living in cities like New York, Chicago, Paris, and London—places where most people on earth would probably agree "significant subsequent developments in human society" were fully in evidence. No contest there. But finding that inheriting friendships were still so astonishingly alive and well on this coast eight decades after Lewis had been there opened our eyes to the reality that it was wrong to call people in this part of the world "primitive" or "savage."

Far from being the kind of place where friendship is too wimpy a phenomenon to play a role in human affairs beyond the immediacy and intimacy of home and local community, we could now see with our own eyes that inheriting friendships on the coast had helped keep a way of life vigorous and productive far beyond our wildest expectations.

It would be years before I would find myself saying that what we had been dealing with back in 1990 was the old Euro-American ghost story about "the savage and the beast." But we knew then nonetheless that we would have to take a much closer look at what it means to be a friend. And we also realized that in challenging conventional wisdom about friendship we would also be questioning conventional wisdom about the nature of human nature.

13

You Can't Get There from Here

WHEN I WAS 16 going on 17, I spent a summer in Great Britain living with a local family in the very small town of Frocester, scarcely more than a crossroads, just below the Cotswold escarpment near the cathedral city of Gloucester. I had come over on an Italian ocean liner from America as a School-Community Ambassador with a small group of other young Americans. I had to write a weekly report on my adventures for my hometown newspaper. These days, in marked contrast, the Frocester Cricket Club has its own Web site, its own Facebook page, and the Annual Frocester Beer Festival featuring more than 100 different cask-conditioned real ales from more than 50 breweries around the United Kingdom is held on the club's grounds every August over the bank holiday weekend. Videos of these evidently rather intoxicating events can be found on the Internet.

After my "home stay," we traveled to Wales and roomed for several days at a youth hostel on the Gower Peninsula. One of our first excursions there was a walk around the coast to find a local delicacy to bring back for dinner, something called lava bread made out of seaweed. (The Internet tells me it is also called laver bread, or *bara lawr* in Welsh.) As you might expect from a bunch of young middle-class American kids off on their own for the first time in a foreign place, we royally lost our way. We never did find the lava bread. Eventually, in desperation, we knocked on a cottage door to ask for help in finding our way back to our hostel at Oxwich on the other side of the peninsula. The kindly woman who answered told us in no uncertain terms: "Oh, you poor dears! You can't get there from here." Fortunately she proved to be wrong, although I can no longer recall how it was we were able to stumble home.

The fact that I can remember this minor adventure after so many years is no accident. Since then I have often felt caught in similar situations, sometimes in the jungles of New Guinea or the Solomons, sometimes in big cities where I am a stranger, but perhaps most often intellectually rather than physically when some problem I am trying to resolve looks desperately unsolvable.

I have also often thought of this minor incident from long ago when I am seeing others, too, who have apparently lost their way: for example, when I am reading something someone has just published that yet once again makes the old claims that down deep inside we would all love to torture, maim, and slaughter our own kind; that the march of human history has been a progressive movement from the simple to the complex, from savagery to civilization; or that once upon a time savages lived in isolated tribes that were constantly at war with one another.

Why do so many still believe in these old ghost ideas?

THERE IS NO disputing that we have the capacity to be nasty, violent creatures. Who could deny, too, that violence has been a decidedly disruptive force in human history? In 1960s the activist H. Rap Brown, also known as Jamil Abdullah Al-Amin, famously observed that "violence is as american as cherry pie." To add insult to injury, he made the "A" in "American" lowercase.[1] In 1924 the renowned 20th century British statesman Winston Churchill began an essay titled "Shall We Commit Suicide?" on a similarly downbeat but more universally dismissive note:

> The story of the human race is War. Except for brief and precarious interludes, there has never been peace in the world; and before history began, murderous strife was universal and unending. But up to the present time the means of destruction at the disposal of man have not kept pace with his ferocity. Reciprocal extermination was impossible in the Stone Age. One cannot do much with a clumsy club. Besides, men were so scarce and hid so well that they were hard to find. They fled so fast that they were hard to catch. Human legs could only cover a certain distance each day. With the best will in the world to destroy his species, each man was restricted to a very limited area of activity. It was impossible to make any effective progress on these lines. Meanwhile one had to live and hunt and sleep. So on the balance the life-forces kept a steady lead over the forces of death, and gradually tribes, villages, and Governments were evolved.[2]

With all due respect, I must observe that Churchill was not an archaeologist. When Jamil Abdullah Al-Amin was writing about the America he knew in the 1960s, he was writing from direct and bitter firsthand personal experience. But what Churchill wrote about us as an eternally godforsaken species was based on traditional hearsay, although let us not forget that these words were written not long after the "war to end all wars"—the Great War in Europe, one of the most costly in human lives on record. The plain fact is nobody knows firsthand or for sure whether human history "long before history began" was or wasn't a story of universal and unending mayhem. Churchill was speaking from received wisdom, not firsthand experience. Therefore, it is not just a rhetorical question to ask why Churchill, or for that matter anyone else, would say such a thing. Yes, Churchill was a politician. But does this excuse his willingness to advance such a depressing claim?

It would be easy to multiply these negative opinions about our human capacity to behave violently many times over. As I noted at the beginning of this book, for instance, the evolutionary psychologist Steven Pinker has insisted that as a species we are not only willing to kill others of our own kind with alarming frequency, but also that we delight in figuring out new ways to do so. Although I disagree with him at almost every turn, I have to agree with him on this point. We all have the capacity and the creativity not only to inflict pain and cultivate cruelty, but we are able to do so with *discretion*. This is his word, not mine, and it is a good choice.[3] What this means is that we do not have to be violent if we feel angry or frightened; nor do we have to feel frightened or angry to be violent. More so than possibly true for other species (but do we really know?) resorting to violence is something we are able to contemplate beforehand, and then perhaps elect to do.

It is certain also that different people respond emotionally to the same kinds of situations, encounters, or events in different ways, and travelers know firsthand that this is also true from place to place around the globe. In some places, it is just fine—perhaps praiseworthy—to jump up and down, scream loudly, and in other ways act out when you are angry. It may even be okay to hit people, or kill someone in a fit of rage. Elsewhere, it is customary, maybe socially necessary, instead to "turn the other cheek" and just "grin and bear it."

Therefore, although I think he vastly overstates the argument, Pinker nonetheless has caught something worth remembering when he says in one of his popular books on how the mind works that our resorting to violence "is a near-inevitable outcome of the dynamics of self-interested, rational social organisms."[4] However, the secret to reading human nature right is to not leap quickly to the conclusion that having the *capacity* to do something despicable is the same thing as having a *predisposition* to do it. Our resorting to violence is

a choice, not an instinctive inclination, although how self-interested or rational such a choice normally is, or has to be, is debatable.

This is a point worth remembering. *Capacity* and *predisposition* are not
just two different words meaning the same thing. To offer a simple but painful
example: all of us are capable of sticking needles in our eyes, but few of us ever
feel the need to do so. And although van Gogh may have cut off an ear (but
some say this isn't the truth), few of us have ever fulfilled any such unaccount-
able desire for self-harm.

The years have taught me that one can never overstate how important it
is to remember that the words *discretion, predisposition*, and *capacity* are not
simply different words having basically the same meaning—especially in the
case of a species as intelligent as *Homo sapiens*. Recall the old saying "ready,
willing, and able," and you will see the drift of what I am talking about.

However, all this does not explain why so many people today apparently
still jumble these three words with their different meanings together and
come to the same old conclusion that there is some sort of bestial Mr. Hyde
lurking within all of us who is dying to get out to misbehave and wreak havoc.
Whichever explanation one is inclined to choose, I would argue that the idea
that human beings are ruled by deep-seated passions and violent biological predispositions shares much in common with another old explanation,
namely the notion that our lives are ruled by the stars. And there is an object
lesson to be gained by reflecting on what finally happened to undermine the
ancient traditional wisdom that we can "find our way home" by following
astrological signs and prognostications.

FOR MUCH OF human history, one of the great mysteries of life was why
certain stars in the sky don't stay put in their appointed place like all the other
stars on a beautiful night. Dangerously, it also seemed that these wandering
stars had a controlling force over the lives of ordinary people and the fates of
their rulers. Hence it was once widely agreed that it was absolutely critical at
all times to know exactly where these rogue stars—we still call them planets, a
name derived from the ancient Greek for "wandering stars"—would be night
after night in the heavens. The mathematics needed to make accurate predictions about precisely where the planets would be at any given time was anything but a piece of cake. Scholars labored literally for centuries to improve
the craft and math for doing so.

As every school child now knows, the irony here is that the mathematics
had to be so convoluted because, as the Polish mathematician and astronomer
Nicolaus Copernicus (1473–1543) finally realized, everyone was accepting as

the gospel truth the mistaken but utterly commonsense notion that the earth sits motionless at the center of the universe while the sun, moon, and planets move around it. It is not hard to understand, therefore, why few people in the 16th century were thrilled to hear what Copernicus proposed instead. Judging by what our eyes can tell us, the claim that the earth moves around the sun is absurd. As the philosopher of science Thomas Kuhn once commented: "Our senses tell us all we know of motion, and they indicate no motion for the earth." It requires no great effort, therefore, to insist that if it were true that the earth moves, then all things not firmly screwed down to the earth's surface would be "hurled from a rotating earth as a stone flies from a rotating sling."[5]

Even after Copernicus had broken with conventional wisdom to argue that the earth spins on its axis once every 24 hours and travels around the sun once each year, it was by no means a sure bet that this improbable idea would win popular acceptance. Why? Because the Copernican view of things was in conflict with a host of other good commonsense ideas then popular explaining, among other things, how stones fall, how water pumps function, and why clouds move slowly across the sky.[6]

I think it is sobering to know that both common sense and good practical (and scientific) reasoning in the 16th century spoke unequivocally *against* Copernicus and strongly in favor of the old Ptolemaic view of the universe—a point of view that we now know was not just a little wrong, but was completely, utterly wrong. A lesser known fact is that for years after Copernicus's death in 1543, some of the world's leading astronomers did their very best to salvage the older world view—efforts that went to the extreme of offering elaborate blends of the old and the new that kept the earth right there in the center of things where it clearly belonged while allowing some of the planets to go around the sun the way Copernicus wanted them to.[7]

THE POINT OF my telling this story is a basic one. Regardless of how sensible and widely believed something seems to be does not make it true. This moral definitely applies also to what philosophers and scientists have all too often said about human nature. However logical and persuasive the claims made by men such as Hobbes, Locke, Rousseau, Pufendorf, Spencer, Boas, and others may still sound to many of us today, what they wrote shows us that when it comes to human nature, like Ptolemy, we can easily start off on the wrong foot.

What is enlightening about this example drawn from the history of astronomy is to see what it finally took to undermine the old Ptolemaic view of the earth and its relationship to the rest of the universe. Basically what was needed *wasn't* a rock-solid accumulation of true astronomical facts and finely wrought mathematical figuring, but instead *a different way of thinking about the problem from the get-go*.

Similarly, what it also took to begin challenging the old conviction that human beings are predisposed to violence and are more than merely a notch or two below the angels in the direction of hell was also a different way of thinking about the natural world down here on earth. I am referring, of course, to Charles Darwin and his theory of evolution by means of natural selection. The irony in this instance, however, is that although what Darwin wrote in the 19th century directly challenged the Bible's story of the Creation, what he had to say about us did astonishingly little to chip away at the ghost ideas of the savage beyond and the beast within. Therefore, it is instructive to ask both what Darwin said about the natural world, and why he (and many of his successors) did not go further than they did in freeing us from the clutches of our old ghost ideas about human nature.

14

The Wizard of Down House

IT IS SOMETIMES said that Charles Darwin discovered evolution. Not true. The basic idea that all life on earth has evolved from one or a few original forms had been around long before Darwin helped make such a view of life on earth both famous and notorious. In fact, experts dispute precisely what Darwin did discover. Nobody contests, however, that what he wrote about evolution in the 19th century has changed how we see the world today, for better or for worse depending on one's point of view.

Although a prolific scientist and author, Darwin's most influential book was *On the Origin of Species by Means of Natural Selection, or the Preservation of Favoured Races in the Struggle for Life*, first published in London by John Murray in 1859. Many scientists talk in terms of "before Darwin" and "after Darwin." They see the year 1859 as an *annus mirabilis*, the miraculous dividing line between the *then* and the *now* of our modern world view.

Legend has it that Darwin began piecing together his theory of evolution by means of natural selection while he was exploring the remote Galápagos Islands in 1835. Yes and no. The Galápagos ("Tortoise") Islands are a group of six major islands, 10 or so smaller ones, and numerous islets and rocks on the equator in the South Pacific about 575 miles (925 km) west of Ecuador. They were discovered by accident in 1535 by Bishop Tomás de Berlanga of Panama. The Bishop found them uninhabited.

Between then and the establishment of the first permanent human colony in 1832, these desolate hunks of ground rising above the ocean's waves were for a time a favorite haunt of pirate buccaneers. History tells us that a hoard of more than a thousand sacks of flour and seven or eight casks of quince marmalade plundered off a Spanish merchant ship were secreted somewhere on these islands by the "Merry Boys," the crew of the pirate ship *Bachelor's*

Delight, in 1684. Hardly your standard pirate treasure, and perhaps not something you might want to find where ✕ marks the spot on an ancient treasure map.[1]

New ideas are not like strange insects, exotic plants, or new comets. You cannot literally pick them off a twig, dig them up, or discover them after dark. Therefore, Darwin neither literally nor figuratively discovered evolution during the five weeks he was exploring the Galápagos Islands in 1835. What he did find there were only the seeds—or rather the birds—that what would one day become his powerful idea.

Today scientists recognize more than 13 species of finches on these islands. As Jonathan Weiner remarks in his Pulitzer Prize winning book *The Beak of the Finch,* "Some of them look so much alike that during the mating season they find it hard to tell themselves apart. Yet they are also spectacularly and peculiarly diverse."[2]

When Darwin came upon these birds during the voyage on the H.M.S. *Beagle* around the world in 1831–1836, he did not see them as particularly interesting. Instead, he thought they were new varieties of perhaps three or four basic types of birds already known to science.[3]

Judging by what he later wrote about the voyage, Robert FitzRoy, the ship's captain, favored the idea that these differing types had been specifically created by God to live on these islands—demonstrating the "admirable provisions of Infinite Wisdom by which each created thing is adapted to the place for which it was intended."[4]

While they were exploring this archipelago together, Darwin did not necessarily disagree with FitzRoy. During the long voyage of the *Beagle*, Darwin was not opposed to finding proof of God's handiwork manifest in nature through her visible wonders. After all, he was an educated Englishman. Like many of his contemporaries, he accepted that the workings of God were revealed in such marvels as the human eye and the exquisite patterning of flowers.[5]

Once home in England at the beginning of October 1836, Darwin never returned to these islands. It is easy to imagine that there were moments when he dearly wished to do so. He commented somewhat poignantly in 1839, for instance, in his *Journal of Researches*: "It is the fate of every voyager, when he has just discovered what object in any place is more particularly worthy of his attention, to be hurried from it."[6]

What makes this statement poignant? While in the Galápagos Islands, he had done something that today would probably have cost him his career in science. He had collected nine of the currently recognized species of what are now called Darwin's finches.[7] However, much to his later dismay—and to the regret of scientists who have tried to make sense of his zoological collections from these islands—he had not been careful about labeling his specimens as to where he captured and killed each one of them.[8] More so than not, as it were, he had put all of his birds in one basket.

Many scholars have tried to account for this seeming scientific carelessness. As Darwin confessed in the first published edition of his *Journal*:

> …the inhabitants can distinguish the tortoises, according to the islands whence they are brought. I was also informed that many of the islands possess trees and plants which do not occur on the others.…Unfortunately, I was not aware of these facts till my collection was nearly completed: it never occurred to me, that the productions of islands only a few miles apart, and placed under the same physical conditions, would be dissimilar. I therefore did not attempt to make a series of specimens from the separate islands.[9]

According to Frank Sulloway, a scholar who spent years figuring out how Darwin was finally able to recover from the mess he had unknowingly gotten himself into, what had evidently misled Darwin in 1835 about these birds is the odd relationship between their beaks and plumage.[10] Elsewhere in the world, closely related species usually have similar beaks but strikingly dissimilar plumage. The opposite holds true for the Galápagos finches. Their plumage varies little between even the biologically most closely related species. What varies a great deal—famously so—are the beaks.

Once home, it took Darwin several years to work out the significance of what he had found in this archipelago. It was eminent British ornithologist John Gould who finally convinced him that the finch specimens he and others had brought back should not be assigned to different kinds of bird species, but were instead all strikingly different but nonetheless closely related.[11] Equally surprising to young Darwin, Gould insisted that 25 of the 26 kinds of land birds that had been brought back from the archipelago, including all the various finches, were forms entirely new to science.

Darwin was stunned.[12] What amazing discoveries! Finches so different they can be classified as different species. Yet finches that are also closely related to one another, biologically speaking, despite their observable physical differences. How on earth could this have happened?

This is, of course, what they used to call many decades ago the $64 dollar question. The really big one. The hard part about the idea of what is now called Darwinian evolution—the idea of descent with modification—is that generally speaking it is incredibly hard to actually see evolution happening right before our eyes. Darwinian evolution takes generations, not days, weeks, or even human lifetimes, to happen. It is usually so slow, in fact, that a shockingly large number of people in an educated place like the United States say they do not believe it happens at all, although to be honest the presence of solid evidence for evolution may have little to do with this human denial in many cases. At least for some it is just a matter of faith.

It was because of the elusiveness of biological evolution as an observable force in the universe that Darwin himself placed a great deal of emphasis in *The Origin of Species* on the solid evidence afforded the subject by the human domestication of plants and animals, including our best friend, the dog.

AFTER DARWIN HAD been more or less successful in sorting out his finches, island by island, with the help of his friends, he set about looking for a down-to-earth solution to the biological mystery they posed—their unexpected diversity. Given that he was facing an intellectual challenge every bit as staggering and maybe even more upsetting than the challenge that Nicolaus Copernicus had faced 300 years earlier, it is not surprising that Darwin waited years to publish his ideas. After all, look what had happened to Galileo when he came out in favor of what Copernicus had claimed. He was forced to recant and was placed under house arrest for the rest of his life—not an encouraging moment in European intellectual history.

There has been much debate about when exactly Darwin put 2 + 2 together to come up with his enduring theory of evolution by means of natural selection. Whatever the timing of the event, his solution to the mystery of how new species evolve turns on some quite elementary facts. First, if you do not reproduce, you cannot pass on whatever it is you have, biologically speaking, to the next generation. Second, if what you have also makes it more likely that you will live to reproduce, then what you have and how successfully you use it may have a direct impact on what the next generation is like, biologically speaking.

In a nutshell, this is Darwin's heretical idea. Given time and the right circumstances, the gradual selective accumulation of even seemingly minor adaptive differences over many generations may add up enough for us to be able to say that what began as one kind, or species, of plant or animal has evolved into two or more different, although historically related, species.

However, as the saying goes, the proof is in the pudding. Today there is abundant evidence of all sorts in support of Darwin's idea available to anyone who doesn't turn a blind eye to it and try to claim that cavemen and dinosaurs walked the earth at one and the same time. Not so back in Darwin's day, and this is where our species' intentional domestication of certain kinds of plants and animals fits into the story of Darwin's personal evolution of the idea of evolution by means of natural selection. To keep it simple, let's just consider the case of the family dog.[13]

DOGS ARE INCREDIBLY skilled at understanding the behavior of their human owners. They are better at this than even our nearest primate relatives.[14] For instance, dogs are less likely to approach a food they have been told not to eat if their human owner's eyes are open than if they are closed, a bit of strategic information about getting what you want when a human being is around and in a way that chimpanzees have not been observed to discover on their own. Since most of us have never kept an ape at home, canine cleverness at "reading" human behavior may not come across to most of us as unexpected and out of the ordinary. Yet it is.

Brian Hare and Michael Tomasello of the Max Planck Institute for Evolutionary Anthropology in Leipzig, Germany have reported in depth on how dogs and humans get along with one another. First we need to know that dogs are descended biologically from Old World wolves (species *Canis lupus*), and wolves are social pack hunters. Consequently, wolves need to be able to follow the behavior of the other wolves they are running with to keep up with the pack. Unquestionably, therefore, some of the social skills that dogs today possess can be traced back to their ancestral wolf heritage.

However, wolves raised by humans evidently do not become as skillful as dogs naturally are at observing and acting on cues given by what the humans around them are doing and saying—a research finding supporting the notion that dogs are not just wolves, so to speak, in sheep's clothing. The conclusion is inescapable that something important happened during the evolution of some ancient wolves into modern dogs.

Hare and Tomasello believe that dogs get along with humans so well because over the course of the many millennia (perhaps for 30,000 years, or longer[15]) that dogs and humans have been intimate and often inseparable companions, our forebears only made room beside the campfire for wolves that were *emotionally capable* of tolerating human closeness. But this is not all. These canines must have also been given to dealing with human attention and solicitations in *a nonaggressive manner*. Furthermore, presumably earlier rather than later in the developing partnership between humans and dogs, these favored individuals began to be capable of working directly with human beings as social partners.[16]

In this regard, it seems particularly revealing that recent research suggests that wolf pups raised in human families exactly the way puppies today are raised never fully develop the social-cognitive skills that come naturally to modern dogs. For example, when as part of an experiment they were denied easy access to food they can see but not get at unassisted, puppies even as young as 5 weeks looked appealingly at their human friends for help. The wolf pups in the same experimental situation apparently never developed this social skill. At 5 weeks they tended to fall asleep defeated; at 9 weeks they just gave up when they could not do it all by themselves.

There are other clues, too, to how remarkable the relationship between humans and dogs truly is. Among wolves, gazing directly at other wolves is a way of threatening them into submission. Hence avoiding eye contact can be a way to avoid conflict. Although for dogs, too, direct staring can trigger aggressive behavior, it also seems that in the course of their evolution, dogs became much more skillful than wolves at "reading" the nonaggressive visual cues that are so much a part of human nonverbal social communication. And then responding to such cues in the socially communicative ways that every dog owner knows and loves so well—including vocalization, tail wagging, and what I personally like to call *canine beseeching* (although I know others who would call it insistent, pleading, or even demanding *visual pressure*).[17] If you have ever had a dog, you know exactly what I am talking about. Cat owners may have a harder time decoding what I am trying to communicate verbally here.

In short, dogs today are ahead of chimps and other apes in the fine art of understanding how humans behave evidently because during the course of our domestication of *Canis lupus familiaris* (the official name today for all dogs) individuals displaying convivial openness to our companionship and adoring gaze were selectively favored by our forebears over beasts that could never quite figure out why they were being given such a warm welcome by those two-legged pack animals of the genus *Homo* whose biological descendants would one day turn out to be you and me.

THIS IS NOT all there is to it, however. As they say in some circles in my adopted hometown of Chicago, this hand washes that hand. Hare and Tomasello are not alone in seeing parallels between the domestication of dogs by humans and the evolution of our own human social behavior. Specifically, they suggest that having a dog-like temperament is a prerequisite for human cooperation and communication. As they infer: "It is only after the human temperament evolved that variation in more complex forms of communicative and cooperative behaviors could have been shaped by evolution into the unique forms of cooperative cognition present in our species today."[18]

If this hypothesis is correct, then an important first step in the evolution of modern human sociability was probably a period of some duration during which our primeval primate ancestors underwent what was—in effect, if not in actual intent—a self-generated process of self-domestication aimed at controlling how we handle our emotions. As the social anthropologist Christopher Boehm at the University of Southern California has argued: "When species are highly social, this means they are constantly making choices about with whom to associate, and this results in potentially powerful social selection effects that have a strong and consistent 'direction.'"[19]

What kind of selective direction? Hare and Tomasello suggest that when our kind was evolving toward becoming what we are like today as human beings, anyone who was seen by others as being too aggressive or despotic may have either been directly done away with, or alternatively, ostracized from society by those around him or her. "Thus, like domestic dogs, this selection for tamer emotional reactivity put our hominid ancestors in a new adaptive space within which modern human-like forms of social interaction and communication could be selected for."[20]

This idea is not far-fetched. There is ethnographic support for it, too. For example, the anthropologist Bruce Knauft at Emory University has reported that the rate of homicides in recent times among the Gebusi of southern New Guinea has been among the highest in the world.[21] Knauft estimates that the rate was an astonishing 39 percent of adult male and female deaths prior to 1963 when effective central government intervention began to have an impact locally in this part of New Guinea.

What is revealing about this statistic, however, is what was behind all these deaths. Between 1940 and 1982, 129 (32.7%) of the 394 deaths documented by Knauft during his field work among the Gebusi were described to him locally as homicides. Significantly, Knauft learned that 86 percent of these listed homicides were the outcome of sorcery accusations. Only 5.5 percent were deaths due to battles or combat staged by the Gebusi themselves.

Why sorcery? Even in the early 1980s when he first visited them, the Gebusi still regarded deaths due to sickness or accident as the work of sorcerers, and it was generally agreed that such evil perpetrators needed to be ferreted out and killed before they could strike again and do others harm, too.

The irony here is that even back in the 1980s, the Gebusi saw themselves as friendly, peace-loving people. Judging by his fieldwork observations and the information Knauft was able to collect then, they were. However, reminiscent of those of us who always must blame someone else when things go wrong, their way of explaining seemingly avoidable deaths in their families and communities was to seek out who secretly was responsible.

What is most relevant about the Gebusi way of life to the hypothesis that our species has domesticated itself to be social and collaborative are Knauft's remarks about who were the people most likely to be singled out to face a death inquest séance, execution, and cannibalization. Children were generally exempt from being so accused. Young women of marriageable age were also usually passed over. Others were not so fortunate. "Men and women who are by temperament more aggressive, outspoken, or assertive appear from my observations to be much more likely targets for sorcery accusations, particularly as they get older. Conversely, persons who are good-humored and accommodating tend to be immune to such accusations."[22] The pattern seems fairly clear. According to Knauft's own assessment: "In sociological terms, this violence acts as a strong leveling mechanism which precludes the emergence of assertive leaders and reinforces commitment to norms of sociality and sharing."

TO GET BACK to the dogs, not everyone agrees with what Hare and Tomasello have proposed about the impact of human selection on their evolutionary domestication, and these researchers freely acknowledge that not enough is currently known, for instance, about the emotional reactivity of dogs in comparison with wolves.[23] Furthermore, it is not certain that our own evolutionary forerunners gained greater self-control over their emotions *before* they went on to evolve more sophisticated forms of social behavior.

However, I think wondering what it is about dogs that makes them so attached to us can be likened to looking in a mirror at ourselves. As another researcher, Juliane Kaminski, has written, dogs are dogs because they have been adapted by human beings to a new and unique habitat—human society.[24] The same holds true for us. Far from being inherently aggressive and bloodthirsty creatures, looking at ourselves in this canine mirror strongly hints that we are where we are today as a species not because we are creatures filled with rage and hostility, but rather because we have evolved over time to become social beings capable of dealing effectively both with our emotions and with one another.

In 1990 Herbert A. Simon (1916–2001), one of the 20th century's true polymaths (and one of my personal heroes) observed that it is of no little moment for the future of humankind to know whether people are necessarily and consistently selfish, as is sometimes argued in population genetics and economics, or whether there is a significant place for altruism in the scheme of human behavior. He argued that what Hare and Tomasello would later call the "new adaptive space" of our species is not just about our modern human forms of social interaction and communication, but about the evolutionary advantages that accrue to us as individuals as a result of our capacity to live with and learn from one another:

> The human species is notable, although not unique among animals, in requiring for survival many years of nurture by adults. In most human societies, the survival and fitness even of adults depends on the assistance, or at least forbearance, of other adults. Leaving aside active hostility from others, even access to food and shelter cannot be ensured in most societies without the consent of others....
>
> Social learning makes two major contributions to an individual's fitness. First, it provides knowledge and skills that are useful in all of life's activities, in particular, in transactions with the environment. Second, goals, values, and attitudes transmitted through social learning, and exhibited in the speech or behavior of the learner, often secure supportive responses from others.[25]

There is more to Simon's argument than what I have quoted here, but the point I want to make stands without need of further elaboration: living socially with others creates many social opportunities for self-domestication.

J. K. ROWLING TELLS us in the *Harry Potter* series of stories that the good and powerful wizard Albus Dumbledore has a long gray beard, one so long that he can tuck it into his belt. Similarly, portraits and drawings of Charles Darwin in later life show that he had a long beard, although certainly not nearly as long as Dumbledore's. Furthermore, whether his many insights into the evolution of life on earth reveal that he was a good wizard rather than an evil one may depend a great deal on your religious views and willingness to credit the reality of descent with modification by means of natural selection.

In the *Harry Potter* series, Professor Dumbledore is the Headmaster of the Hogwarts School of Witchcraft and Wizardry. Darwin wrote the *Origin of Species* while similarly secluded from the normal demands of urban life. In 1842 he moved his family from London to Down House in what is now the London borough of Bromely, but that was then called Kent. He died there on April 19, 1882. Between 1907 and 1922, Down House served as the Downe School for Girls, but this boarding school was never anything like the establishment known as Hogwarts. Currently Down House is under consideration as a UNESCO World Heritage Site.

Considering his decided impact on our modern views about the Book of Genesis and the origins of life, it has struck many as ironic that after a state funeral on Wednesday, April 26, 1882, Darwin was buried in Westminster Abbey next to the mathematician and astronomer Sir John Herschel and only a few feet away from the renowned Sir Isaac Newton. In a memorial sermon at Westminster on the Sunday, May 1, the Bishop of Carlisle observed: "It would have been unfortunate, if anything had occurred to give weight and currency to the foolish notion which some have diligently propagated, but for which Mr. Darwin was not responsible, that there is a necessary conflict between a knowledge of nature and a belief in God."

Many would agree with this assessment, and many, too, would concur that Down House should be a World Heritage Site. In any case, unlike Dumbledore, Darwin was certainly no wizard. Nor was he a saint. He held views that were absolutely typical of the Victorian era in which he lived, especially about people whom he saw as savages. These views should not be passed over in silence.

In *The Descent of Man*, first published in 1871, Darwin gave us his most complete statement on the subject of ourselves. In a chapter comparing the mental powers of humans with those of other animals, he reports:

> The chef causes of the low morality of savages, as judged by our standard, are, firstly, the confinement of sympathy to the same tribe. Secondly, powers of reasoning insufficient to recognize the bearing of many virtues, especially of the self-regarding virtues, on the general welfare of the tribe. Savages, for instance, fail to trace the multiplied evils consequent on a want of temperance, chastity, etc. And, thirdly, weak power of self-command; for this power has not been strengthened through long-continued, perhaps inherited, habit, instruction and religion.[26]

These prejudiced remarks sound a lot like Herbert Spencer speaking, not like the Charles Darwin many of us who call ourselves evolutionists hold up as our hero and intellectual godfather.

Even so, it would be unwise to take Darwin too firmly to task. After all, that was then; this is now. What bothers me more is that similarly thoughtful evolutionists today may hold similar views. The ghostly apparition of the bloodthirsty and morally deficient savage has been much more difficult to exorcise than you might think.

15

The Numbers Game

WE LIVE IN a four-dimensional world. Psychics, mystics, ghost hunters, and some modern physicists may want us to see things differently, but the simple truth is that as a species we have been adapted by Darwinian natural selection to deal with only four dimensions. If truth be told, for most of us—and I include myself here—these four are more than enough to cope with.

Mathematicians, of course, can have as many dimensions as their equations and computer simulations can handle. Therein lies a tale that needs telling. In the early decades after World War II, with the threat of thermonuclear war hanging over all of us during the Cold War, many people working in the so-called "soft sciences" such as biology, economics, ecology, geography, psychology, political science, and sociology enthusiastically adopted mathematics, quantitative methods, and the use of formal mathematical modeling to substantiate and invigorate their ways of doing science.[1]

Among the motivations behind what has been called the postwar "quantitative revolution" was unquestionably a desire to counter accusations made by "real scientists" such as physicists and engineers—as well as government funding agencies such as the National Science Foundation, which was established by an Act of Congress in 1950—that these "lesser sciences" were too atheoretical, too descriptive, too qualitative, too statistically lax in their choice of methods and research strategies. Hence too often research findings and conclusions could be lampooned as too impressionistic, too historical, too particularistic. What was badly needed, it was said, was more in the way of solid and reliable quantitative data leading to sound conclusions supported perhaps by inspiring mathematical models involving, say, a couple of highly apropos differential equations.[2]

Just how successful this quantitative revolution in the sciences was after the war is debatable.[3] The impact of this revolution, however, on the study of evolution was profound and lasting. Today all serious discussion about how evolution happens must be conducted using the language of mathematics. Yet as every scientist knows, there are lies, damn lies, and statistics. Similarly, however elegant, mathematical models are only as useful as they are insightful.

Although it would be hard to prove, I suspect that the enthusiasm back then for mathematics in combination with the real threat of thermonuclear war encouraged many evolutionists to write impressive equations showing that even when it comes to our own undeniably thoughtful and inventive species, the Enlightenment scholar Thomas Hobbes had been right after all. In the great game called life, self-interest and selfishness rule the day.

Let's just face it, many in effect said. No individual in any species, including our own, would willingly help or collaborate with anybody else for the good of others. Check out the math. Collaboration and altruism make no evolutionary sense at all. When it comes to evolution, the cry is not "one for all, and all for one" famously associated with Alexandre Dumas' *Les Trois Mousquetaires* (The Three Musketeers). Not on your sweet life. It's a dog eat dog world out there in the natural world. There the Darwinian battle cry is "me, myself, and I." So don't be a chump and help others to survive and reproduce. Hell, no, don't you see that evolution is war? The name of the game of evolution is *competition*.

However mathematical and scientific, this Hobbesian view of nature is every bit as depressing these days as it was during the Enlightenment. This dismal view also overlooks a simple fact that is painfully obvious once you take it into account. Mathematics isn't limited to the realities of space and time. Mathematics doesn't have to conform to or take into account the real-time demands and challenges of our four-dimensional world.

Hence what should have been obvious even to mathematically inclined scientists is that anything as truly widespread in the biological world as social collaboration cannot be the great *exception* to an evolutionary rule that says natural selection favors only the survival and reproduction of individuals who are solely out for themselves. There simply must be some way for evolution to look with favor on altruism and cooperation among individuals, perhaps also between species.

Plainly evolutionists during the early decades after World War II had taken themselves down a blind alley, and had—to mix metaphors—painted themselves into a corner. Phrased succinctly: "If natural selection followed the classical models exclusively, species would not show any behavior more positively social than the coming together of the sexes and parental care."[4]

Fortunately or unfortunately, depending on your point of view, down this alley in 1964 came a gifted biologist and mathematician named William D. Hamilton (1936–2000).[5] Much like a highly talented Medieval scholar intent on improving on the Ptolemaic view of the universe, Hamilton showed mathematically how social cooperation could evolve in the dog-eat-dog world of postwar Darwinian evolutionism despite the apparent inconsistency that individuals (or, as some would argue, genes) are putting themselves at a competitive disadvantage if they help others out in the struggle for existence.[6]

Hamilton's two benchmark scientific papers published back-to-back in 1964 showed mathematically that individuals can act as if they are capable of caring for the welfare and biological success of others if such altruism is self-serving—if it aids or comes to the rescue of close biological relatives such brothers and sisters, uncles and aunts, nephews and nieces. With mathematical elegance he showed how it would be assisting their own individual evolutionary self-interest to help such people. In this way at least some of their own biological traits, their own genes, would still thereby be favored in the nasty Darwinian struggle for existence.

What to call this watered-down form of evolutionary selfishness has been much debated since Hamilton's seminal papers appeared in the *Journal of Theoretical Biology* a half-century ago.[7] Some have proposed, as did Hamilton, that this peculiar but still competitively rational form of natural selection should be called "inclusive fitness" to signal that looking after one's own reproductive success (i.e., "fitness") can include relatives who may also share the same genes that are giving you whatever edge you have over others in the struggle for existence.[8] Other experts have suggested the label "kin selection." Still others say inclusive fitness is what kin selection leads to. No matter, this mathematical explanation for the evolution of altruism and cooperation throughout the animal world is now one of the cornerstones of modern evolutionary theory.[9]

For example, in his book *The Social Conquest of the Earth* published in 2012, Edward O. Wilson, Pellegrino University Professor Emeritus at Harvard University, agrees along with most other modern evolutionists that "selection at the individual level tends to create competitiveness and selfish behavior among group members—in status, mating, and the securing of resources."[10] But nowadays he is no longer as willing as he once was to say that Hamilton showed everybody how to back out of the blind alley of postwar Darwinian competitive evolutionism to explain the fact of cooperation among individuals in some species—notably, social insects such as ants, bees, wasps, and termites, and our own species. It is Wilson's current opinion that something more than what Hamilton called inclusive fitness is needed. He now favors the older minority scientific view that natural selection between *groups*, not just between individuals, can lead to selfless behavior—which can have the added side benefit, he says, of strengthening group cohesiveness and the competitive prowess of the favored group.[11]

Ironically, there is reason to think that if he were alive today (he died in 2000), Hamilton would probably agree with Wilson, at least when it comes to human beings. He wrote in 1971 that vicious and warlike tendencies come naturally to our species, and added: "The atrocities recorded in human history appear to bear witness to the existence of a spontaneous drive to imagine and carry out cruelty which, at least in some people, in some circumstances, has been given free play and public approval."[12] Setting mathematics aside, he was willing to grant precisely what Wilson many years later would newly embrace. As Hamilton observed somewhat parenthetically in 1971, "a really appropriate term" for the mode of selection at work in many human situations may well be group selection, not individual inclusive fitness.[13] Ironic, indeed!

AT THE RISK of being firmly excluded from the group that sees itself as the rightful heirs of the Wizard of Down House, I need to point out at this juncture, perhaps like the critics of the Ptolemaic view of the universe, how it is actually not necessary to invoke either inclusive fitness or group selection to explain the evolution of friendship and social cooperation in our species, or in any similarly intelligent species such as dogs and dolphins. I am not, however, going to go so far out on a limb here as to suggest that inclusive fitness or group selection is never an appropriate way to account for the evolution of social cooperation in the biological world. In the following remarks I will stick to my own kind.

As I see it, there are four major flaws to the argument that the evolution of human friendliness and social cooperation make little sense in the competitive world view of Darwinian evolutionism without invoking inclusive fitness or group selection.[14]

The first flaw is to insist that genes, individuals, or groups are out to maximize their evolutionary fitness, that is, their reproductive success.[15] As Thomas Malthus pointed out at the end of the 18th century, it is an observable biological fact that population growth tends to be exponential—and hence, as Darwin added to the equation, in life there is a struggle for existence.

Consequently there is little need for anyone to say that all life forms are competitively striving to *maximize* the number of the offspring they sire.[16] All that is required for any species to stay active in the evolutionary game of life and not go extinct is for it to be *capable enough* to sire a *sufficient number* of offspring for it to stay in the running, generation after generation.[17] As Hamilton himself observed several years after the publication of his famous set of papers: "The animal part of our nature is expected to be more concerned with getting 'more than the average' than with getting 'the maximum possible.' "[18]

Second, Hamilton's mathematical treatment of his theory of inclusive fitness may be elegant and sound, but it underplays the four dimensions of the real world we live in. These dimensions cannot be ignored.[19] Specifically, *geographic distance* is a limiting factor on human collaboration even if we human beings are currently showing ourselves to be remarkably inventive in coming up with distance-defying ways of getting from point *A* to point *B* both practically (e.g., trains, planes, and automobiles) as well as virtually (smart phones and the Internet). A recent political scandal in the United States involving an elected official sending sexually charged pictures of parts of himself to knowing or unsuspecting recipients may be a form of distance-defying flirtation and infidelity, but for the most part, both human social life and biological reproduction are still achieved by people engaging in what social scientists call "face-to-face interaction."

One consequence of the face-to-face reality of human existence is that even today in the world of Facebook and Twitter, biological similarities and differences among individuals are strongly shaped by geography. Even now, when modern forms of transportation make it much easier than it used to be to move people from place to place either as tourists or as immigrants, the old geographic rule-of-thumb still applies that the closer any two individuals are to one another geographically, the more likely they are to share similar genes. The technical term for this patterning of human biological diversity by geography is *isolation-by-distance*.[20]

Another name for this same phenomenon, one favored by statisticians, is *spatial autocorrelation*, a designation that underscores the fact that observations about similarities and differences between individuals made at neighboring locations are not necessarily statistically independent observations. This is an indirect way of saying that if you know what *A* is like, then there is a good chance you already know what *B* is also like due to the spatial patterning of variation.

Hence there is little mystery about why natural selection under the right geographic circumstances might favor the evolution of friendliness and collaboration in any species, including our own. As Hamilton recognized and wrote about, if neighbors are likely to be like one another biologically speaking because of isolation-by-distance, then you do not have to love thy neighbor to be helping your own genes by lending them a hand across the back fence, so to speak.[21] In his own somewhat begrudging words: "Human generosity seems also to depend partly on idealism and partly on correspondences of personality that encourage friendship."[22] Tellingly, Hamilton acknowledged, too, that the mathematical challenges of such true-to-life situations—what he labeled as "the analytical complexity of the models"—can be daunting. Or as another mathematically inclined researcher has phrased the dilemma, models that are realistic enough to model nature may not be "mathematically convenient."[23] Such is real life.

Third, although I don't want to spend too much time on the issue, Darwinian natural selection is *not* just about individuals, groups, or species competing with one another in the struggle for existence. Mother Nature is a big and often heavy-handed player in the game of life. Species have to cope not just with *biological* competitors, be they relatives or not, but also with a world that can rain down upon them fire and brimstone, not to mention disease, droughts, floods, tsunamis, volcanic eruptions, climate change, and other assorted natural afflictions. Having friends as well as relatives to help you get through a disaster, or for that matter, get through the day, can make all the difference in the world.[24]

Lastly, despite the elegance of Hamilton's mathematical approach, I think he underestimated how two heads (and four legs or hands) can be better than one. Who could doubt that we have evolved as social animals because there is strength and sometimes also wisdom in numbers?[25] I think it is fascinating that recently published defenses of Hamilton's idea of inclusive fitness and the dog-eat-dog competitive evolutionism of modern Darwinism have so watered down and extended the notion of "inclusive fitness" that these days being "a relative of mine" can be taken to mean just about anybody who happens to share whatever it is that you have, genetically speaking, that would make helping them worthwhile, genetically speaking.[26] This is a loophole big enough for just about anyone to get through it, so much so it sounds like someone in Washington might have written the legislation for it.

IN 2010 EDWARD Wilson and his colleagues Martin Nowak and Corina Tarnita at Harvard got themselves in a great deal of hot water with most evolutionary biologists around the world for daring to question the value and usefulness of Hamilton's way of playing the evolutionary numbers game.[27]

They daringly concluded that there is no need at all in modern evolutionary theory for this particular mathematical idea.

This was extremely brave of them, but the nobility of their attack on one of the central tenets of modern Darwinism was tarnished in the eyes even of those who happen to agree with them (I am definitely on their side, at least when it comes to explaining human evolution) because they came out strongly instead in favor of the old idea of group selection described earlier.[28]

At least in the case of human beings, invoking this explanation to account for the evolution of our capacity to be friendly and work with one another makes sense only if it is true—shades of the Enlightenment yet again—that once upon a time we lived in separate isolated groups that were given to crushing other human groups whenever the opportunity to do so came up or could be cleverly orchestrated—say by inviting everybody in another village over to dinner, and then having them for dinner instead.

Several years earlier Nowak had published an extremely insightful paper in which he had noted how commonplace cooperation is in nature, and in particular how humans are "champions of cooperation." Though nearly everybody today agrees that the two most fundamental principles of evolution are mutation and natural selection, he went out on a limb and boldly proposed not only that "cooperation is the secret behind the open-endedness of the evolutionary process," but also that we should add "natural cooperation" as a third fundamental principle of evolution right up there along with these two.

This is a strong and decidedly unconventional suggestion entirely in keeping with what I am calling the friendship hypothesis. But before jumping on Nowak's bandwagon, a fundamental question needs to be asked and answered. What is cooperation?

PART FOUR

The Social Baseline

16

Animal Cooperation

ENLIGHTENMENT PHILOSOPHERS USED their sense of imagination to try to figure out what life would be like for our species in a "state of nature." Ever since Darwin, however, scientists have looked instead to nature herself for clues about the evolution of our human ways. The logic is simple. If our species has not been cut out of whole cloth, or made all in one glorious day by God Himself in the Garden of Eden, then we have to pin down what was on hand for evolution to work with to create our kind, step by step. Specifically, and much to the point, take our well-documented willingness to collaborate with others of our kind to get things done. Where did our capacity to do so come from? And is this worthy human talent in some way unique to our species?

As Harvard's Martin Nowak has observed, evidence of cooperation is everywhere—from the level of genes on up to whole organisms, and throughout the awesome sweep of the earth's remarkable diversity of species. Yet on this broad field of cooperative players, as Nowak has written, humans "are the champions of cooperation: From hunter-gatherer societies to nation-states, cooperation is the decisive organizing principle of human society."[1]

Even so, scientists have known for years that cooperation is commonplace throughout the biological world. The fact that cooperation is *not* a unique characteristic of humans may make it easier to figure out why we have ourselves gone down this particular evolutionary path. Consider, for example, the kind of interspecies cooperation called mutualism where two or more species are able to survive and reproduce only if they coexist.[2] A classic example of such evolved cooperation is the survival partnership that exists between fig trees and fig wasps that is apparently many millions of years old.[3] Minute wasps pollinate the fig tree's flowers that line the interior of the fig-to-be, thereby initiating the production of seeds. The figs then serve as the protective wombs, so to speak, for the eggs and young of these tiny wasps (something to remember, or perhaps forget, next time you are eating a fig and you come across crunchy bits).[4] A fine example of "you scratch my back, and I return the favor."

Commonly, however, the survival mutualism that exists between different species is not this coldly *obligatory*. From an evolutionist's point of view, for example, the relationship between human beings and domesticated maize is mutualistic, but not compulsory, at least not on the human side of the association. After all, there are foods for us to eat other than corn, whether fresh, frozen, dried, ground, hominy, or succotash.

However, the type of cooperation we need to look at more closely is not of this type. If I wanted to sound like a biologist, I would call this other type *facultative mutualism* since I am referring to the kind of collaborations in which two or more individuals or species engage with one another because they *can*, not because they *must*. Yet I don't like using such language because this terminology makes it sound like human beings cooperate with one another largely because they can see intellectually that they will somehow benefit in a direct and tangible fashion. I am confident that weighing the gains, or benefits, of collaboration may sometimes be part of human social life, but I am equally certain that people often collaborate with one another because they can and like to do so. Simply put, because it feels right, and it feels good.[5]

With this thought in mind, it is instructive to find that the primatologist Joan B. Silk has said that experts in her field of study are extremely skittish about using what she calls "the F-word" (aka "friendship") perhaps because of a narrow-minded preoccupation with the more negative aspects of animal behavior, such as competition, conflict, manipulation, coercion, and deception. She knows that the word "friendship" is not an easy one to define. Yet, as she notes: "There is a general consensus that friendships are intimate, supportive, egalitarian relationships. Companionship, trust, loyalty, commitment, affection, acceptance, sympathy, and concern for the other's welfare are also important components of friendship." Especially important—since it runs counter to the kind of cost accounting that is at the heart of modern evolutionary theory—what she calls "tit-for-tat reciprocity" is not fundamental to human friendship and may even jeopardize it. "Friendship seems to transcend an obligation to repay favors, loans, and other forms of help in kind, while less intimate relationships are based on balanced tit-for-tat exchanges."[6]

Phrased another way, it is hard to see how human friendships fit the costs-and-benefits logic of postwar competitive Darwinian evolutionism. But here's a good evolutionary question. Can we use this same word with this very same benevolent meaning when we are talking about nonhuman animals?

When it comes to what other animals do socially together rather than all on their own, we are hampered by the obvious fact that watching the behavior of other creatures does not get us into their minds and motivations. Therefore, how wise and worthy it is to talk about chimpanzee friendship, say, or whether pair-bonding in birds is anything like human marriage are open questions. As Joan Silk has said, our knowledge of friendships in nature is still extremely limited.

Let's step back, therefore, from the loaded and obviously challenging word *friendship* and tackle instead the seemingly more mundane word *cooperation* (Figure 12). Logic suggests that since cooperating calls for at least two or more of us or any other kind of creature to be involved somehow with one another, a minimal definition of this word might be that creatures that cooperate are likely to be seen in one another's company. For instance, all monkeys and apes, except orangutans, live in stable social groups. But as we all know, they are not the only animals to do so. Two of my own favorite examples of social animals are meerkats and dolphins.

FIGURE 12 A group of banded mongooses (*Mungos mungo*) on the alert, Kenya, Africa. Just moments before this picture was taken they had succeeded in driving off a martial eagle that had tried to take one of their number. This species plays a role in the animal world of East Africa similar to that of meerkats of southern Africa. (*Photograph:* Bruce Patterson.)

MEERKATS (*SURICATA SURICATTA*) are cooperative mongooses living in groups of 2 to 50 individuals in arid regions of southern Africa. According to the evolutionary biologist Tim Clutton-Brock at the University of Cambridge, a typical meerkat group comprises a dominant female, a number of subordinate females that are usually related to the dominant female, one or more immigrant males (one of which is dominant over the other males in the group), and a number of subordinate males that are usually offspring of the dominant pair.

Baby meerkats ("pups") are initially unable to find their own prey to feed upon, and even after their first month of life when they begin to venture out with foraging groups, they are dependent on older meerkats ("helpers") to give them something to eat in response to their begging calls until about the age of three months, when at last they have grown skilled enough to forage successfully for themselves.[7]

What is perhaps most fascinating about the collaborative social behavior of these creatures is that older meerkat helpers actively teach pups prey-handling skills, and do so by increasingly giving them opportunities as they mature to interact with live prey.[8] This "opportunity teaching" is important. Meerkats eat a variety of things, and many of the species they consume are hard to handle. Some are potentially quite dangerous—such as scorpions of the genera *Parabuthus* and *Opistophthalamus*. The former can deliver neurotoxins potent enough to kill a human, and the latter, although not so deadly, are armed with large powerful pincers, and can be quite aggressive. As reported by Alex Thornton and Katherine McAuliffe at Cambridge:

> After a helper gave a pup a food item, it normally remained with the pup and monitored its handling of the prey (87.5% of recorded feeds; $N = 10,479$ feeds). If pups did not attempt to handle a prey item, helpers sometimes nudged the item repeatedly with their nose or paws (8.3% of occasions; $N = 5343$ feeds). After nudging occurred, pups normally consumed the prey successfully (99% of occasions; $N = 446$ feeds). The duration of monitoring and the probability of nudging both declined with pup age, suggesting that helpers modify their behavior in response to improvements in pup competence.

I cannot resist adding that Thornton and his colleagues have also reported finding persisting differences between neighboring groups of meerkats in the wild. More than a decade of observations has established, for example, that some groups are given to being earlier risers in the morning while other groups prefer to sleep in longer. This is so despite significant overlap in the foraging territories of neighboring groups, immigration between them, and different groups sometimes living in the same burrows, although not at the same time.[9]

BOTTLENOSE DOLPHINS (*Tursiops truncatus*, the common bottlenose dolphin, and *T. aduncus*, the Indo-Pacific bottlenose dolphin, both in the family Delphinidae) live in what has been called "fission–fusion societies"—while individuals swim with other dolphins in schools, they often move around from one school to another. What this comes down to in the case of any particular individual dolphin varies a great deal. Some dolphins are more or less constant companions; others form acquaintanceships that may last only a few hours or a few days. Even so, research by David Lusseau and his colleagues at the University of Aberdeen has established that bottlenose dolphins living off the east coast of Scotland appear to be divided into two more or less discernible social units that have only limited interactions with one another. There seems to be one community of individuals seen only in the inner Moray Firth, and another outer community of individuals that are seen both in the inner firth and farther afield.[10]

Therefore, although dolphin social life can be characterized as being for the most part decidedly fluid, and although the availability of food probably plays a major role in determining the size of any given school of individuals that are swimming together at any given time, what stands out is that dolphins are unquestionably social creatures that both like the companionship of others of their kind, and whose social life is not only free-form but can also be quite far-reaching.

What stands out as well is that dolphins obviously have no trouble forming and leaving social associations and alliances. Recent research has also shown that dolphins can remember for years—at least 20 years or more—the individually distinctive calls, or "signature whistles," of those they used to hang out with regardless of kinship relatedness, sex, or duration of association.[11]

Why are they so good-natured and friendly if—given current thinking in evolutionary biology—life is all about me, myself, and I? Hanging around others without clear commitments is asking for a lot of trouble, or at any rate for a lot of competition in the game of life where the rewards are getting enough to eat and enough quality time to procreate.

Two things are certain in our uncertain world. Dolphins can communicate with one another even if they may not do so as richly as we can. They also have quite large brains. Hence I would be prepared to argue that caution needs to be observed when trying to explain what they do and why. Call it what you may, for example, but in March 2008 there was much press attention around the world for a story out of New Zealand about a local, and locally well-known, dolphin that had helped New Zealanders rescue two beached pygmy sperm whales, a mother and her calf. As the National Geographic Web service reported: "Most days Moko the bottlenose dolphin swims playfully with humans at a New Zealand beach. But this week, it seems, Moko found his mojo."[12] Witnesses have reported how they saw this locally much beloved dolphin swim up to the stranded whales and guide them to safety after all human attempts to intervene like good Samaritans on their behalf had failed. "Moko just came flying through the water and pushed in between us and the whales," Juanita Symes, one *Homo sapiens* would-be rescuer told the Associated Press. "She got them to head toward the hill, where the channel is. It was an amazing experience."

I think these two examples of cooperation as seen in other species are enough to establish that even if we are reluctant to use the F-word, cooperation in the animal world can mean more than just being seen in one another's company. Not all that is evidently social behavior, therefore, is necessarily the same in its motivations and performance. Minimally it looks like we need to make a distinction between animals that are just running with the herd, perhaps as a way of avoiding being singled out by predators, and animals that are actually engaging with one another in some friendly way. Yet even given this more focused definition of what it means to be "social," it is obvious that we are not the only intelligent, caring, and compassionate social creatures on earth, although how far it would be appropriate to extend this observation to other species is by no means resolved by looking just at these two.[13]

YET LET'S BE honest. Acknowledging that something at least resembling human-like sociality can be found elsewhere in the animal kingdom is skirting around an important issue.[14] Okay, there are other species that behave in surprisingly human-like ways when it comes to hanging out together. But why is it that we are the champions of the social graces?

This is a surprisingly difficult question to resolve, and unfortunately the trouble with many scientific theories about why we do what we do as a species is that they are often what I like to call smoking-gun theories.[15] They are purportedly about the big reason, the precise cause, for why we have evolved the way we have. Not an easy answer to pin down.

Classic examples of this bias in favor of big but simple answers are two currently popular explanations for why most of us are proficient at working well with others. The first explanation is the plausible inference that most of us are able to do so because our prehistoric forefathers hunted big game together during the Pleistocene. The second, or flip side, of this popular explanation is the counterclaim that long, long before the Pleistocene began a few million years ago our forefathers and mothers had already opted for social living to keep from being singled out individually and eaten by hungry predators with a penchant for primate flesh.[16]

Both of these explanations may have their merits, but the problem is— as hackneyed as it may sound—something like evolution that takes a long time to happen rarely happens for just a single cause.[17] Consider, for example, the proposition that we are social creatures because our forefathers needed to work together to kill and carry home big game. Relying on what is known about modern-day hunter-gatherers, the anthropologist Christopher Boehm has tried to figure out what life would have been like during the Late Pleistocene around 45,000 to 50,000 years ago when our forerunners finally began leaving Africa to colonize the rest of the world. Boehm has found— in keeping with the first hypothesis—that although hunter-gatherers today invariably both hunt and gather, they do have a preference for bagging big animals. Commonly they also subscribe to a strong social ethos against anyone coming across as overbearing and instead in favor of communal sharing of the spoils of the hunt: "their social preferences include not only a dislike of interpersonal domination and self-interested deception, but an active appreciation of those with generous traits."[18]

In light of this modern ethnographic information, Boehm reasons that Pleistocene hunter-gatherers may well have subscribed to a similar social ethos. This suggestion is a good example of what has been called the "Man, the Hunter" hypothesis about the driving force behind human biological and social evolution. Unlike Boehm's fairly benevolent phrasing of this idea, however, other versions of this popular hypothesis have usually also taken it for granted that in order to promote hunting as a viable way to make a living, evolution has had to nurture within our hearts a deep-seated instinct for killing rather than just an ardent commitment to sharing and social equality.[19]

Beyond the fairly obvious fact that "killer" versions of the Man-the-Hunter hypothesis seem to be equating what Enlightenment philosophers called the state of nature with the state of things during the Late Pleistocene, it is not obvious why our human willingness to collaborate with (or kill) one another dates back only to the Pleistocene—particularly since almost all of our living primate relatives (lemurs, lorises, tarsiers, monkeys, and the great apes) are animals that devote between 3% and 10% of their waking hours to active social interactions, most of which can be characterized as coordinated, cooperative, peaceful, and friendly.[20]

In light of this kind of observation, the anthropologist Robert Sussman at Washington University in St. Louis, an expert on the ecology and social structure of primates, has given the Pleistocene hunting hypothesis a novel twist, one he calls (somewhat tongue-in-cheek, I think) the "Man, the Hunted" hypothesis. According to this reading of human evolution, our capacity to cooperate with one another evolved not just to facilitate bagging big game, but also to help our prehistoric ancestors avoid becoming the medium-sized game bagged by predator species such as saber-toothed cats, hyenas, eagles, and crocodiles.

Less whimsically, Sussman and his colleagues have also emphasized that "cooperative behaviors, associated with collective action, are widespread across primates and include prey flushing and other forms of hunting, communal infant care, food sharing, vigilance and predator protection and group defense."[21] In other words, the benefits of social life can be more than nutritional.

I think one of the real strengths of Sussman's more encompassing way of thinking about the evolution of human sociality is that he and his colleagues are taking not just thousands of years into consideration. They are talking about millions of years. Seen from this comprehensive time perspective, it seems probable that gathering rather than big-game hunting has been one of the main driving forces behind the evolution of our species. And however whimsical the thought may be, it also seems likely that over the course of millions of years of living socially, our forerunners must have had countless opportunities to experience firsthand the survival value of having as many eyes and ears around you as you can garner when big predators are "out there" on the hunt—especially given that our species did not invent the fine art of making fire, and therefore did not have the security of cozy campfires at night, until around 400,000 to 300,000 years ago.[22]

ON THE FACE of it, these differing ideas about the evolution of our human capacity to collaborate with one another may appear to be just different answers to the same evolutionary question, but they are not. They are largely answers to different questions. Sussman's perspective may account for why we are able to tolerate being near one another and generally favor communal living over solitary roaming about here and there for food, shelter, and the occasional sexual encounter, but this is only Step 1 in being social in the ways that we humans are able to be social. In contrast, Boehm's fairly benevolent

YBP Library Services

TERRELL, JOHN.

TALENT FOR FRIENDSHIP: REDISCOVERY OF A
REMARKABLE TRAIT.
Cloth   302 P.
NEW YORK: OXFORD UNIVERSITY PRESS, 2015

EXAMINES INTELLECTUAL, SOCIAL, & CIVIC ASPECTS OF
FRIENDSHIP.
LCCN 2014019311
ISBN 0199386455   Library PO# FIRM ORDERS

	List	29.95	USD
8395 NATIONAL UNIVERSITY LIBRAR	Disc	14.0%	
App. Date 2/04/15 COLS-PSY 8214-08	Net	25.76	USD

SUBJ: FRIENDSHIP.

CLASS BF575   DEWEY# 302.34   LEVEL GEN-AC

YBP Library Services

TERRELL, JOHN.

TALENT FOR FRIENDSHIP: REDISCOVERY OF A
REMARKABLE TRAIT.
Cloth   302 P.
NEW YORK: OXFORD UNIVERSITY PRESS, 2015

EXAMINES INTELLECTUAL, SOCIAL, & CIVIC ASPECTS OF
FRIENDSHIP.
LCCN 2014019311
ISBN 0199386455   Library PO# FIRM ORDERS

	List	29.95	USD
8395 NATIONAL UNIVERSITY LIBRAR	Disc	14.0%	
App. Date 2/04/15 COLS-PSY 8214-08	Net	25.76	USD

SUBJ: FRIENDSHIP.

CLASS BF575   DEWEY# 302.34   LEVEL GEN-AC

Man-the-Hunter hypothesis basically takes our communal predispositions for granted and tries to explain why we are not just herd animals like caribou or gazelles but are instead also able to work together to make ends meet and tackle life's many challenges, fears, and disappointments—including tackling game animals many times our size in body weight and mass.

Should we, nonetheless, prefer one of these explanations over others? In my opinion, the answer is yes. François Jacob, the French biologist and a winner of the Nobel Prize for Medicine in 1965, once famously observed that evolution "works like a tinkerer—a tinkerer who does not know exactly what he is going to produce but uses whatever he finds around him whether it be pieces of string, fragments of wood, or old cardboards; in short it works like a tinkerer who uses everything at his disposal to produce some kind of workable object."[23] Jacob added that evolution is unable to create new things from scratch. Instead, in its own piecemeal fashion, evolution makes a wing out of what was once a leg, part of an ear out of a piece of jaw bone. No wonder evolution takes a long time.

If so, then it is entirely relevant to take note of the fact that the last common ancestor we shared with chimpanzees and bonobo before we went off to write our own evolutionary story roamed the earth around 6 to 8 million years ago. Between then and the time Boehm's explanation would begin to kick in to play a role in our evolution as social beings was a matter of literally, not just figuratively, millions of years and millions of ancestral generations. Living together over the course of such an immensely long period of time meant that our ancestors had literally millions of daily opportunities to tinker with what was at hand and work out how to act collaboratively, not just live collectively. Given such innumerable opportunities, it would surely have been remarkable indeed if our ancestors had not tried to make something out of at least some of these many opportunities to work together. Evolutionists generally insist that evolution is blind. What this basically means is that natural selection has to work with what is immediately at hand and cannot anticipate future needs or developments. There is no reason to quarrel with this basic premise. Yet as every business entrepreneur knows, success is not just a matter of having the right opportunities to do something. Success depends also on being *aware* of promising opportunities when they arise. Is Darwinian evolution always an exception to this rule?

We have now seen that human cooperation is unusual but not entirely unique in the animal world. What about human awareness? How much did evolution have to tinker with our ancestral animal sense of awareness to turn it into modern human social awareness?

17

The Question of Animal Awareness

PRIMATES HAVE UNUSUALLY large brains relative to their body mass even by mammalian standards.[1] One explanation for this, and one in keeping with the current Darwinian supposition that competition is the name of the game of life, is the *Machiavellian intelligence hypothesis*. According to this argument, since they are intensely social animals, primates need really big brains to help them outwit those they are living with tooth-to-jowl in the lifelong struggle for resources and reproductive opportunities. Big brains are also handy, it is said, when forming strategic alliances with others in the group to achieve these same personal goals, and they have inestimable value, too, for keeping track of who is actually pulling his or her weight in the struggle for survival and reproduction, and who is just being a self-serving freeloader.[2]

This particular modern Darwinian argument has also been called the *social brain hypothesis* since it does not take a great deal of Leslie's powers of imagination (Chapter 4) to see that the rewards of being able to be with others might be many, not just Machiavellian: food, security, comfort, companionship, love, friendship... the list goes on.[3] This more generous labeling for the idea in question seems like a step in the right direction, but I think it is worth adding that sometimes doing something can be its own reward, and it doesn't have to be for some other reason or reward. We could think of all sorts of reasons why someone plays golf or climbs a mountain, but please let's not entirely overlook the likelihood that golf can be fun, and convention has it that rugged outdoor types climb mountains just because they are there. It is hard to imagine that either golf or mountain climbing adds much to one's evolutionary reproductive success, but since I engage in neither, perhaps I am missing something obvious I ought to know about but don't.

I am not trying to suggest that it isn't worth inquiring about the possible payoffs of why humans or other animals do what they do. Far from it (Chapter 22), but I happen to think that an equally important question is to ask not just *why*, but also *how*. What does it take, for instance, for an individual to be able to cooperate with others of its kind, or for that matter, with those of other kinds?

There are many ways to approach this fundamental question. One of the most revealing can be to ask how well and how accurately individuals are (a) *aware* of what others around them are thinking and doing, and (b) *understand* what would happen if they worked together with others rather than all on their own. However simple sounding, these are huge questions. Scientists have been working on them for years. Since it takes (a) to get to (b), let's now take a closer look at the question of awareness.

I SUSPECT MOST of us take it for granted that animals are aware of what they and others are doing, and have sensations, feelings, and intentions. Not every scientist does. When I was an undergraduate at Harvard in the early 1960s, one such skeptical researcher was the behavioral psychologist and Harvard professor Burrhus Frederic Skinner (1904–1990). For B. F. Skinner, the mind was an impenetrable "black box" that nobody could open and look into. Consequently he saw little value in talking about such "mentalistic explanations" as wants, fears, desires, feelings, and purposes. Not even in the case of sophisticated animals like you and me. A black box is a black box regardless who or what is carrying it around on their shoulders or up there at their front end.

For a great many years during the last century, experts like Skinner pretty much ruled (and reigned in) the study of animal awareness and intentional (purposeful) behavior.[4] Not so today, thanks in particular to the late animal behaviorist Donald R. Griffin (1915–2003) at Rockefeller University, who is widely credited as being the founder of the modern field of cognitive ethology—the comparative study of animal thinking and consciousness.

As Griffin explained in 2001 in *Animal Minds: Beyond Cognition to Consciousness*, we now realize that from a Darwinian perspective, conscious thinking could well be a core function of *any* creature's central nervous system.[5] How so? Chiefly because any creature able to consciously ponder alternative actions and their likely outcomes *before* making a move has an obvious advantage over any creature lacking such insight into achieving whatever it is that it needs to achieve (or obtain)—or alternatively, what it needs to avoid. If we grant that this kind of thinking in human beings is Laurence-thinking

(Chapter 4), then we probably need to accept that other animal species, too, may have such capabilities.

While Griffin and others would agree with the average man or woman on the street that human consciousness must be vastly more complex, versatile, and interesting (to humans, at least) than how thinking is done in other animal species, there is now a strong and growing scientific consensus that in one way or another all animals are probably capable of acting consciously and hence intentionally to achieve their desires and improve their chances of survival in a hostile world. By the same token, however, there is also scientific consensus today that it is unwise to credit people with anything approaching omniscience. Just as there is scant reason to believe that animals are fully aware of everything that is going on around them, so too, it must be granted—as I discussed in Chapter 4—that human beings are aware only of what might be called the "tip of the iceberg" of what is going on. Or, for that matter, what is happening also inside their bodies.[6]

Therefore, while acknowledging that words like "awareness" and "consciousness" can mean different things depending on the species in question, there is little to be gained by limiting the existence of both solely to the species *Homo sapiens*.[7] As Griffin wrote in *Animal Minds*, the capacity to be consciously aware of being in the world may well be so essential to survival that "it is the sine qua non of animal life, even for the smallest and simplest animals that have any central nervous system at all."

MY FATHER WAS brilliant at reading other people. Within minutes after we had come into a restaurant, for example, he would have our waitress—we now say server to acknowledge that gender is not an obligate part of the role—in the palm of his hand, not only laughing at his jokes, which were often risqué, but also nudging my dad affectionately on the shoulder. It takes real talent to make someone who was a stranger only moments ago feel this comfortable with you so quickly.

Technically what he was really good at is often labeled as having a well-developed "theory of mind," or ToM for short. ToM is generally defined as the ability to reason about the mental states of others—such as their beliefs, desires, and intentions, and to use such reasoning to predict and explain what others have done or are going to do.[8] Hence these days ToM is also called "mentalizing."[9]

Although exactly what a ToM is and how it works is often debated, the capacity to reason in this way about other minds, as the psychologist Adam Waytz at Harvard University and his colleagues have remarked, is an impressive tool that nearly all humans possess.[10] Calling this capacity a "tool" is a wise choice, because this terminology underscores that having such a talent can be both beneficial and purposeful. Beneficial in the sense of helping you to do something, and purposeful in the sense of helping you figure out how to get what you want to do done. For both reasons, it is not hard to see how Darwinian natural selection might favor the evolution of such a talent not only in our species but in other sentient creatures, as well.

Importantly, these same researchers note, too, that our being able to mentally find common ground with other individuals increases the perceived similarity between ourselves and others, thereby making them less strange and more predictable, or at any rate, more seemingly so. Hence the ability to have a ToM about what others are thinking and planning may be crucial to being able to say hello to strangers and initiate the social give-and-take that together can turn a stranger into a friend. I would argue, in fact, that a good part of what is called "making friends" or "becoming a friend" is precisely this—reasoning about the mental state of others to discover or develop common ground with them. Furthermore, on the reverse side of this same coin, those with whom we intellectually cannot find common ground may be seen as dull-witted, uninteresting, and perhaps suspiciously unpredictable, as well.

BUT WHAT ABOUT other animals? Do at least some other species have ToM abilities? Josep Call and Michael Tomasello at the Max Planck Institute for Evolutionary Anthropology in Leipzig, Germany, have concluded that when it comes to chimpanzees, for instance, it is time for us to quit thinking that our nearest primate relatives read and react only to the behavior of others that they can see. All of the evidence to date, they suggest, points to the conclusion that chimpanzees understand to some degree both what others perceive and know as well as the goals and intentions of others. "There is much less evidence overall, but it is possible that other non-human primate species also have a similar understanding, and as do, perhaps, some bird species."[11]

They may well be right, but a few reservations are needed. As their research colleague Brian Hare at Duke University has reported, it seems that chimpanzees are not good at reading social cues in cooperative and communicative contexts. This is a vastly important skill for humans that begins to develop in early childhood. It is possible, therefore, that this ability evolved in our human ancestors *after* they had split off the evolutionary family tree from chimpanzees and bonobos six to eight million years ago.[12]

One difficulty in figuring out what ToM is and how this talent works in our own or other species has been noted by Ian Apperly at the University of

Birmingham in England. Researchers interested in ToM are not always talking about (or so it would seem) the same thing.[13] Yes, there is no doubt that most adults and older children are able to intuit in an often coherent, organized way what others are thinking and planning. As they get older, children between the ages of two and five become increasingly competent at doing so. Whether the same holds for even younger children is far less certain. More to Apperly's point, however, the recognition that humans clearly possess ToM abilities does not in itself tell us much about how these abilities actually work either in our own species or for other kinds of animals—assuming that at least some other species may have the same or at any rate comparable socially perceptive abilities.

Confusing? Absolutely, and just to make matters more so, I should add that Apperby and his colleague Stephen Butterfill suggested recently that humans may use the two-tiered approach to reasoning that Daniel Kahneman and others have written so much about—and we discussed in Chapter 4—to make inferences about the minds of others.[14] Sometimes, he says, we arrive at ToM conclusions quickly and as efficiently as possible (that is, in a "Lou" way) using fairly rote techniques—quick-and-dirty knee-jerk tactics needed, say, when we find ourselves being suddenly confronted by a potentially dangerous foe. In other situations, however, we need to reason carefully (in a "Laurence" way) to arrive at solid and workable understandings of what and why others are behaving the way they evidently are.

Both approaches, they suggest, are equally important and necessary for human survival and social life. Seen from this perspective, currently available evidence hints that young children and some other nonhuman animals make use of abilities drawn from the first tier of ToM skills since it is known that they can quickly, efficiently, but rather inflexibly arrive at fairly good judgments about what others know and believe at least in relatively uncomplicated situations. It may only be later in life for human beings, and possibly not at all in the case of other species, that a second, more insightful tier of ToM judgments can be mastered—judgments about others based on more established life experiences and perhaps requiring facility with language skills, as well.

AT PRESENT, RESEARCH on animal and human awareness and social cognition is growing rapidly. Such research, however, is still dealing with many uncertainties, and often, too, with results that are sometimes simply bewildering, sometimes openly contradictory. And Ian Apperly has underscored one of the crucial unresolved issues. How do people set aside what they think and know so that they can reason successfully from another person's point of view, however seemingly erroneous?

This may be a bigger issue than Apperly suspects. Being able to say hello even to strangers, for instance, is not just a matter of quickly and efficiently sizing them up on first encounter. How well we do so may critically depend also on what we already believe we know about strangers in general, not just the stranger in particular who happens to be down the hall or in that poorly lighted alley.

A common way of talking about this vital issue is to say that to know others, you must first know yourself. But if this is true, then what we need to know about ourselves includes knowing what we falsely know or wrongly fear that can interfere with how we think or suspect others are feeling, believing, thinking, or intending to do. Needless to say, such a degree of self-awareness and objectivity is wonderful to imagine but can be difficult to achieve. Nonetheless, having an evolved capacity to be aware not just of others around you, but also of what they may be thinking and are likely to do is more than just a neat intellectual blessing. Guessing wrong about what someone else is thinking and planning could mean ending up dead. But misreading the thoughts and intentions of others because of one's own prejudices and false assumptions could mean they are the ones who end up dead instead. We need to be careful how and why we stand our ground.

18

Babies and Big Brains

ONCE UPON A time it seemed easy and straightforward to say what makes us unique as human beings. For hundreds of years the answer was that God had created us to be special and rule over all the rest of His earthy accomplishments. Ever since Darwin, however, the game has been on to discover instead precisely what is it that makes us more than just another great ape that either must go around naked, or cover itself with a suitably large fig leaf or some other fashionable article of clothing.

What has often been lost in this quest for what it is that makes us special and possibly also still worthy of God's undivided attention is the simple fact previously discussed that evolution creates something new out of something old by tinkering with something already available. Given this limitation on how creative evolution can be, what defines us as a species apart from other species is far more likely to be a matter of degrees than of absolutes.

In the previous chapter we looked at how fully animals other than ourselves are likely to be aware of what others are doing and thinking. But I mentioned there briefly, too, that working with others also calls for understanding what could happen if instead of working alone, whatever needs to be done is done collaboratively. In this respect, the difference between us and other primates may actually be quite extreme.

This is, at any rate, the opinion of Michael Tomasello at the Max Planck Institute, who sees that our having both the ability and the motivation to share goals and intentions with others in collaborative activities is basically unique to our species.[1] In his own words: "Underlying humans' uniquely cooperative lifeways and modes of cultural transmission are a set of species-unique social-cognitive processes, which we may refer to collectively as skills and motivations for sharing intentionality."[2] Furthermore we are born, he suggests, with the fundamental skills and motivations needed to be so cooperative—or at any rate we are born with the capacity to develop during childhood the skills and the motivations required.

If Tomasello is right, we should be careful when talking about animal cooperation and awareness to distinguish at least three sorts, or perhaps more accurately degrees, of social behavior in the animal world. Some animals are social in the sense that individuals normally hang out together, perhaps because there can be safety in numbers. But the individuals involved may be only minimally aware of one another, and may interact together rarely or only in quite rudimentary ways. Examples would be schools of fish swimming in unison and herds of reindeer or dairy cows that move together from place to place—but do so with little or no social coordination beyond perhaps follow-the-leader.

Then there are social animals that travel together in groups within which individuals actively interact with one another at least in certain fairly stereotyped ways—for example, social grooming by monkeys and apes, which appears to be one of the ways that these animals maintain their social alliances or dominance rankings, and which may sometimes lead to sexual encounters. And in the case of bonobos, these may often include same-sex encounters, so the objective is not always biological reproduction to enhance one's own inclusive fitness.

Then there are the sorts of fully collaborative activities that Tomasello and his colleagues see as being particularly, and perhaps uniquely, human that involve sharing goals and intentions with others—that is, the kinds of social interactions they call "shared intentionality."[3] Examples abound: parades on the 4th of July, rallies and political conventions, prayer groups and church services, Ginger Rogers or Eleanor Powell dancing with Fred Astaire, a symphony orchestra. All are witness not only to our capacity to share intentions and goals, but also to how pleasurable we apparently find our activities shared with others. And sadly, I think we would have to include here even public lynchings and military maneuvers.

IT IS NO skin off our teeth to grant that other creatures may have their wants, needs, and passions as well as varying degrees of intelligence, geniality, and perhaps compassion. In addition, although acknowledging that words like "awareness" and "consciousness" may have somewhat different meanings depending on the species in question, there is little to be gained by limiting the existence of both solely to the species *Homo sapiens*—a point already noted in the previous chapter. Yet while granting that we have all this in common at least to a degree with other creatures on earth, there are two characteristics of our species that although perhaps not entirely unique to us are nonetheless absolutely compulsory when it comes to our kind of primate. These two evolved characteristics are matters of utter necessity, not elective choice—that is, they are both *obligate* rather than *facultative* traits.

First, *we are obligate social learners*. Although there are those who would make the list longer,[4] beyond such basics as smiling, blinking, and breathing, almost everything we are able to do in the course of getting through life as human beings is something that we have learned from others even if our own personal experiences play an important role in how we conduct ourselves and how we handle particular situations, novel or routine. As the Australian philosopher of science Kim Sterelny has phrased the argument, human survival is dependent on "high volume, high fidelity cultural learning."[5]

Second, *we must invest a great deal of time and effort in caring for our young*, for without our intervention and love, human newborns and young children die. There are no exceptions to this rule.

These two basic characteristics of our species are intimately entwined with one another. But before exploring later how this is so, let's first consider each of them in turn, beginning with obligate social learning.

AVERAGE BRAIN SIZE across the primate order varies from less than 2 cc in mouse lemurs to more than 1,200 cc in humans.[6] More than half of this variation is largely a function of body size. All other things being equal, the bigger the body, the larger the brain. But this is not the whole story. Elephants and whales have brains several times larger than our own, but we are the ones who study them, not the other way around. Therefore, intelligence, however you wish to define it, is not just a matter of brain size, although even in this instance, our outstanding level of intelligence appears to be an enhancement of physical properties also seen in nonhuman primates rather than a set of unique characteristics that only human beings possess.[7]

Our brains are roughly three times larger than those of our nearest primate relatives, the great apes.[8] Many plausible evolutionary explanations have been offered for why our brains are this big.[9] One clue is that our brains are not just big in volume. They are also notable for the size of the neocortex, which in our species is significantly larger than expected for a nonhuman primate of the same brain volume.[10] The neocortex is the outer area of the brain usually said to be the seat of higher brain functions such as sensory perception, spatial reasoning, conscious thought, and speech, as well as the ability to make tools, make friends with strangers, and keep the friends we already have reasonably friendly and willing to be around us, just to name a few. These are all capacities, according to anthropologist Robin Dunbar at the University of Liverpool and his colleague Susanne Shultz, that are critically needed for the successful conduct of human (and primate) social life—an inference, you will recall, that has been nicknamed the social brain hypothesis.[11]

Dunbar and Shultz have also pointed to the fact, discussed in Chapter 4, that our brains are one of the most energetically expensive organs in the body, second only to the heart. The cost of having a head on your shoulders worthy of our species is roughly 8 to 10 times higher than the cost of maintaining muscle tissue.[12] Given this disparity, it is a bit of a mystery why our brains are so big, a question that I have found often comes to mind soon after election day when I learn that the candidate I voted for didn't win. With an organ this big and costly on their shoulders, why on earth would anyone have voted for the candidate who won? Mystery of mysteries.

While Dunbar's social brain hypothesis has much intuitive appeal as an explanation if for no other reason than that highly social animals like ourselves and other primates do spend a lot of time in the company of others, there seems little reason to put all our explanatory eggs in one basket. As Dunbar himself acknowledges, the payoffs of being intelligent are many, not just social. In keeping with this observation, a number of experts have proposed a more general version of Dunbar's hypothesis, one they call the *cultural intelligence hypothesis*.[13]

In any case, it is not easy to say precisely what the word *intelligence* means. One simple definition would be that intelligence is the ability to deal flexibly with new or complex situations, to learn, and to innovate. To this reasonable definition some would wisely add that what is biologically inheritable about intelligence that can be tinkered with by natural selection is only the *capacity* to invent effective new solutions to life's problems (that is, the intellectual aptitude I have called Leslie thinking), *not* the solutions themselves.

But this is not all. Having to individually reinvent over and over again clever ways of handling challenging situations is not nearly as effective as being able to draw upon the solutions that others have previously devised. Therefore, it is only to be expected that along with intelligence, evolution might also try to promote a biologically inheritable capacity to teach and to learn from others. I think this is in part what Tomasello means when he talks about our species having the ability and motivation to share goals and intentions with others while engaging in collaborative activities. Through social teaching and learning, the rewards of any given individual's intellectual creativity can be shared, and may potentially also be stockpiled over time—assuming the memory capacities of the human brains socially linked with one another are large enough—in the form of socially (rather than biologically) inherited ideas, ideals, and the like. In the jargon of some today: *intelligence + social learning = socially inherited knowledge.*

THERE IS NO undisputed evidence suggesting that individuals in any great ape species intentionally engage in teaching others in their social group.[14] Needless to say, this is decidedly not true of our own species. Nobody is quite sure how long both social learning and social teaching have been human characteristics. Tomasello reports that among nonhuman primates (and in the case of at least a few other species, as well), social learning is essentially individualistic. "In contrast," he notes, "human culture and cultural transmission are fundamentally cooperative," and "human social life is more cooperatively structured than that of other primates."[15]

To this I would add an important qualification. It is not necessary to be an Enlightenment philosopher to think that without the support of social learning and teaching, individual human beings would have very little chance of survival. For this reason, I think we have to accept that one of the defining characteristics of our species, as I have already suggested, is that we are obligate social learners. Thankfully we have the brains for it, although this still does not account for why some people don't vote for the candidates I like who are so obviously head-and-shoulders above the rest.

WHAT ABOUT THE other obligate characteristic of our species I mentioned earlier, namely, that we have to invest a great deal of time and effort in caring for our young since without such dedication and hard work newborns and young children will die? My colleague Robert Martin at Field Museum of Natural History in Chicago has written extensively on the evolution of all primates (lemurs, lorises, tarsiers, monkeys, apes, and humans). From this unusually broad perspective, he sees us as being unique in another way, too, one that is closely tied to social learning as an obligate characteristic.

Although the correlation, he says, between brain size and body size in the case of a human fetus or newborn fits the usual primate pattern, human brain growth differs markedly following birth from that of every other primate, indeed from that of any other mammal. Rather than merely doubling in size as in other primates, a human baby's brain increases in size almost fourfold following birth.

Why is this significant? The slowing down of brain growth that usually starts around the time of birth in nonhuman primates does not occur in human babies until around the end of the first year of life. Said another way, a child's brain continues to grow for about a year after birth at basically the same rapid rate characteristic of the mammalian fetal (i.e., pre-birth) stage of development. As Martin relates, the length of human pregnancy should actually be reckoned as 21 months: 9 months inside the womb followed by another 12 months outside of it. This helps explain, he says, why human newborns are so helpless in comparison with other primate young.[16]

Another reason for this strange human pattern of fetal-like brain growth both inside the womb and then for a year thereafter is that during our evolution as a species, our ancestors did not just develop bigger brains. They also began walking around upright on what would one day be called feet rather than hoofing it about on all fours. The biomechanics of assuming this upright posture led to the reshaping of the human pelvis where our thigh bones meet our bodies. Unfortunately, for women this also meant narrowing the birth canal.[17]

Although this change complicated things, even without this narrowing of the birth canal, our babies could not be born alive and kicking if their brains at birth were further along in their growth toward adult size—and therefore bigger—than they are. So something had to give, and it could not be the birth canal. Hence that something was the size of the human brain at birth.

Although it is debatable exactly when the shift to upright body posture and mobility happened, the bigger our brains got during the course of the last four million years or so since our early ancestor *Australopithecus* was wandering around some parts of Africa, the more difficult and dangerous giving birth became. Evidently the only way for evolution to pave the way for our forebears to take advantage of both (a) having a big brain and (b) walking upright— thereby freeing up what we call our hands for doing lots of neat things well beyond just walking (although I am confident that texting-while-driving was not intended to be one of the skills we humans would one day rather stupidly master)—was to force our babies out of the womb and into the real world well before their brains have finished growing and their skulls have finished swelling to a suitably solid and workable dimension. Another word for this condition is called being born premature.

In this instance, however, it is only a baby's brain at birth that is lagging behind the standard and usual primate norm. As Bob Martin explains, a newborn's brain is not unusually large in comparison with that of other primate species given that our babies are also on the large size all around at birth, not just in brain size. Instead what is unusual about our offspring is that the brain continues to grow for so much longer following birth than is true for other primates, and becomes so much bigger, again in comparison with our primate relatives.

This whole topic strikes home for me most intimately. My twin sister and I were born four weeks premature during World War II. Jane arrived five minutes before I did. She was a few ounces bigger than me, but we each weighed barely more than three pounds. So we completed the last month of my mother's third trimester outside the womb and under oxygen tents in the hospital where we had greeted our first day of freedom from her womb. This is why I like to claim occasionally that my twin and I had been womb-mates for eight months before we were kicked out perhaps for nonpayment of rent.

I don't know why I am laughing at this wisecrack even if you are not. When my mother was alive she told us often enough that nobody back then had thought I was going to live to see the completion of my first month of life, although the prospects for the survival of my twin sister were rosy. My sister has also reminded me that our mother loved to tell people that as preemies, we had looked a lot like plucked chickens. But here is what is relevant about this personal rumination. In truth, all of us who are human are in a way born premature—at least when it comes to the human brain. As twins often do, my sister and I were simply jumping the gun.

Hence, although human babies are born with their eyes and ears open and ready for them to begin mastering the fine arts of human social life by paying attention to those around them, our newborns and infants are utterly and totally dependent physically for their survival (and hence the survival of our species) on the kindness of strangers—or at any rate, on the commitment, good will, and unselfish labors of the primary adults who come into their lives. And make no mistake here, as everybody knows, infants are not just a little dependent on others; they are totally, absolutely dependent on what others do for them.

WHILE MINDFUL OF my own caveat that we must be wary about believing singular "smoking-gun" theories of evolution, I think it is impossible to ignore that from an evolutionary point of view, the utter helplessness of human infants makes our species exceedingly vulnerable to extinction. As I have already said, if the adults in their tender lives were to walk away from them, human newborns and infants would die. And with them, our species.

Therefore, it was absolutely essential that evolution should nurture within us whatever it takes to make adults bond strongly with, and possibly lay down their lives for, this weakest link in the pipeline of our survival as a species. It is now time, therefore, to move on to take a closer look at why is it so easy for most of us to fall in love with babies. The fact that most of us do so has an impact on more than just the survival of our species. Our willingness and capacity to commit ourselves to rearing our young also has a lot to show us about how we deal with each other as adults, why we are willing to play ball or Frisbee with the dogs we bring into our lives for our children to play with, and why we are able to make friends even with strangers.

19

Mission Impossible

ALTHOUGH I AM USUALLY at the Field Museum in Chicago during the work week, on weekends I live at home on 11 acres of rolling farmland in southwestern Wisconsin. Awhile back I was in the garden harvesting basil leaves for pesto. I heard an unexpected although immediately recognizable sound coming from somewhere under our house. It was a small kitten's meowing—plaintive, insistent, repetitive, continuous, and strongly appealing. I couldn't see the kitten, but it was obvious that although it could see me, it wasn't about to come any farther toward me across the open lawn.

I went into the house with my basil cuttings. The loud, rapid, and persistent meowing continued. Eventually I caught sight of a tiny black kitten sitting in the woods and looking in our direction just a few feet behind the house. The meowing continued. Clearly it wasn't about to give up on me. I went out and sat on our front steps. Much to my surprise, the kitten was already sitting on the stone garden wall an arm's reach away from the steps. Was it reading my mind? I waited a minute or two and then went back into the house feeling like I was at risk of losing my heart to this incredibly cute little thing even though I am truly allergic to cats.

The meowing continued. I went out and sat down on the steps again. By then the kitten was even closer. Since I am not a cat fancier, I have to say I was honestly surprised at its boldness. And from an evolutionary point of view, how reckless. There are hawks and coyotes in our neck of the woods. Bringing such loud and obvious attention to itself was foolhardy. Yet it was certain that this cat couldn't resist approaching me.

I sat still to see how close it would come. To make this story short, within minutes it was rubbing back and forth around my legs, purring contentedly, and in quick order climbing in a surprisingly gentle way up my leg to nestle in the crook of my arm. This was a very happy stranger indeed. Needless to say, we had to find it a place to call home even if that couldn't be our place.

Given that I had always thought cats are not terribly social creatures, this kitten's behavior astonished me. I have since learned that such behavior is typical of kittens only a few weeks old. At that age they actively seek out companionship.[1] It is only later that they are likely to become feline imperious.

What about my own reaction to this kitten? Conventional wisdom would probably have it that I was immediately taken by this little animal because it was little; because it was plaintively calling for food, comfort, and companionship; and yes, because it was really cute. For comparable reasons, I would argue, this kitten was drawn to making its appeal to the nearest receptive individual—however large, inedible, and unattractive—it caught sight of, namely me—although I have to wonder if it had already tried to make the same appeal to one or more of our dairy heifers without success. We were both hard-wired by evolution to be this way, although evidently mine is a life-long predisposition while the average cat may get over such susceptibility sooner rather than later.

The psychologist Matthew D. Lieberman has proposed that "we think people are built to maximize their own pleasure and minimize their own pain. In reality, we are actually built to overcome our own pleasure and increase our own pain in the service of following society's norms."[2] Saying this in some respects begs the question. Or actually two. Are we really wired to have this kind of reaction to small, cute, and clearly needy creatures? If so, why are human beings wired this way? Let's take the first question first.

IT MAY COME across to you as avoiding the issue, but there is no simple explanation for how I reacted to this kitten. One thing is certain, nonetheless. I responded as positively as I did not simply because of how I was wired by evolution or because I experienced some kind of automatic hormonal rush attributable to an instinctual response to its size, appearance, and plaintive cries. It is clear, for instance, that how I was raised as a human being by others around me is definitely part of the explanation. I learned quite early in life that cats and kittens are to be seen as pets, not potential menu items. It never occurred to me that day when I was in the basil patch I could opt to raise this kitten in a cage, say, to adulthood and then make dinner *with* it rather than *for* it. My failure to consider this culinary option had nothing whatsoever to do with my biology or biochemistry, but rather is attributable to my social upbringing.[3] After all, it is not just an urban legend that there are places on earth where people are more than willing to add cat (or dog) to the family stew pot.

Part of the explanation is also that this kitten had an advantage over other similarly small, cute, and needy creatures. Although it is common knowledge that cats can "escape into the wild," house cats are domesticated animals even where they may be served for dinner. In other words, this kitten had the evolved capacity—partially as a product of its domestication by human beings—to appeal directly to me both vocally and physically (rubbing up against another creature is about as physical as you can get except perhaps when making babies is the aim in mind). Although it is possible to tame individuals belonging to a broad range of animal species, doing so is often not easy and usually takes more than a degree of dedication on the part of the human who is intent on forming something more than just a passing relationship with the adorable object of his or her affection. Not so with domestic cats and dogs. They understand us better than most, and know well how to get through to us, as unquestionably this kitten did.

Similarly, how we evolved socially as a species at least partially through our own self-domestication made it possible for me to "understand" that this kitten needed something from me.[4] Said another way, I found it easy to sympathize with its evident plight. The topic of empathy has long been a focus of research in psychology and allied sciences, and continues to be the subject of much disagreement.[5] Saying that I could easily empathize with this kitten may not be saying a great deal that is crystal clear, but empathy is undoubtedly part of the reason, nonetheless.

IF EXPLAINING HOW I responded is complicated and perhaps confusing, so too is accounting for why evolution gave me the capacity to do so regardless of any uncertainty about the precise details involved. Nobody these days would contest the claim that individuals in all gregarious primate species have in one way or another evolved the capacity to develop strong social attachments to one another.[6] Why? One plausible and rather self-evident reason, as discussed previously (Chapter 15), is that being able to live together makes it easier and safer to meet life's challenges (collectively keeping predators at bay would be one example). Without denying that this may be one of the reasons why human beings, like so many of their primate relatives, are such committed social creatures, I think there is another compelling reason behind our sociality. We are strongly predisposed to be cooperative and collaborative because we must bond ardently with—and possibly even lay down our lives for—the "weakest link" in our survival as a species: infants from a mammalian point of view are markedly immature because, as a species, we have invested so heavily in having big brains.

I think this last observation is so important that it should definitely be put on a bumper sticker (Figure 13).

FIGURE 13 Big brain = warm heart. (*Source*: author.)

Like any good bumper sticker worthy of the back of a car, this particular one has several layers of meaning, and those layers are tied up with the possibly cryptic thought that positive feedback has had a hand in the evolutionary creation of our kind of primate.

Assuming that this thought does indeed come across as rather cryptic, let me hasten to explain what I mean by such a statement by first repeating what was said in the previous chapter about babies and big brains: (1) as evolution gave us bigger and bigger brains, it became *increasingly important* to postpone most of human brain growth until after rather than before birth; (2) as a consequence, parental commitment to childcare and tender nurturance of the young also became *increasingly indispensable*, so much so that eventually long-term parenting became an *obligate* requirement for the survival of our species; and (3) to fulfill this obligate requirement, human beings have to be (a) *motivated* to care for infants and young children through thick and thin; (b) *aware of* and *attentive to* the needs of these helpless individuals who start off being much too young to tell us themselves what they need us to do for them; and (c) *successful* at meeting their needs despite the rather ironic truth that our species has so strongly committed itself to social learning that knowing precisely what to do to achieve this worthy and essential goal *does not come naturally to us*—despite what popular wisdom may say about the alleged naturalness of our species' supposed "mothering instincts."[7]

When spelled out in this lengthy fashion it does not seem at all surprising that some people consider it the better part of wisdom to avoid going down the road to parenthood. What's required seems enormously challenging, a veritable mission impossible. So let's ask the same question again one more time: Why on earth would anyone accept such a challenging assignment?

THE POPULAR TELEVISION series *Mission Impossible*, which first aired in September 1966 and later inspired several movies starring Tom Cruise, was based on the dramatic premise that a small task force of secret agents would be willing to accept seemingly impossible assignments and, week after week, would be able to triumph over dictators and evil-doers of all kinds. Beyond the obvious premise that the Impossible Missions Force was deeply motivated by a noble desire to see truth, justice, and the American way of life triumph against all odds, I do not now recall all these many decades later whether the issue of motivation was ever addressed in any meaningful way. Nevertheless, I do not think we should overlook the simple likelihood that part of the explanation for why many people may be willing to become parents despite the obvious drawbacks and challenges involved may often be comparable to what we saw back then on the television screen. We may do so because we can see that it is the right thing to do, because other people are expecting us to do it, and because we can see that parenting is the adult's role that has been written into our socially learned script called "life" as it should be properly performed on our way from the cradle to the grave.

However, before we pat ourselves too dramatically on the head for being such thoughtful souls, I think we need to get a better perspective on how "impossible" the job of human parenting actually is. Even if it is true (as indeed it is) that human babies are born more helpless and dependent than other primate babies, in part because they come into the world with brains that are only about 25 percent finished growing, how does a human child's striking vulnerability compare with that of babies in other species? Is our assignment truly extraordinary? Or are we just making a mountain out of a mole hill to make ourselves come across to one another as special, perhaps even divinely so?

EVOLUTION HAS COME up with an incredible number of ways for species to reproduce their kind generation after generation. Some species simply bank on the odds that if they bring into the world a great number of offspring, then at least some of their progeny will survive long enough to later mate and reproduce. At the other end of the spectrum of reproductive strategies are species such as our own that opt instead to invest heavily both before and after birth in the nurturance of just one or two new individuals at a time. Between these two extremes are countless other ways of going about it. In fact, the known diversity of the ways of being a parent is so astonishing that I need to watch myself. I would love to explore this intriguing side of nature with you, but we need to stay focused. Here are only two rather extreme examples: North American deer and rattlesnakes.

Fawns of the North American deer species *Odocoileus virginianus*, the white-tailed deer, and *O. hemionus eremicus*, the mule deer, survive pretty much on their own for the first three to four weeks of life by hiding and keeping a low profile while waiting for their mothers to return to nurse and groom them one to three times a day from wherever they have gone off to forage for food—although starting around two weeks of age, fawns may begin to forage for themselves for short periods, and by two months of age, they are generally able to handle their own nutritional needs.

These two closely related species of deer differ somewhat in their behavior as adults. Mule deer are adapted ecologically to more open habitats than whitetails, and at least partly as a consequence, they differ from the latter both in their social behavior and survival strategies. For instance, adult mule deer can reduce the risk of predation by coyotes (*Canis latrans*) by foraging in groups, and they may aggressively confront attackers, which can result in fewer fawn losses and possibly greater population growth. Whitetails, on the other hand, are more likely to run for cover when a predator comes along, which means that their offspring are left pretty much on their own to fare as best they can by staying hidden or running off—although there are reports of female whitetails sometimes confronting or attacking predators such as coyotes, foxes (*Vulpes vulpes*), and bobcats (*Lynx rufus*) that come too near their young.[8]

Experts suspect the behavioral difference between these two species in how they confront or don't confront predators probably reflects differences in their evolutionary history. Whitetails have been around for about three million years, and as such, are the older of these two species. Before the end of the last Ice Age around 10,000 to 11,000 years ago, whitetails shared North America with 15 predators larger than coyotes. It has been suggested that the strategy of abandoning their young and running quickly off had earlier made much more sense than it does today now that there are fewer predator species around bigger than coyotes.[9] However, there are also differences in the gaits of whitetails and mule deer—the former gallop, but the latter have a springing gait—differences that affect how well they can act aggressively. Because of their gait, mule deer are able to pounce on predators more effectively than whitetails can. So the explanation for why they differ in their parenting styles is not a simple one.[10]

What about rattlesnakes? How do their babies deal with life? Unlike many kinds of snakes, rattlers actually give birth; they don't just lay eggs. It used to be thought that their young are not only born live, but since they are born venomous, they are also quite dangerous from the moment they see the light of day. However, recent studies both in the field and in the laboratory have shown that understanding the social and reproductive behavior of these often misunderstood and much maligned creatures is far more challenging than previously believed.

Using remote time-lapse cameras, Melissa Amarello at Arizona State University and her colleagues have made great strides in documenting, for example, the social life of two communities of Arizona black rattlesnakes (*Crotalus cerberus*). They find that different individuals vary a great deal in how willingly they associate with others of their kind, and they can be choosy, too, in the individuals they are willing to deal with. Some like to be alone or in small groups; others are inclined to hang out with a crowd of adults and juveniles.[11]

Newborn rattlers have clouded eyes until their first shed, which happens 7 to 14 days after birth. This condition, combined with their lack of experience with the world and its risks, makes them particularly vulnerable to predation by birds and other predators.[12] Field observers report that when newborn rattlers venture out on their own, adult females—presumably their mothers given their obviously reduced body-weight appearance and the fact that they are basking nearby—may keep an eye on them, and may get them to turn back to the safety of their shelter if they venture too far away. Adult males have also been seen visiting the sheltering places where rattler newborns and their mothers are staying, where they then rested with the young (even letting them crawl and coil on and near them), and made no defensive or sexual advances against the adult females. However, despite such evident willingness on the part of adult rattlers to deal at least in such minimal ways with newborns until after their first shed, observations of adults defending the young in the wild or of parent–offspring associations lasting more than a week or so after birth are rare.[13]

Given these two such remarkably divergent reproductive strategies, where do we fit into this intriguing range of possibilities? We are clearly not doing the job of reproduction in the ways that either deer or rattlesnakes do, although we are obviously closer to the former than the latter. And as any human parent knows, our babies are definitely not as easy-going and quiet as fawns. In fact, we would have good reason to be quite alarmed if they were. Why then are so many human beings willing to take on such a demanding and prolonged assignment?

IT IS CONVENTIONAL wisdom that whether and how deeply a parent is captivated by a child is somehow a matter of hormones and perhaps how the brain is rewired when a child comes along.[14] However, there is no one brain area or specific hormone that can be pinned down as the chief biological contributor to social bonding among humans or other animals. Different brain regions, hormones, circumstances, and experiences all help foster whether two people (in this case of such divergent ages) form a trusting relationship, or instead feel they are basically incompatible.

Research on animals does suggest that the mammalian hormone *oxytocin* and neurotransmitter *dopamine* are involved in attachment and caregiving. For example, oxytocin evidently helps mothers overcome any reluctance they may feel to being near their offspring, and together with dopamine, may make maternal caregiving rewarding.[15] More generally, studies in animals and humans have suggested that oxytocin is released in the body in response to positive social interactions, such as social support or social proximity, and may thus be one way in which our bodies in general respond to the stress-protective effects of sociality. In support of this inference, oxytocin may also assist in social cognition and how we interpret social signals—perhaps, therefore, helping to facilitate pair-bonding, social closeness, empathy, and friendship.[16]

In some journalistic circles, oxytocin has been dubbed the "love hormone." However, although hormones may modulate the expression of behavior, they are not causes of behavior.[17] Moreover, Jennifer A. Bartz at the Mt. Sinai School of Medicine in New York and her colleagues have cautioned that close scrutiny of the published research literature indicates that the impact of oxytocin on social behavior is often weak and inconsistent.[18] Perhaps this observation should come as no surprise given the complexities of human psychology and behavior. In any case, oxytocin's effects on any given individual are probably dependent on who the person is and on what the situation is like that she or he is dealing with.

For instance, it has been found that increased levels of oxytocin may increase the social effectiveness of individuals who are socially less adept, but may have little impact on people who are socially skillful. Similarly, although this hormone has been said to have an effect on trust and cooperation, it was recently found that the positive effects of oxytocin on whether people trust one another may vanish if someone involved is seen as untrustworthy, is not personally known, or is perceived to be a member of a marginalized and allegedly dangerous social group. Thus though research on this and other hormones is showing us that body chemistry certainly does have a hand in how we deal with the world around us and how we interact with one another, including with infants and young children, the basic truth is we are not automatons led around by the nose by our hormones.

WHEN PEOPLE TALK about how mothers are hard-wired to fall in love with their babies, I believe they are nowadays usually talking about the brain, not about the biochemistry of our bodies, however neatly "hormones" once may have seemed an easy and persuasive way to explain our behavior. Unfortunately, if it is the wiring of the human brain that we need to know about to explain what people mean by mothering, then it must be confessed that the neuroscience needed is still only just on the research horizon.[19] It hasn't arrived yet. In this regard, experts today are not even sure they are asking the right questions.

Take mothering again as an example. I was engaged to a New Zealander in 1971. When this relationship did not work out, two friends gave me a seven-week-old puppy from Angel Memorial Animal Hospital, a famous Boston dog pound, as an alternative route to happiness—an adorable Shepherd mix I named Kathleen. She came to me unspayed, and went through several heats before I could bear to do something about that. But before doing so, we facilitated an encounter with a friend's dog she liked to romp with in a small Hyde Park neighborhood playground in Chicago where our local community of dog walkers rendezvoused daily with their pets. Just before Christmas that year, Kathleen gave birth to seven of her own.

Although I had read about it beforehand, what amazed me as I watched from a respectful distance was how Kathleen knew *exactly* what to do. As soon as a pup appeared, she would lick it ravenously, eat the placenta, and then just as rapidly repeat the same process on the arrival of the next pup. Seven times over.

Kathleen was a perfect mother until shortly after Christmas, when she may have decided she had had enough of their sharp little claws. Nutritionally, she totally abandoned her offspring. They had to be hand-fed until they were able to make it on their own, although thankfully she was still willing to consume the by-product of their meals when they deposited it in the whelping box.

Sarah Hrdy, Professor of Anthropology Emeritus at the University of California at Davis, has written extensively about mothering in a comparative evolutionary perspective. While the behavior involved varies a great deal depending on the species, the kind of instinctual care displayed by Kathleen years ago is basically standard and par for her canine species (except perhaps the sudden abandonment of her offspring). And Hrdy has vividly related, to offer another species example, how a colleague had once seen a gorilla mother set aside her newborn to eat its placenta with both hands like a slice of pizza before attending further to her infant's needs.[20]

Obviously, however, there is nothing quite like this evidently hard-wired gorilla behavior in our species. Yes, human mothers experience hormonal changes associated with birth and lactation that others around them do not feel, at least not nearly to the same degree. But neuroscience has been able to find no secure evidence so far that mothering in our species is based on mothering-specific brain wiring. As Hrdy says, there is "no species-typical suite of behaviors all women engage in right after birth, say licking off the amniotic fluids or eating the placenta, before placing the baby on our breasts to suckle there."[21]

Hrdy has examined in historical and cross-cultural detail how even something as seemingly uncomplicated as a woman's decision whether to accept or reject the assignment of motherhood is determined by much more than just the hormonal changes associated with being pregnant and giving birth. As she describes the situation: "More than in any other ape, a mother's love is contingent on her circumstances." And she adds: "wherever assistance in rearing infants is in limited supply and other forms of birth control are not available, mothers in all societies practice infanticide."[22]

Phrased in my own words, despite conventional wisdom to the contrary, there is nothing especially "natural" about motherhood in our species beyond the fundamental biological facts of ovulation, conception, parturition, and lactation. And yet our species has not gone extinct, and babies do live to tell the tale. How so?

I AM NOT a woman, nor a mom in the usual sense of the word. Yet in 1990 at the ripe old age of 48, I decided I did not want to go through life childless. I knew I would end up being a very sad and rather bitter old man if I didn't at least try to do something to change the situation I was in. As things turned out, I was fortunate enough to be able to adopt a baby boy from Paraguay who was just over a year old when I went down there to complete the legal adoption process (Chapter 30). His mother had clearly done the best she could to care for him for the first 5½ months of his life. Thereafter, however, he had spent the rest of the time before we met one another in late July 1991 in a crib in private foster-care facilities in Asunción. His impoverished background meant that judging by standard Western growth charts, as a rule 97 percent of children are taller and heavier than he was at the age of 12 months. It wasn't until he was two years old that he finally entered the 50th percentile. As for height, he had not quite reached this same mid-way value when we stopped charting his growth progress at the age of five years.

Knowing this, you can see why I bridle whenever I read anyone asserting too easily that human mothering comes naturally to mothers when they are caring for their own biological offspring. For example, it strikes me that there is something not quite on the mark about how Hrdy tells us in her book *Mother Nature* that instincts to care for others "slumber" in the hearts of primates, including men, and then asks: "Under what circumstances are they activated?"[23] I do not want us to be sidetracked by the issue of gender politics, but I think there is another way of looking at why human beings of either sex may be predisposed to accept the mission impossible assignment of child-care allegedly "slumbering" within them. Stated simply, it is likely that we do so because we are human.[24] I realize saying this may sound superficial, glib, or both. What's the evidence for making such an apparently outrageous claim?

JAMES COAN AT the Department of Psychology at the University of Virginia studies the neurological processes underlying the expression and social regulation of human emotional responses. With his research colleague Lane Beckes, he has developed a highly promising approach to the psychology of empathy and human sociality that they call *social baseline theory*.[25]

Their working premise is that being a social animal gives us a real and practical advantage in the struggle for existence—namely, a social baseline of emotional support and security. So much so that perhaps far more than most of us realize, *our social connections with others are in effect an extension of the way our brain interacts with the world.* And as a consequence, when we are around others we know and trust, we are able to let down our guard and relax.

This may seem both obvious and self-evident. However, the payoffs are not just emotional. When we find ourselves thus secure in life with its inevitable risks and threats, we are quite literally able to devote less energy to staying alert and being prepared for possible threats and uncertainties. Coan and Beckes argue, in fact, that *the human brain has evolved to assume the presence of other people*. In their own words: "In our view, the human brain is designed to *assume* that it is embedded within a relatively predictable social network characterized by familiarity, joint attention, shared goals, and interdependence."[26]

Their recent research using functional magnetic resonance imaging (fMRI) of the brain suggests that their way of analyzing human sociality applies to more than just what has traditionally been called "emotional attachment"— say, between a parent and a child. They have found, for instance, that holding another person's hand when facing a threat, even the hand of a stranger, can actually reduce the neurological threat response observable within the brain (specifically, the "neural threat matrix" in the insular cortex, anterior cingulate cortex, and subcortical affective regions).

If your reaction to this research finding is a dismissive "gee whiz, I would have never thought of that myself," please think again. I would argue this observation shows us that, as animals, we are so attuned to being around others of our kind that in a pinch even a stranger may do.

If so, then is it any wonder that holding a child not just at a mother's breast but in anyone's willing arms might prove to be as seductive, appealing, and nurturing as finding a small kitten rubbing back and forth between your ankles, purring contentedly, and nestling soon thereafter in the crook of your arm? Or that, barring allergies or other contending contrary circumstances, we human beings might want to take on the mission impossible assignment of parenthood, litter box cleaning, or twice-daily urban dog walking?

PART FIVE

Social Being

20

Alone in a Crowd

THE PHRASE *SEPARATION anxiety disorder* (SAD) refers to the psychological distress that individuals may experience when they are separated from a preferred companion or group.[1] Feeling this way is not restricted to our own species. Veterinarians have observed it in a wide variety of other species including birds, dogs, horses, pigs, sheep, goats, cattle, cetaceans, and primates other than ourselves.

Although domestic cats are commonly seen as asocial or even antisocial creatures, there is growing evidence that cats, too, form social bonds and may experience symptoms comparable to SAD in humans—and as a dog lover, I hasten to add also comparable to similar symptoms in dogs. As Stephanie Schwartz at the School of Veterinary Medicine, Tufts University, reports: "Separation reactions in dogs and cats have much in common with phobic disorders and panic attacks in people."[2] Such reactions in household pets may be characterized, for example, by excessive grooming resulting in serious self-inflicted injury.

Schwartz suggests that being susceptible to separation-related distress can be seen as a measure of a species' predisposition toward sociality—the tendency to seek out others, a phenomenon seen in kittens, for instance, between 2 and 7 weeks old, and in puppies between 6 and 13 weeks. Thereafter, individuals in both species usually become defensive on encountering strangers and less given to being social. Significantly, however, just like human infants, kittens and puppies truly thrive only when raised in a nurturing social environment. Even a few minutes a day of gentle handling, for instance, can help kittens and puppies grow up to become not only socially attuned companions, but also better at dealing with change and stress generally.

Unlike most dogs, however, cats are famously better than their canine counterparts at living more or less on their own as adults. Yet their tolerance for doing so varies widely, more so than in dogs, which may be telling us that we have not had as active a role in their domestication as we have apparently had for dogs.

Recognizing that different species as well as different individuals within any given species may vary widely in their tolerance and commitment to social living brings into sharper focus the fact that people, too, vary in this regard. One way to arrive at a better understanding of how important friendships in particular and social life in general are to the success of our species is to ask what happens to people when circumstance, illness, or disability undermines their capacity for social awareness or their willingness to engage socially with others. This topic is a huge one.[3] We cannot do it justice here. Let me offer, therefore, only three examples.

First, let's consider the complicated psychological condition called depression. Then I would like to turn, briefly also, to the detrimental effects that violence can have on the human psyche, specifically on the lives and happiness of children forced or in other ways recruited into direct involvement in military and rebel conflicts as child warriors. Finally, we will look at how autism spectrum disorders (ASD) can shape the lives of people dealing with such social and cognitive deficits. Each of these examples underscores how committed we are as a species to being social.

THE CLASSIC MOVIE *It's a Wonderful Life*, produced and directed by the legendary director Frank Capra, opened just before Christmas 1946. This picture was not a box-office success. Hollywood legend has it that Capra was never able to regain the full confidence of those who saw movie-making as a way of making money big time. Although it is heartening that this film is nonetheless now seen as one of the best ever turned out by Hollywood in its halcyon days, there is no denying that it is sentimental to its core in its celebration of family, friendship, and the value of doing more than just half-heartedly showing concern for others. No wonder it came under suspicion at J. Edgar Hoover's FBI soon after its original release as a bald-faced example of how Communists had taken over Hollywood and were trying to turn Americans against true-blue American values.

The film was also unusual for its time in its portrayal of the emotional struggles and eventual despair of George Bailey, its central male lead, played by James Stewart. As the plot unfolds, we learn how every time George has tried to go down the road to individual achievement, financial success, and personal fulfillment something has happened to call him back into service for the greater good of others. It literally takes a miracle in the form of divine intervention by a more than suitably human and ordinary guardian angel named Clarence to keep our hero from committing suicide.

It is thought that the incidence of depressive disorders in adults in any given year is about 9.5 percent, and lifetime rates on the order of 18 percent have been reported. The highest rates are evidently among women during the years they are bearing and raising children. However, just how true these figures are around the globe is uncertain.

Depression great enough to call for medical and psychological intervention is something that I have personally experienced during two separate and thankfully brief periods in my own adult life. I know firsthand how a major depressive disorder (MDD) can affect a broad spectrum of human behaviors. Most relevant here is the marked effect that depression can have on social functioning—notably on a person's capacity to understand and respond to the thoughts and feelings of others, an ability that is central to most human social interactions.

A few findings in particular are worth noting. People who are acutely depressed may not read faces well for their emotional content. Happy faces are likely to be ignored; sad faces are likely to be given selectively close attention. Furthermore, faces that are neutral—neither happy nor sad—are likely to be read as sad faces.[4] In short, people who are depressed are prone to look for comparable sadness in others even when it isn't there.

Needless to say, not being able to read how others are feeling can socially distance people who are depressed from others, which in turn may lead to a heightened sense of isolation and loneliness. Research has also shown that depression can run in families. A child with a parent or caregiver who is depressed is evidently at much greater risk than others of developing depression and other cognitive and medical difficulties such as impaired academic and social functioning. There is some evidence, too, suggesting that having a depressed parent can be one of the factors contributing to adolescent conduct problems as well as later chronic violence, although it is not clear why this might be so.[5]

Fortunately depression can often be treated, and the quality of life and social functioning generally improves for about 60% to 70% of depressed individuals who seek help. It also seems likely that depression can be self-limiting. Even without treatment, in other words, individuals may pull out of their depression given time and the right circumstances.

CURRENTLY AN ESTIMATED 300,000 young people younger than 18 years old are caught up in military and rebel conflicts around the world. These "child soldiers," both male and female, are performing a wide variety of military services. They are cooks, messengers, spies, combatants, sex workers, diamond miners, nurses, garbage men, housekeepers, and the list goes on. They are involved in conflicts of often extreme violence, and they may witness revolting human atrocities.

The psychological and health effects on these children are clear and seemingly all too predictable. One study, for instance, of war-affected youth in Sierra Leone who got caught up in the civil war there between 1991 and 2002 found that both girls and boys had witnessed comparable high rates of beatings, injuries, torture, and violent deaths. Although some of these young people joined the conflict voluntarily, many were forcibly recruited—roughly 50 percent of the latter were abducted when they were 15 years old or younger. Young women had been just as likely to witness bomb explosions and massacres, and had been more likely than males to have seen stabbings and shootings. In the incidence of sexual abuse, 5 percent of the boys but 44 percent of the girls had been raped.[6]

Theresa Betancourt and her colleagues at the Harvard School of Public Health in Boston report that although more boys (42%) than girls (28%) had been trained as soldiers, girls and boys alike had experienced almost equally high rates of abuse by armed groups that included being beaten, threatened with murder, shot, deprived of food, and forced to take drugs. Furthermore, boys and girls had been equally likely to have been involved in injuring or killing others.

Face-to-face discussions with survivors conducted in 2004 established that the mental health impact was substantial, especially for the young women interviewed. Losing a parent, in particular, was associated with high levels of depression and anxiety. Killing or injuring others was found to be strongly correlated with severe depression, anxiety, and hostility. Being a victim of rape or sexual abuse was linked with anxiety and hostility, but evidently not clinical depression.

While gender alone was not found to be a significant statistical predictor of anxiety, depression, or hostility, it was apparently much more difficult for girls than boys to reintegrate into society after the civil war. For example, Ugandan and Sierra Leonean men often refused to marry women who had been associated with the armed forces on the grounds that they had become sexually tainted, unpredictable, and aggressive.

One unexpected finding of the study reported by Betancourt and her colleagues was increased vulnerability to depression and anxiety among males who had lost a caregiver. Since generally speaking Sierra Leone is a highly patriarchic society, these researchers had assumed beforehand that females would be more dependent on caregivers to help protect and support them, and would thus be more psychologically afflicted by the war and its disruptions. They found that for males, however, the loss of caregivers may have shifted family economic and social burdens onto the shoulders of young men returning from the war, which may have added considerably to their risk for depression and anxiety.

The one positive observation made by Betancourt and her colleagues is that going back to school had a discernibly positive effect on the sociality and confidence of the young people they interviewed. "Qualitative data attest to the ways in which school access was a universally important goal for most youth in our study: *Yes, [school] was very important and beneficial to me because with education I will be able to help my family* (female, older adolescent)."

The archaeologist Danielle Ribbe—then a graduate student at the University of Illinois at Chicago who took my course there on the friendship hypothesis in 2011—surveyed the issue of violence and human evolution for her term paper. She found that the available evidence clearly establishes that violence has a strong psychological impact on child soldiers and their adult counterparts regardless of age. Depression, anxiety, posttraumatic stress disorder, drinking dependencies, and the like all show us the real limitations of our human capacity to carry out violent acts against others. Furthermore, the positive support of family, friends, loved ones, and community can all help protect individuals from the psychological shock of the atrocities of war. "This suggests that as a species, humans mentally benefit more through cooperation and positive interactions with one another than through violence. If violence was an action that humans were evolved to carry out on a regular basis, then a mental capacity to handle the atrocities of war would have simultaneously developed, as well."[7]

"AUTISM" REFERS TO a range, or spectrum, of neurological and developmental difficulties in communication and social engagement associated with repetitive and stereotyped behaviors that taken together have a characteristic course of development beginning in early childhood. The American Psychiatric Association has revised its clinical definition of what constitutes an autism spectrum disorder (ASD). Among the diagnostic criteria, which are not all that dissimilar from the criteria formerly used, there must be observable and persistent deficits in social communication, interaction, and reciprocity.

Kevin A. Pelphrey and his colleagues at Duke University have underscored the realities of the first area of disability.[8] They have found that people with autism may not spontaneously look at faces in the same way others do, and that children with autism may even have difficulty recognizing faces. Although they can be intellectually gifted, people with autism may also be strikingly literal in how they handle social situations and conversations. Furthermore, they may have difficulty using spoken language as well as facial expressions and body language in socially nuanced ways.

These deficits can be disabling. Not being attentively aware of what others are saying and doing can make it exceeding difficult to sense the likely actions and responses of others—something that is fundamental to negotiating the complexities of social life. Not being good at this skill can be both stressful and psychologically isolating. Moreover, people with autism may be naïvely trustful—taking people at their word unchallenged by any "gut" sense of how honest or dishonest they may be, which can sometimes lead to confusing, unfortunate, disturbing, and possibly dangerous encounters with others.

For most people establishing new friendships can be challenging, but this may be especially true for those with ASD. Elyssa Cherney, then a journalism undergraduate who took my course on friendship at Northwestern University in 2012, succinctly summed up the situation in her final research paper: humans are hard-wired to connect, and children without friends are at risk of loneliness, stress, and psychological difficulties because friendship quality is correlated with healthy levels of self-esteem and well-being.[9]

For most children, loneliness commonly spurs them to reach out to their friends or initiate new friendships. In contrast, although children with autism may see themselves as having friends, they may feel their friendships are somehow wanting when it comes to trust, companionship, security, and helpfulness.[10] They may also define friendship differently. For them, friendships may be judged more by physical closeness than by emotional closeness—which may partly explain why they may be so prone to high levels of anxiety and loneliness. Although children with ASD commonly self-report their desire for increased peer interactions, the social difficulties they experience—especially during interactions with same-age peers—may become even more aggravating as they mature. Since the challenges of social life tend to increase in middle school and later, they may become acutely aware of their social disabilities, which may further contribute to mood and anxiety problems.[11]

A FORMAL AND rather impersonal definition of social interactions would be that they are the give-and-take during which individuals effectively initiate and respond to the presence, verbal and nonverbal exchanges, and actions of others.[12] Considered separately or together, clinical depression, the devastating impact of violence and bloodshed on the mental health and happiness of child warriors, and ASDs alike testify to how powerfully evolution has committed our species to collaborative social life. This is a fact. We are hard-wired to be this way.[13] For better or for worse, few of us can readily accept or easily handle loneliness, social isolation, or brutality and violence.

There is still much that remains poorly understood about how depression, traumatic stress, and autism affect the psyches and lives of those dealing with such social deficits. It seems likely, for example, that autistic individuals may experience more intense levels of loneliness than their more typically developing peers since they may want to initiate new friendships and be around those they value as friends, yet they may not be sure how to do so.

The author John Elder Robison was not diagnosed as having ASD until he was 40 years old. He tells about his life with Asperger's (a type of ASD) in his biography *Look Me in the Eye*. Robison eloquently relates what it feels like to want friends but not know how to go about making them:

> Many descriptions of autism and Asperger's describe people like me as "not wanting contact with others" or "preferring to play alone." I can't speak for other kids, but I'd like to be very clear about my own feelings: *I did not ever want to be alone.* And all those child psychologists who said "John prefers to play by himself" were dead wrong. I played by myself because I was a failure at playing with others. I was alone as a result of my own limitations, and being alone was one of the bitterest disappointments of my young life. The sting of those early failures followed me long into adulthood, even after I learned about Asperger's.[14]

21

A State of Mind

IT WASN'T ALL that long ago that evolutionary biologists were saying that what Darwin called natural selection means all living things, including ourselves, must conform—that is, adapt—successfully to the world around them or face defeat in the struggle for existence.[1] When I tried to reconcile this view of life with what I knew as an anthropologist about *Homo sapiens* and what people are capable of doing, I became discouraged. This view is such a one-sided way of thinking about evolution. Just a moment's reflection will affirm that people are amazingly adept at modifying the world to suit their needs. It is simply not true that we can only adapt ourselves to fit into the world and whatever it demands of us—a reading of adaptation and Darwinian evolution that could be called "conform-or-die adaptation." We are also masters at what might similarly be called "give-and-take adaptation."[2]

It is not difficult to point to other species that survive like our own by engaging in give-and-take with Mother Nature. For example, there are at least 235 known species of attini (leaf-cutter) ants.[3] All of these species live in the New World, including the southern United States. What is most intriguing about these ants is that they practice a kind of farming, or agriculture. They grow fungus gardens inside their nests on tiny pieces of leaf they remove from plants and carry back home especially for this purpose—one of the rare examples of farming by nonhumans. According to the authors of one recent study: "Mature leaf-cutter ant colonies contain millions of workers ranging in size from small garden tenders to large soldiers, resulting in one of the most complex polymorphic caste systems within ants."[4] Equally startling, it is now known that at least some of the species studied have been each exclusively associated with their own particular fungal species for millions of years— even though alternative choices are readily available.[5]

A decade ago the evolutionists John Odling-Smee, Kevin Laland, and Marcus Feldman gave us an entire book on give-and-take adaptation—except in their book they call it environmental "niche construction." This they define as all the ways in which creatures go about modifying our planet to make it a more suitable, more accommodating place for them to live on (or in).[6]

What often gets overlooked even by advocates of such a give-and-take view of evolution, however, is that our humanly constructed planetary niche includes more than just what we do to make the earth at least seemingly a better place to live.[7] Unlike ants or other creatures such as beavers and many kinds of birds, we construct niches that also reach beyond the elemental necessities of food, shelter, and reproduction. How so? Because our human niches are not just physical and tangible places in nature, but also *imaginary cognitive places between our ears.*

What I am talking about, of course, is the mental realm I have previously called Leslie thinking—that private cerebral world where we all spend such a goodly part of our lives (Chapter 4). As noted earlier, whether there are other species on earth that are sometimes similarly able to detach mentally from their physical surroundings, its demands and risks, is still an open research question.[8] But there can be no doubt that human beings excel at the fine art of escaping into their inner thoughts—a skill that I reckon can be likened to holding conversations between Laurence and Leslie inside the biological labyrinth called the mind during which we create virtual worlds within our skulls.[9] And these worlds (perhaps we should call them "cognitive environments" to sound more erudite?) may be as intricate and improbable as we want to imagine them being, a facility that I think gives a whole new twist to the meaning of the word "being" in human being.

Some other writers have recently also begun talking about cognitive niche construction, but what they may have in mind is somewhat different. Harvard's Steven Pinker, for instance, defines cognitive niche construction as "a mode of survival characterized by manipulating the environment through causal reasoning and social cooperation."[10] Other scholars have evidently more or less gone along with Pinker's definition.[11] However, his way of thinking about cognitive niche construction puts it squarely in the camp of Lou and Laurence, where I don't think it always, or even often, belongs. I definitely think cognitive niche construction is something Leslie does masterfully, although when it comes time to consciously applying what Leslie has been doing to the real world, undoubtedly Laurence needs to lend a direct hand.

More critically, however, Pinker's definition overlooks what we have identified previously as the Leslie effect, and thereby glosses over how difficult it can be for each of us to apply what we may see so clearly in the mind's eye to the realities of life—which seems to be the preoccupation of Pinker's interpretation of the words "cognitive niche construction." To each his own, but if we were to adopt Pinker's definition focusing so much on reality rather than on fantasy and imagination, then how does Leslie's way of thinking fit into the picture? More to the point, such a definition glosses over both the great strength as well as potentially the greatest weakness of cognitive niche construction. What goes on between our ears when we are engaged in Leslie thinking does not have to be rational at all—at least not if by "rational" we mean thinking that actually makes sense in the real world "out there" outside our bodies.

IF THERE WERE some way we could take a look at what is going on between their ears in the cognitive niches of other people—if we could see what their Leslie minds are imagining and constructing up there inside their skulls—my suspicion is that we would find that what's there is far from neat and orderly, and probably comes and goes in and out of focus fairly rapidly depending on what they "have in mind" and how long they can afford to stay out of touch with reality.[12] As my friend Nancy Bailey has said to me about her own way of seeing and imagining the world: "my niche is constructed out of all sorts of notions, beliefs, traditions, personal world views, and people who affirm how I see myself with and without words. Those other people mirror me, and contribute to my sense of myself, and help me sustain a stable view of myself over time."

Currently, however, as the neuroscience researchers Alexander Schlegel and his colleagues at Dartmouth College have observed, we do not really know how the brain mediates complex and creative behaviors such as artistic, scientific, and mathematical thought. It has been suggested that these critical human abilities somehow take place in a diffuse and quite extensive neural network, or "mental workspace," but evidence for such a network has been hard to obtain using current neuroscience techniques.[13] Yet regardless how eclectic and variable the content, or how far from logically constructed, perhaps you agree with me that what is in a person's cognitive niche—their Leslie world—plays a critical role in how she or he deals with other people and with the real world around them.[14] Consider this example.

While taking a walk, we happen to see a small child and her parents on a playground one beautiful sunny afternoon having fun together, say, on the swings, or playing Frisbee. Nobody knows for sure who came up with the famous "duck test," but if we were to apply the rule "If it walks like a duck, quacks like a duck, swims like a duck, it must be a duck," then it takes little imagination to decide that we are watching a happy family at play. But would this still be the conclusion if I were to tell you that the two adoring parents are of the same gender? Two moms, say. Does the duck test still lead us to the same inference? Depends on what we think a family is, doesn't it?

We all know that at least a sizable minority of Americans, particularly those age 60 or older, would currently say that despite what they would be seeing right there in front of their eyes, this obviously contented family is not really a family. Or at any rate should not be called a family. Many of those holding such an opinion might add that the only right way to refer to these two adults and their delighted child would be to label them as a gay or lesbian family—a label that, if applied logically, would seem to be saying that the child herself is also lesbian, or at any rate is destined to grow up and become one sooner or later. Such an inference might make absolutely perfect sense in the realm and logic of the cognitive niches of some people, but does this view of things really reflect the world we live in? And in any case, where does such a view of life come from?

Needless to say, I just asked several leading questions to make a point. While we humans are *obligate* social learners, we are also *facultative* teachers. How much time and deliberate effort any one of us invests in trying to inform, fill in, or shape the cognitive niches of others, particularly those who are young, varies widely. Yet this may not really matter all that much. A great deal of social teaching—say, about what the word "family" means—goes on when nobody is intentionally playing the role of teacher.[15]

Why is even passive (unintentional) teaching often so effective? The cognitive psychologists Chris and Uta Frith have extensively explored the broad gambit of mental skills that human beings have been gifted with by evolution, skills that we may be mostly unaware most of the time, that enable us to be taught by others simply by watching what they are doing and what they are dealing with. For example, humans are quite gifted at imitating what other people do, and at mirroring the emotions of others, often with almost uncanny perceptiveness. According to Frith and Frith, even something that sounds as demanding and complicated as group decision making can happen without any deliberate attempt by those involved to arrive at a collective decision.[16] Just as we are social learners, so too, we are social teachers whether we like it or not.

ALTHOUGH PROCLAIMED BY famous evolutionists back when it was first being talked about a decade or so ago as a massive reorientation of evolutionary theory, other scientists then were doubtful that the notion of niche construction was really all that new. To a certain degree, of course, these skeptics were right. Is there really ever anything new under the sun (actually, yes, but let's not go down that road)? Despite such skepticism, those promoting this view of Darwinism did have something useful to offer, and today talk about niche construction is commonplace in the evolutionary sciences.

I think, however, something important gets lost when the phrase "niche construction" is used to label the evolutionary give-and-take of life on earth. Advocates for this view of evolution rightly point out that adaptation seen from this perspective becomes a two-way street.[17] But the label *niche construction* turns this back-and-forth into something that sounds rather one-sided. Rachel L. Day and her colleagues Kevin N. Laland and John Odling-Smee, for instance, wrote in a benchmark paper in 2003: "There are two routes to the fit between organisms and their environments: (1) organisms may, as a result of natural selection, evolve characteristics that render them well-suited to their environments; or (2) niche-constructing organisms may change their environments to suit their current characteristics."[18] Does this sound like give-and-take to you? It doesn't to me.

In any case, when I read that the mutual relationship between leaf-cutter ants and their fungal friends arose around 50 million years ago, and that these natural partnerships have been going strong ever since, I am not sure why some evolutionists see the idea of niche construction as a massive reorientation of evolutionary theory.[19] This does not sound like much of a give-and-take to me. Call it niche construction if you like, but it is obvious that there is something massively different about what humans do when they are engaged in their own forms of niche construction—be it building a humble little hut in the woods associated with a small vegetable garden and perhaps a cow, some chickens, and maybe a pig or two, or great skyscrapers in a place like downtown Chicago that are within convenient walking distance to a supermarket. (As an aside: Do you think Herbert Spencer or Franz Boas would agree with me that shopping for food is just the modern urban dweller's version of ancient hunting-and-gathering?)

It is not just the scale of the constructions and the methods used to complete them that strike me as different about what human beings are capable of doing. Despite the appealing or appalling (you choose) similarity between attini ants and our species when it comes to niche construction, it is hard enough for human beings to maintain a monogamous relationship over the course of a lifetime. The thought of doing so for millions of years, as these ants and their fungal partners evidently have been, is surely beyond even Leslie's free-form powers of comprehension. Why so? Because unlike other species of almost any description, the hallmark of human behavior is its astonishing versatility.[20] Take friendship. How behavior even this close to human nature gets expressed varies remarkably around the world.[21]

Therefore, calling what some ants do "farming" and calling what they and we both do "niche construction" may nicely underscore the fact that evolutionary adaptation does not just have to be a case of conform-or-die to whatever Mother Nature decides to throw at us. But my despair decades ago when reading what evolutionists back then were writing about Darwinian evolution would be still justifiable today. Human beings do not just engage in niche construction, but also in cognitive niche construction. And it is the creativity of the human response to Mother Nature that has helped make us human, and which has also presented us with that quintessentially human dilemma I have labeled the Leslie effect. If it is true that this dilemma is uniquely our own, what kind of a niche do we have to construct to deal with this remarkable but challenging human facility?

22

It's Who You Know

I LOVE THE word *conundrum* partly because of how it sounds when you say it. I also like the fact that the answer to such a puzzler may be a pun, a play on words, an unexpected twist. All joking aside, however, one conundrum we must all deal with as human beings is that the imaginative freedom our Leslie minds can enjoy when we are able to decouple our brains at least awhile from the cares and woes of life would be of no earthly use (except perhaps to keep us individually entertained) if there were no way for us as individuals to share our thoughts, impressions, dreams, and brilliant ideas openly with others—and then at least sometimes get others to work with us to turn our personal insights (and fantasies) into public realities. What better way could there possibly be for us to remake the world in novel ways attesting to our resourcefulness as a species? What other way would distinguish our kind of niche construction so incontrovertibly from that pursued now for millions of years by leaf-cutter ants, apparently driven only by instinct rather than by well thought out clever new ways to select and carry home tiny fragments of leaf to be used as manure in subterranean fungus gardens? But if the Leslie effect truly is a genuinely human dilemma, then what is the answer? How do we resolve the conundrum posed by our remarkable ability to engage in Leslie thinking—a talent that we and perhaps we alone as a species possess?

In the mid-19th century, while writing about the power of education to change the world, Ralph Waldo Emerson observed that the maxim of tyrants is "if you would rule the world quietly, you must keep it amused." Maybe yes, or maybe no. In any case, Emerson's words can be rewritten as "if you would rule the world, you must first have a circle of friends."

Friends are by no means the only people we need to have available to us to confront the Leslie effect head on, but I think it is fair to say that most of us hope that at least our friends are ready and willing to listen to our struggling attempts to put our private Leslie thoughts into understandable public words, images, sounds, and smells even if others less committed to us socially and emotionally may be all too willing to walk away when they see us struggling to find the right words, the right musical note, the right brush stroke, the right camera angle, the right flavoring or fragrance, or the most compelling argument for why others should pay attention to us and accept the wisdom and perceptiveness of our brainstorms, suggestions, proposals, schemes, collages, and demands.

Most attempts by evolutionists to pin down how people are able to communicate their inner thoughts and visions to others focus on language as the quintessential human acquisition and facility.[1] Certainly on point, but this is far from a startling observation, wouldn't you agree? Furthermore, focusing on language may lead to the belief that Leslie thinking depends somehow on grammar, syntax, and vocabulary.[2] This presumption strikes me, however, as unlikely because if this were so, then wouldn't putting our ideas into words be a walk in the park? Yet we all know how finding the right words to use can often be anything but a picnic. So let's grant that while resolving the Leslie conundrum frequently involves putting ideas into words, let's also consider what else we commonly do to cope with this dilemma. Let us shift our attention instead, therefore, to the issue that playwrights, novelists, and scientists, too, may all similarly refer to as "audience."

Stated as a series of questions: How do we all—not just stand-up comedians, but the likes of you and me regardless how skilled we are at tickling the ol' funny bone—generally deal with the Leslie effect, find an audience willing to listen to us, and then keep that audience attentive to our words and deeds once we have found it?

For starters, it is a good idea to have the social capital to do so.

THE INFLUENTIAL FRENCH sociologist, anthropologist, and philosopher Pierre Bourdieu, who died at the age 71 in 2002, did much to popularize the idea of what has been called *social capital*. This expression does not refer to a place like Paris, San Francisco, or Las Vegas, but rather a measure of social worth. In this sense, this is one of those ideas the meaning of which may seem so intuitively obvious that no formal definition would appear to be needed—which means this is also one of those ideas that commonly mean different things to different people.

Nonetheless, it has long been recognized that being part of a group can be a good thing both for the individuals involved and also for the group they are a part of. I am tempted to call this a capital idea. Bad pun aside, if you want to win friends and influence people, something called social capital is part of the equation. Even those who believe wholeheartedly in the idea that evolution is a Hobbesian war of all against all acknowledge this to be true. The sticking point, however, is trying to pin down what "being a good thing" amounts to, since we are talking about something that is a lot like trying to put your finger on a melting ice cube that's on a hot griddle.

Bourdieu defined social capital as "the aggregate of the actual or potential resources which are linked to possession of a durable network of more or less institutionalized relationships of mutual acquaintance or recognition."[3] Wow, say this again only quicker than last time! If nothing else, this rather convoluted definition suggests that it is a decided challenge to define, weigh, and measure social capital. Let us begin bravely, therefore, with a more conventional definition: "It's not *what* you know, it's *who* you know."

The late sociologist James Coleman, a pioneer in the use of mathematics in sociology, emphasized a critical side, or dimension, of this familiar old saying. The worth of any person's social capital, however defined, is not just a matter of who you know, but also how knowing them helps get things done. Needless to say, being a sociologist, he didn't express it quite this way. What he actually said was: "Like other forms of capital, social capital is productive, making possible the achievement of certain ends that in its absence would not be possible."[4] I believe these words probably mean the same thing. Or maybe not?

Luckily Coleman gave us a terrific example of what he was talking about. In one public school district in the United States—one where textbooks had to be paid for by a child's family—school officials were surprised to discover that many immigrant families were buying two copies of every required text. They learned that the second copy was being purchased for the mothers in these families so they could help their children do well in school. "Here is a case in which the human capital of the parents, at least as measured traditionally by years of schooling, is low, but the social capital in the family available for the child's education is extremely high." Because their mothers were both willing and able to invest time and effort in their children in this way meant they were playing a direct role in their lives that was perhaps unconventional by the standards of others in America, but that was unquestionably a direct "investment in the future," as any good banker would say it. Or as Coleman said it in this instance: "The social capital of the family is the relations between children and parents (and, when families include other members, relationships with them as well)."

Said another way, social capital is about the rewards, both tangible (e.g., getting ahead in life) and less tangible (e.g., having someone willing to help you get ahead in life) of having and maintaining social relationships with other human beings.

Friendship, as I have said before, isn't wimpy.

BUT WHAT EXACTLY is social capital, and can we bank on it? You have perhaps noticed that I have been dragging my feet on getting around to this basic point. After all, we have already seen how evidently easy it is to come up with vague and convoluted definitions. With hesitation, therefore, I would like to approach this topic from as far away from it as I can get—specifically, I'd like to draw on what has been said about it on the other side of the earth—in New Zealand.

The word *maori* in New Zealand Polynesian can be translated into English as "normal," "usual," "natural," and "common." It can also mean "native," and it is in this sense that this term is commonly used today to refer to the first settlers of New Zealand—the Maori—who arrived in this beautiful archipelago of islands in the South Pacific around 800 to 1,000 years ago from somewhere in tropical Polynesia to the northeast.

The Maori have a word *mana* that is usually translated as "power," "prestige," "dignity," "authority," "control," "influence," "status," "spiritual power," or "charisma." However translated, this is a word that can be easily misunderstood, much like the paired words *social capital*.

David Robinson and his colleague Tuwhakairiora Williams at Victoria University of Wellington in New Zealand have looked at Bourdieu's concept of social capital from a Maori perspective. They have concluded that to understand the notion of social capital, it is important to keep in mind what they call the "whole story" of the social setting within which people give and receive aid, support, and the like from one another—including what people know about other peoples' interests and resources and the opportunities that exist for sharing, giving, and receiving.[5]

Like most people who have written about social capital, Robinson and Williams accept the point of view made popular by Bourdieu that when we are talking about social capital, we are talking about resources, but they take the step (perhaps toward even greater ambiguity?) of defining what they mean by "resources" as knowledge, ability, and opportunities to participate and communicate with others, not just connections that give a person access to physical resources or useful information—in other words, precisely the kinds of "resources" that Leslie's potent imagination can contribute to what it means to be human.

An essential feature of their definition is their focus on having "a capacity to associate for mutual benefit or common purpose." I think once again that this may be in part what the primatologist Michael Tomasello means when he talks about our (probably) unique human capacity for shared intentionality (Chapter 18).

The paper by Robinson and Williams discussing this way of thinking about social capital appeared more than a decade ago, before the era of social networks, social media, Twitter, and Facebook. While they make reference to networks and human relationships as enabling the flow of information between individuals, their treatment of both seems relatively tame and perhaps a little understandably naïve by current standards. Even so, at the time they were writing, important steps were already underway to add modern analytical ideas about social networks to the study of social capital (I discuss some of these modern analytical ideas about social networks in Chapter 28).[6]

In any case, like the idea of social capital, it is easy to think about the Maori word mana as a thing or some kind of substance rather than as a kind of relationship. The late anthropologist Roger Keesing, however, in the mid-1980s argued convincingly that this Polynesian word is best translated as "potent" and "potency" rather than "power" and "powerful."[7]

To a certain extent Keesing was playing around with words, but if he were alive today (I knew him when he was still a graduate student at Harvard), I would ask him if he would now consider the idea that mana is about the *potency of relationships between people* (or things, since in New Zealand and elsewhere in the Pacific, things and people can both have mana), as well as between people and the less apparently tangible forces of the universe—that is, to say it perhaps too crudely, between people and the gods who are from a Maori point of view the sources of earthly promise and potency.

Saying that the word "capital" in the expression "social capital" is less about what we know or what we can literally get our hands on, and more about who we know and the potency of what can be made of knowing them is why every time I hear someone talking about social capital I think of the Maori word mana. Social capital is less about resources as such, and more about having the potency or potential for access to—and often, therefore, some kind of relationship with—people, places, knowledge, and yes, sometimes stuff like material wealth, useful resources, and the willingness of others to give you the time of day, listen to your woes, pat you on the back, or give you a much needed kick in the butt to help you get on the right course.

Lauren Schwartzberg, a journalism major concentrating in anthropology at Northwestern University who took my course on the friendship hypothesis in the spring of 2012, independently came around to the idea that, like Keesing's reworking of the meaning of the word mana, social capital is about *potential*. As she wrote in her paper for me that term: "All social capital is potential. Every person and every relationship has the potential to be used for an advantage in achieving certain goals."

Reflecting on what she and Keesing have written, I might step even further back from the notion that social capital is about something equivalent to the economic sense of capital as something having to do with wealth (money or goods) that can be used to generate income. Social relationships are "a good thing" to bank on instead because they extend the reach, productivity, and creative potential of our Leslie minds beyond what we as individuals acting alone are able to accomplish.

I SUPPOSE IN part because it is an altogether too obvious play on the word "capital," I cannot resist offering you a concrete bricks and mortar example of how *cognitive niche construction + social capital* can lead to substantial and enduring instances of *environmental niche construction*. The example I have firmly lodged in my own cognitive niche is none other than the US Capitol building on the Mall in Washington, DC.

This noble edifice is much more than just a constructed physical niche made out of walls, floors, and roofing materials designed to keep those within it safe, sound, and occasionally agreeable enough to sometimes do successfully what those who voted for them sent them to Washington to do. This building makes both visible and tangible the cognitive bicameral structure of our American system of government. And when its history is taken under purview, it is also a physical reminder of just how difficult it can be to translate what is in our cognitive niches—our Leslie thoughts—into public realities.

Although the current track record of the US Congress as a governing body amply attests to this often painful truth, the Capitol itself has been witness to the test of wills ever since Thomas Jefferson proposed a formal competition for its architectural design in 1792. Perhaps most famously, this clash became more than conceptual during the War of 1812 when the British tried to burn it down on August 24, 1814 during their military dispute with their former American colonies over how they both ought to be conducting their relationship with one another as sovereign nation states.

23

Bloodlust, Fear, and Other Emotions

THE IDEA THAT savages are cruel, violent beings did not originate with the Enlightenment. The belief, the wild conviction, that human monsters walk the earth had haunted the European mind long before Columbus set sail. According to the historian Margaret Hodgen, these frightful legendary beasts "could not be exorcised, but appeared and reappeared for centuries, in the work of would-be scientists, in the sermons of the clergy, and in poetry and the drama."[1] As she observed half a century ago:

> ...we still know too little of the ways and means conjured up by the human mind to meet its problems. One fact alone seems certain. It is usually agreed that man has resisted innovations in thought. When confronted with a new question, he has preferred to resort to old answers, old organizing principles, old presuppositions and procedures ....[2]

In the years following Columbus's voyages to the New World, writers, travelers, and commentators under the influence of such ageless Medieval horror fantasies were predisposed to describe the newly encountered inhabitants of Africa and the Americas as half-human, hairy wild men degraded by fears, doubts, suspicions, and barbarous cruelties. Around 1505, for example, the Portuguese explorer, soldier, and cartographer Duarte Pacheco Pereira in his *Esmeraldo de Situ Orbis* portrayed people on the west coast of Africa as dog-face satyrs, wild men, and cannibals.

Now, centuries later, when the claim is still made that savages are predisposed to violence and on meeting strangers may try to kill them, it is not entirely clear how literally factual such allegations are supposed to be. After all, recall what Brian Hare and Michael Tomacello have written about the domestication of our canine friends. Dogs get along so well with humans because our forebears befriended only dogs that were emotionally capable of tolerating being close to us and were able to handle our attentions in appropriately nonaggressive ways. If so, then why would people act differently when dealing with one another rather than with dogs? Are we supposed to believe that human civility and compassion are only skin deep? And that despite all appearances to the contrary, underneath we are all werewolves whose domestication has been, at best, superficial?

Are there answers to such questions? The comparative psychologist Jack Panksepp has written extensively about the emotional life of humans and other animals.[3] In a recent summary of available evidence, he reports that although science today knows approximately where affective states are generated in the brain, little is currently known for sure about how the neural mechanisms involved actually work. Even so, it is now widely accepted that the emotions of humans and other mammals are ancient functions operating deep within the brain, not higher cognitive processes taking place within our more recently evolved human neocortex.

According to Panksepp, it is now possible to recognize at least seven deep-seated primary mammalian emotions—*seeking, rage, fear, lust, care, panic/grief* and *play*, all of which may be associated with specific subcortical networks of the brain. *Seeking*, which generates approach and explorative behavior, is thought to be evolutionarily the oldest and most widespread of these emotional systems in the animal world, followed somewhat more recently in evolutionary time by *rage, fear*, and *lust*. In contrast, *care, panic/ grief,* and *play* are social emotions that are characteristically most fully seen in mammals rather than in other vertebrates.

Precisely what these terms mean, however, in the case of any given species is still an open question. Considering the complexity of the topic, it is no surprise that other experts have come up with yet other ways of talking about our emotional lives.[4] As Panksepp acknowledges: "Because of evolutionary diversification, we may never be able to objectively describe the precise nature of affective feelings in either humans or animals, but we can at least have confidence in the existence of meaningful similarities in the anatomies, neurochemistries, and psychological functions of these systems across mammalian species."[5]

IF WE LIMIT the inquiry to our own species, which of the primary mammalian emotions listed by Panksepp would you say is likely to be the most probable one that most people will experience when they suddenly encounter strangers in their midst? I do not think I am being overly optimistic to suggest that the answer is less likely to be *rage* or *lust*, and more likely to be *fear*, although I would agree that much depends on where and when. Here's my argument for this claim.

According to Panksepp, the subcortical emotional neural system that can be labeled *fear* specifically organizes natural danger-escape and avoidance behavior patterns such as freezing and flight that help animals stay out of harm's way. The *fight-or-flight response*, which has a number of alternative names including the familiar *acute stress response*, was apparently first identified as such by the American physiologist Walter Cannon at Harvard Medical School. In the preface to his classic study *Bodily Changes in Pain, Hunger, Fear and Rage: An Account of Recent Researches into the Function of Emotional Excitement* (1915) he observes:

> Fear, rage and pain, and the pangs of hunger are all primitive experiences which human beings share with the lower animals. These experiences are properly classed as among the most powerful that determine the action of men and beasts. A knowledge of the conditions which attend these experiences, therefore, is of general and fundamental importance in the interpretation of behavior.[6]

One of the consistent distinctions Cannon draws in this book is that between fear and anger, or as he identifies them, "the belligerent emotion of anger or rage and its counterpart, fear." Anger has often been described as one of our three primal emotions—the other two being love/lust and fear—that are marked by changes in body temperature, heart rate, glandular activity, and so on that can alter a person's actions or conduct.

It is also commonly said that as we grow up, the causes of the internal changes supposedly associated with anger may not be only such seemingly straightforward infantile conditions as hunger or discomfort (which most of us would probably agree are good enough reasons for being angry), or similarly conventional reasons outside us, such as a schoolyard bully, or a parent who won't let us play a favorite video game. As we mature, the grounds for being justifiably or irrationally angry may be less easy to isolate as being either inside or outside our bodies.[7] Our reasons for getting angry may evolve to become as seemingly intangible as a remembered or anticipated situation, encounter, or event. And as we all know, merely because the reasons for being angry are "only in our heads"—only in our cognitive niches, in our Leslie minds—may not make them any less provocative.[8] In short, our emotions are *not* just biologically induced, and some would go so far as to say that they may not be even basically, or fundamentally, biological.

Now like me, I am sure you know some people who appear to be angry about one thing or another most of the time. But these people are rare enough that they stand out from the crowd—perhaps because the crowd has moved away from them to get out of their line of fire. This doesn't mean that the rest of us are deliriously happy most of the time. It is just that most of us don't go around being angry 24/7/365.

Given this, why would anyone believe the suggestively medieval horror fantasies authored by Herbert Spencer about conflict and cannibalism in the early days of our species, or the claim by Franz Boas that long ago it was an act of high merit to kill a stranger? Unquestionably, angry people can become violent, but surely "savages" weren't always angry people? Why, therefore, should crossing paths with a stranger have automatically condemned him or her to instant death? Or is the emotion called anger mostly beside the point, and what these two scholarly gentlemen may really have had in mind instead is the emotion called fear?

THE ANTHROPOLOGIST RUTH Gerber has remarked that North Americans generally associate emotions with internal body sensations. We seem to be wedded to the idea that accurately describing our emotions means talking about what is allegedly going on inside us. We may devote considerable time and energy to the job, and often favor metaphorical language to accomplish the task. For example, we may try to capture our sense of "happiness" using words such as "a bubbly feeling that makes you feel warm all over." Or when we are angry, we may say that we are "boiling inside." Taken literally, such statements seem to imply that inside each of us there are different kinds of emotional bubbles waiting to be released into the air.

In contrast, according to Gerber—to offer a counterexample she has written about—it seems that American Samoans in the South Pacific have a great deal of difficulty talking about their emotions as internal states or sensations. Instead, they are likely to put their feelings into words by detailing the kinds of typical social situations and human relationships that they see as giving rise to different emotions. In Gerber's words, the Samoans she has talked with "tended to describe emotions in terms of the actions the feelings called forth, the stereotyped scenarios in which the feelings would be an appropriate response, and the specific relationships with close associates (e.g., parents, siblings, and friends) common to those scenarios."[9] (I should add here that there is now neuroscience evidence seemingly confirming the wisdom of their way of talking about emotions.[10])

Gerber also found while she was living in American Samoa that even when prompted by her questioning to do so, the Samoans she was interviewing had a hard time finding ways to put emotional "body feelings" into words, some going so far as to deny that emotions are linked with inner body sensations. She discovered that such denials were so common that when she wrote up and published her research findings, she felt it necessary to include this rather astonishing disclaimer: "I believe, however, that Samoans experience internal sensation in association with emotions, although they are generally unable to express it verbally."[11]

Gerber has further related that at least when she was in Samoa in the 1970s it was considered decidedly poor form to express anger toward your parents, and performing work and service for your relatives was seen as a primary expression of love.[12] I can imagine that many American parents on hearing this testimony might experience a certain degree of envy. However, Gerber goes on to explain: "When I asked Samoan informants about the feeling of *alofa* 'love' which exists between parents and children, I was surprised to learn that many of them believed a father's beating was an appropriate sign of his love."[13] Hearing this, many Americans might also experience a certain level of shock, if not outrage.

The explanation Gerber offers for why many Samoans were drawing a connection between parental love and fatherly beatings is rather convoluted, and turns chiefly on the fact that in Samoa in the 1970s (some Samoans tell me this may still hold true today), children were closely identified in the public eye with their father. Hence if children misbehaved, their father took the public heat. Fathers, therefore, felt they needed to teach their children right from wrong, and at least in American Samoa when Gerber was there, it was widely felt that with children, especially young children, a little pain was an inducement to learn. "Concerned fathers, who worry about their children's capacity to shame them and wish to make their children good people, therefore beat them. This logic is so compelling that several informants told me that if their fathers failed to beat them, they would be sad, since it would be a proof of parental indifference."[14]

SAMOA ASIDE, IN North America in recent decades it has been popular to assert—and not just by feminists—that the men in our society should stop being so "bottled up" emotionally. Men should be more "open," more accessible, more emotionally expressive. The evident implication is that by "putting their emotions into words," they would be making it easier on others to deal with the Leslie effect and feel their pain or hear their rage. I think what has been taken for granted, at least in recent years, however, is that it is genuinely possible, if not necessarily always easy, to describe not only to others but also to ourselves what we are feeling and why. At least Gerber's remarks about Samoan emotional life hint that such expressive honesty may be more difficult to come by than most North Americans may popularly believe. If so, then what I have called the Leslie effect may have its counterpart in that more intuitive, emotional, and habitual "inner world" that in Chapter 4 I labeled as "Lou."

In any case, it should not be assumed that being open and expressive about one's feelings is always a good thing. For instance, in 1976 I spent several weeks in the Fiji Islands scouting out the possibilities for doing anthropological research there using museum collections as a starting point. One Saturday while I was in Suva, the capital city, I walked by the sports field in the afternoon just as a rugby football game was letting out. I passed by two very unhappy and disgruntled Fijian rugby fans—their home team had just been royally trounced by the visiting team from New Zealand or South Africa, or some other foreign place. I caught only the tail-end of their conversation, but the words that reached my ears were memorable. "Well, you know in the old days we would have killed and eaten them."

Talk about being emotionally expressive!

PART SIX

Principles to Live By

24

The Lady or the Tiger?

If you don't know where you're going, you might not
get there.

— YOGI BERRA

IT IS LIKELY that people have been trying to decide how wild or civilized
we naturally are as human beings for as long as humankind has been trying to
put up with the new neighbors who just moved in next door. Hence the following question should come as no surprise. If we could knock on the door of
our early primate forerunners, what would we find there? Something good or
something unpleasant, if not necessarily truly bad?

The famous late 19th century short story by Frank R. Stockton titled "The
Lady or the Tiger?" ends with the reader not being told whether the accused
man has found a beautiful woman waiting for him behind the door he had to
open to prove his guilt or innocence, or alternatively that a tiger, "the fiercest
and most cruel that could be procured," was there eager to spring out and rip
him apart. What about our own human story? If we opened the door to our
past, which would it be? Metaphorically speaking. The lady or the tiger?

It has long been conventional to say that the choice would be between
the aggressive and sometimes ill-tempered chimpanzee or the more peaceful and sexually uninhibited bonobo. Which one of these apes you favor,
however, may have more to say about what you think of us as a species than
about what science today can concretely tell us about what our ancient
predecessors were like.[1] In this regard, I think it is appropriate to add that
Stockton begins his famous story this way: "In the very olden time there lived
a semi-barbaric king, whose ideas, though somewhat polished and sharpened

by the progressiveness of distant Latin neighbors, were still large, florid, and untrammeled, as became the half of him which was barbaric." Here yet once again we find ourselves dealing with the classic old belief that people who are not like you and me must be barbaric in both kind and deed.

As noted in an earlier chapter, however, the last time we humans shared a common ancestor with our evolutionary cousins the chimpanzees and the bonobos was about 6 to 8 million years ago. By anyone's measure, that was more than enough time for a lot to have happened not only in our own human ancestral line, but also in the evolutionary lineages of modern chimps and bonobos.[2] Hence it is not a foregone conclusion that these two primate species, although they are our closest cousins, can tell us all that much about how our own forebears may have behaved millions or even just thousands of years ago.

Therefore, is there any sound scientific reason to prefer one of these two species over the other as the best prototype for what our own ancestors may have once been like? And more to the point, does studying either of them really tell us anything of actual substance about ourselves today?

Ask no simple questions.

WHEN IT COMES to aggression, chimpanzees are evidently more the exception than the rule for primates generally. The anthropologists Robert Sussman and Joshua Marshack report, in fact, that most apes are remarkably nonaggressive.[3] Consequently, it is questionable whether it makes much sense to look only to chimps or bonobos to help us figure out how wild we "naturally are" as a species. It is entirely conceivable that we ought to cast our species-net farther afield and look to other primates, too, for clues to our ancestry and inherited predilections as social beings.

In any case, it is now thought that chimpanzees and bonobos split from their own common evolutionary ancestor about 2 million or so years ago.[4] Therefore, although it is perhaps not surprising that both of these primates display similar traits differentiating both of them from us, 2 million years has also clearly been sufficient time for our closest relatives to develop conspicuous behavioral and psychological differences *between* themselves as well as in comparison with us.[5]

For example, bonobo aggression evidently does not reach the levels of severity seen in chimpanzees, and unlike chimps, there are no confirmed cases of lethal bonobo aggression in the wild. Furthermore, although both species are known to hunt and consume the flesh of various species, hunting is fairly rare for both. In addition, it is becoming increasingly apparent as field research continues that variation in the behavior of social groups within each of these species may partly reflect differences in their locally transmitted traditions—social traditions that would be called *cultural* or *tribal* if we were talking about human beings rather than about these apes.[6]

Moreover, and perhaps most notoriously, as I alluded to earlier, there are significant differences between these two primate species in their sexual behavior. Research on bonobos both in captivity and in the wild has found that they are inclined to use sex even for "nonreproductive purposes"—to use the impersonal language generally favored by scholars when writing for scientific publications. Bonobos also use a variety of sexual positions, and often have same-sex partners. Will wonders never cease?

It has been suggested by some experts that bonobos use sex to relieve social tension, reconcile with one another following aggressive encounters, show one another who is boss (sounds familiar, doesn't it?), and promote bonding between females, group mates, and even during encounters between different bonobo social groups. Perhaps most unexpected of all, it is reported that bonobos have significantly more sexual partners than chimpanzees do, and they have more same-sex than opposite-sex partners. Furthermore, apparently "even as infants, bonobo use socio-sexual behavior, whereas the same behavior is completely absent in chimpanzee infants."[7]

Based on such information and informed speculation, it is beginning to look like chimpanzees might reasonably be characterized as confrontational prudes, while bonobos are laid-back philanderers. Certainly I'd rather have a bonobo living next door than a chimpanzee. Nevertheless, should we accept the conventional old wisdom that these are at least the right two alternative role models for us to choose between when thinking about our own ancestors back when they were living in an Enlightenment "state of nature"? Not necessarily.

WITH REGARD TO the puzzle at the core of his storybook fantasy, Stockton wisely observes toward its conclusion: "The more we reflect upon this question, the harder it is to answer." Similarly, given that there is no reason to think that chimpanzees and bonobos stopped evolving after our ancient forerunners parted company with them 6 to 8 million years ago, hesitation before deciding whether it should be (a) the chimpanzee, (b) the bonobo, or (c) none of the above would seem justifiable. Even if we want to see the chimp as a closer relative to ourselves than the bonobo (as some experts would insist), why assume that ancestral chimps long ago were behaviorally identical to today's living chimpanzees? After all, maybe their current less than pleasant behavior toward others was not always a personality trait inherent in the chimpanzee evolutionary line.

The primatologist Frans de Waal has suggested that "perhaps the most successful reconstruction of our past will be based not on chimpanzees or on bonobos but on a three-way comparison of chimpanzees, bonobo, and humans."[8] He may be right, but if it is our past and not just our anatomy we are trying to fathom and understand, does he really believe this task would be easy to accomplish?

There is still a lot to be learned about what it means to be human, and about how we evolved the biological capabilities that—with much added social learning and considerate parental nurturing—make us human. Given what is now known about evolution, biology, and human behavior, nonetheless, there are several things that can be said about *Homo sapiens* as one of nature's more remarkable creations that will probably withstand the test of time. Yes, Virginia, there is something that can be called human nature.[9]

First, as we have discussed, *we are hard-wired to be social creatures, however much we may vary among ourselves in how well we tolerate or may even seek out solitude.* Humans want to connect with others of their kind, and often, too, with other species—be they dogs or cats, whales or dolphins, fish, or fowl (or fuzzy teddy bears, for that matter). As we have also discussed, *we are obligate social learners* (and at least unintentional teachers). Equally important, *we are obligate caregivers.* Our species wouldn't survive if we weren't prepared as a species, if not necessarily as individuals in all cases, to care for the young.

Second, if James Coan, Lane Beckes, and other experts in neuroscience today are right, our brains have evolved over time to assume that we are embedded in social relationships characterized by familiarity and interdependence. As Coan and Beckes have argued, from the perspective of the human brain, our friends and loved ones are in effect if not in actual fact part of who we are as individuals.[10] In other words, the *basic unit of human social life is the individual plus his or her social relationships, not the individual alone.*[11] To understand an individual, therefore, you must see him or her as part of this larger social realm. Or as I like to say it, *to see the whole individual, you have to connect the dots* (Figure 14).

Third, people are not fools. Trust in others must be based on reason and experience, not just on emotion. Fear may be an emotion that is rooted deep within the vertebrate brain rather than being a uniquely human phenomenon, but fear can rule the human head as well as the human heart. Therefore, *even though we are predisposed to connect with others, we also need and desire safe ways to do so.*

FIGURE 14 To see the whole individual you have to connect the dots. (*Source*: author.)

Fourth, and possibly most important, when we connect socially with others, the connections are not just "of the mind," but also "of the body." Surely there is not a living soul who doesn't know this, and yet many contemporary ideas about how the mind works—for example, theory of mind, the Machiavellian brain hypothesis, the social brain hypothesis, and the cultural intelligence hypothesis—look more to the head than the heart when trying to explain human sociality. Yet far more than we may be aware of most of the time, *we invest our hearts as well as our minds in our social relationships* even when the connections involved may be as brief and seemingly inconsequential as buying a cup of coffee or a pack of chewing gum from another human being rather than from a vending machine.[12]

IN HIS FAMOUS *Discours sur l'origine et les fondements de l'inégalité parmi les hommes* (Discourse on the Origin and Basis of Inequality Among Men, 1754), Jean-Jacques Rousseau asked:

For how shall we know the source of inequality between men, if we do not begin by knowing mankind? And how shall man hope to see himself as nature made him, across all the changes which the succession of place and time must have produced in his original constitution? How can he distinguish what is fundamental in his nature from the changes and additions which his circumstances and the advances he has made have introduced to modify his primitive condition?[13]

We can disagree with Rousseau and other Enlightenment savants—and I have vigorously been doing so throughout this book—about what we were like when we were all supposedly living in a state of nature, but these thoughtful scholars were right to believe that there is something called human nature. However, I think we need to take the word "nature" to mean not something we left behind in the past, or something we must reject as brutish and inhuman. Instead this word refers to *our evolved baseline of abilities, talents, and needs that help define us as human beings, to one degree or another, and which for the most part we also share, to one degree or another, with other species on earth.*

This book rests, therefore, on a different way of understanding what it means to be human. Human nature is not something that we must struggle with or fight against to become civilized. Quite the contrary, *human nature is what evolution has endowed us with as human beings that we work with to do what needs to be done not just to survive and reproduce as a species, but to make the choices that in many ways we and only we have the evolved capacity to make as individuals and as communities.*

In short, I firmly believe there are lessons to be learned from knowing ourselves better as a species. And as in Stockton's story, there are choices to be made—although they may not always be as definitive as deciding which is the right door to open. In the following (and final) six chapters, I am going to try to boil some of these lessons down to six simple principles to live by, as illustrated by six stories that will, hopefully, make these principles memorable. The principles themselves are straightforward. My stories are not always as uncomplicated. When we are talking about our species, how could they be other than this?

25

A Kiss Is Just a Kiss?

Principle 1: It is easy to be misunderstood.

THE AMERICAN SONGWRITER Herman Hupfeld wrote "As Time Goes By" for a Broadway musical in 1931. A decade later this song and its haunting melody became a popular hit when it was sung by Dooley Wilson in the role of Sam, the piano player, in the 1942 Hollywood movie *Casablanca*. The original lyrics famously declare that a kiss is just a kiss. Time has gone by, and others have given this song their own interpretations. The lyrics have evolved somewhat—clarifying perhaps some of the ambiguity of the wording. Whether this has also changed their meaning is uncertain. Even so, this is a classic example of evolution at work, except in this case in the realm of words and popular culture rather than in biology and genetics.

In an essay called "Thick Description" in a collection titled *The Interpretation of Cultures* published in 1973, the late American anthropologist Clifford Geertz not quite so famously took exception to such seemingly undeniable human truths.[1] However, it wasn't a kiss but rather a wink that he took aim at. Following the lead of the British philosopher Gilbert Ryle, Geertz asks what, if anything, is the difference between the rapid closing of an eyelid—an involuntary twitch—and a genuinely conspiratorial wink. As an elemental although minimal body movement, both are similar. Yet the difference between a twitch and a wink is immense. After all, someone who winks is intentionally signaling, not just batting an eyelid, and is obviously, although perhaps surreptitiously, seeking to communicate with someone else in a precise and special way. But when it comes to a wink, as Geertz observes: "That's all there is to it: a speck of behavior, a fleck of culture, and—voilà!—a gesture."

Now suppose, as Ryle and Geertz also do, that there is someone else present who witnesses this sly wink and decides to mimic it deliberately in some comic fashion. Again, blinking an eyelid in this instance is effectively the same as a twitch or a conspiratorial wink, except now the intent, the meaning of it all, is entirely different—the goal is not furtive conspiracy but humor.

And having gotten this far in reinterpreting the possible significance or insignificance of moving an eyelid why stop? Suppose this would-be humorist is unsure of the quality of her winks—what is the chance the comic winks come across to others as just odd, involuntary tremors perhaps? So before engaging in them in public, she first practices them before a mirror. When doing so, this would-be standup comic is not twitching, winking, or parodying, but simply rehearsing. So a wink is just a wink is evidently not the same thing as a rose, is a rose, is a rose. A different kettle of fish altogether, assuming Gertrude Stein wasn't just pulling our leg when she penned her famous words about this thorny flower.

Geertz's point in drilling down further and further to expose winking as a thorny issue—or more correctly, to see what can be made out of the rapid blinking of a human eyelid—is to convince us that reading the meanings or intentions of what we see others doing can be far from simple or straightforward.

WHILE EVOLUTION HAS tinkered successfully enough with the genetic traits and behavioral characteristics of our ancient as-yet-not-human forebears to turn us into the intelligent social creatures we are today, this natural tinkering has gotten us only so far as a species. As we have previously discussed, there was nothing in our ancestral evolutionary heritage for natural selection to tinker with to turn us into genuine mind-readers, although there are plenty of times when being so biologically endowed would come in handy at home as well as in the public arena. Just imagine, for instance, how difficult it would be for anyone to be a politician if we could all read his or her innermost thoughts while he or she is making extravagant promises just before Election Day. Or how useful this talent would be when you were chatting with someone who takes your fancy.

But sadly, to repeat, we are not mind-readers. The best that evolution has been able to do for us is to give us certain biological and learned workarounds to deal with this shortcoming so that we can at least try to intuit with some degree of accuracy what other people (and domesticated animals like dogs, cats, and horses) may be thinking and planning to do. Hence, as we have discussed, the real limitation on human collaboration and friendship is not that secretly down deep inside we all loathe one another, or at any rate, wouldn't mind killing anyone who isn't biological kin, but rather that we aren't mind-readers. And as I am confident you know well from your own personal experiences, this problem can become critically acute when we are confronted by people and situations that are way out of our comfort zone and well beyond the range of our own previous experiences.

A wonderful example occurred centuries ago at the dawn of the Enlightenment in a far off place now called New Zealand (or in Maori, *Aotearoa*). In this instance, it wasn't a wink or twitch that was hard to read, but rather a trumpet call at the dawn of European exploration in that Great South Sea now more commonly called the Pacific Ocean.

IN THE CHRONICLES of history, the 16th century belongs firmly to the Spanish and the Portuguese, and their conquests in the New World. Not so the 17th century. That was when the Netherlands came into its own, not so much in the Americas but more exotically in the South Pacific.

The *Vereenigde Oost-Indische Compagnie* (the VOC, or Dutch United East India Company) was established in 1602 as virtually a nation-state unto itself having extraordinary powers of war and commerce, justice, and retribution.[2] Forty years later the Company had grown to become a fabulously successful mercantile concern holding a near monopoly over the rich European trade with Malaysia and island Southeast Asia in nutmeg, cloves, pepper, and other spices.[3]

In 1642 those running the Company set their sights on further expanding its gains, opportunities, and corporate holdings. They chose one of their ablest employees, Abel Janszoon Tasman, then in his late 30s, to take charge of a new venture—ascertaining what there was to see and exploit over on the as-yet-unexplored southern side of the world where public rumor and cartographic logic alike declared there had to be a great southern continent, a fabled land referred to as *Terre Australis Incognita*, waiting to be discovered by those who would know how to make the most of the riches that it undoubtedly possessed and could somehow be induced to part with.

Tasman was issued his official sailing instructions by the Company on August 13, 1642.[4] In addition to spelling out in detail the practicalities of the trip he was to undertake, the document he was handed contained sage advice on how to behave properly toward strangers. He was also forewarned therein about the kind of stranger he was likely to encounter on the southern side of the globe:

> In landing with your small craft great caution, circumspection and prudence will have to be used, since, as aforesaid, it has repeatedly been experienced that Nova Guinea [New Guinea] is inhabited by cruel, bloodthirsty men, and it remains quite uncertain up to now, with what sort of men the South-lands are peopled, though it may well be presumed that, so far from being civilized or polite persons, they are rude, wild, fierce barbarians, for which reason you will always have to be well armed, and to use every prudent precaution .... [5]

How successful was Tasman in sticking to the Company's instructions? On November 24, 1642, the two ships sailing under his command—the war yacht *Heemskerck* and the sleek flyboat *Zeehaan*—sighted land that Tasman elected to call Anthony van Diemen's Landt "in honor of the Honorable Governor-General, our illustrious master, who sent us to make this discovery." Nowadays, the world calls this same place Tasmania, the beautiful large island off the southeast coast of Australia.

On the 1st of December, good anchorage was finally located near a small island—Green Island—off the Tasmanian coast. Men were sent ashore "to ascertain what facilities (as regards fresh water, refreshments, timber and the like) may be available there." They found "high but level land covered with vegetation (not cultivated, but growing naturally by the will of God)," an abundance of excellent timber, and a gently sloping watercourse of good quality in a barren valley. Those who had gone ashore heard "certain human sounds and also sounds nearly resembling the music of a trumpet or a small gong not far from them." But they saw no one. Nonetheless, by a process of reasoning that to this day remains obscure, Tasman and others deduced from what was later reported to him that these unseen inhabitants must have been more on the order of giants than men of normal stature.

On December 13, the Heemskerck and the Zeehaan found the west coast of a land they christened *Zeelandia Nova*. They had reached the west side of New Zealand's South Island, a coastline unwelcoming then, as now, to anyone seeking to come ashore. Sailing northward along this forbidding coast, on the 17th they finally sighted smoke rising in several places behind the shoreline. The following day the decision was made to see if it would be possible to land. Two boats were sent off from the ships to reconnoiter closer to shore.

In his journal, Tasman described what happened next in words that he may have chosen carefully to reassure the Company that he and all those with him had made every effort, as instructed, to behave in a kindly fashion toward the local inhabitants:

> At sunset when it fell a calm we dropped anchor in 15 fathom, good anchoring-ground in the evening, about an hour after sunset, we saw a number of lights on shore and four boats close inshore, two of which came towards us, upon which our own two boats returned on board; they reported that they had found no less than 13 fathom water and that, when the sun sank behind the high land, they were still about half a mile from shore. When our men had been on board for the space of about one glass the men in the two prows [canoes] began to call out to us in the rough, hollow voice, but we could not understand a word of what they said. We however called out to them in answer, upon which they repeated their cries several times, but came no nearer than a stone shot; they also blew several times on an instrument of which the sound was like that of a Moorish trumpet; we then ordered one of our sailors (who had some knowledge of trumpet-blowing) to play them some tunes in answer. Those on board the Zeehaan ordered their second mate (who had come out to India as a trumpeter...) to do the same; after this had been repeated several times on both sides, and as it was getting more and more dark, those in the native prows at last ceased and paddled off.

During the night, the men on board the two Dutch ships were ordered to keep double watch and have in readiness necessaries of war, such as muskets, pikes, and cutlasses. The following morning the drama became more serious and more deadly (Figure 15):

> Early in the morning a boat manned with 13 natives approached to about a stone's cast from our ships; they called out several times but we did not understand them, their speech not bearing any resemblance to the vocabulary given us by the Honourable Governor-General and Councillors of India, which is hardly to be wondered at, seeing that it contains the language of the Salomonis islands, etc.... We repeatedly made signs for them to come on board of us, showing them white linen and some knives that formed part of our cargo. They did not come nearer, however, but at last paddled back to shore. In the

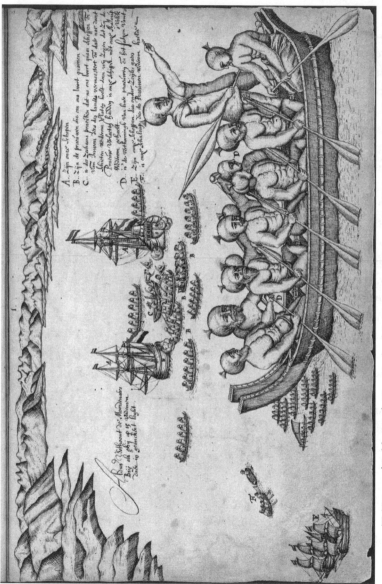

FIGURE 15 Te Taitapu (Golden Bay), New Zealand, in December 1642—called "Moordenaers Baij" (Murderers Bay) by Abel Tasman. (*Source:* http://upload.wikimedia.org/wikipedia/commons/6/6e/Gilsemans_1642.jpg).

meanwhile, at our summons sent the previous evening, the officers of the Zeehaan came on board of us, upon which we convened a council and resolved to go as near the shore as we could, since there was good anchoring-ground here, and these people apparently sought our friendship.

However, in this regard the captain and his crew were in error (or so Tasman elected to tell the tale):

Shortly after we had drawn up this resolution we saw 7 more boats put off from the shore, one of which (high and pointed in front, manned with 17 natives) paddled round behind the Zeehaan while another, with 13 able-bodied men in her, approached to within half a stone's throw of our ship; the men in these two boats now and then called out to each other; we held up and showed them as before white linens, etc., but they remained where they were.

A boat was sent across from the Heemskerck to the Zeehaan with six paddlers in it to caution the crew to be well on guard and not let too many of these people on board. This boat was rammed by one of the local canoes "so violently it got a violent lurch, upon which the foremost man in this prow of villains with a long, blunt pike thrust the quartermaster Cornelis Joppen in the neck several times with so much force that the poor man fell overboard." Thereupon, other natives with short clubs and their paddles fell upon the rest of the men in the boat, killing three of the sailors and giving another a mortal blow. "After this outrageous and detestable crime the murderers sent the [Dutch boat] adrift, having taken one of the dead bodies into their prow and thrown another into the sea."

Seeing what had happened, Tasman tells us, his men "diligently fired our muskets and guns and, although we did not hit any of them, the two prows made haste to the shore, where they were out of the reach of shot. With our fore upper-deck and bow guns we now fired several shots in the direction of their prows, but none of them took effect." Then the Heemskerck and the Zeehaan weighed anchor and set sail, "since we could not hope to enter into any friendly relations with these people, or to be able to get water or refreshments here."

By then, 11 of the local canoes were making for both ships. "We kept quiet until some of the foremost were within reach of our guns, and then fired 1 or 2 shots from the gun-room with our pieces, without however doing them any harm; those on board the Zeehaan also fired, and in the largest prow hit a man who held a small white flag in his hand, and who fell down." The canoes retreated, and hung near shore.

A council was convened on the Heemskerck, and a resolution was drawn up and agreed upon:

> Seeing that the detestable deed of these natives against four men of the Zeehaan's crew, perpetrated this morning, must teach us to consider the inhabitants of this country as enemies; that therefore it will be best to sail eastward along the coast, following the trend of the land in order to ascertain whether there are any fitting places where refreshments and water would be obtainable; all of which will be found set forth in extenso in this day's resolution.

Tasman named the location of this historic first known meeting between Europeans and Maori people "Moordenaers Baij" (Murderers Bay). This name, however, did not withstand the test of time. Today this part of Aotearoa is called Golden Bay, or in Maori, Te Taitapu.

THE ARCHAEOLOGIST AND ethnohistorian Ian Barber at Otago University in Dunedin, New Zealand, recently offered a compelling explanation for what went wrong at Murderers Bay. The Dutch arrived at the midpoint of the growing season in an agriculturally marginal part of the country. Despite Maori warnings and expressions of concern, these strangers seemed intent on coming ashore right where the local community's gardens had been placed under a sacred *tapu*, or injunction, against intrusion. As time went by, their continued presence could only be interpreted as an act of war, and those who were native to the place, and therefore had much lose, reacted accordingly. Ramming the Zeehaan's boat was possibly just a preemptive strike against a perceived threat both to the local food supply and also to the sovereignty and political standing of the local landowners and their community leaders.[6]

Barber's explanation makes a great deal of sense and seems to be in accord with what each side reportedly did during this ill-fated encounter (admittedly as reported only from the European point of view). In their own ways, since they came from radically different backgrounds, both sides had made a sincere good-faith effort to communicate with the opposite side instead of reacting either by hiding away (as evidently happened with the "giants" on Green Island near Tasmania), or immediately resorting to violence to drive the strangers physically away.

A troop of chimpanzees would have unquestionably reacted to the arrival of strangers from overseas or the sighting of odd-appearing people on the beach quite differently. Judging by what Tasman reported back to the Dutch United East India Company, everyone on each side was apprehensive and watchful. Therefore, a plausible guess is that at least some of the standard physiological changes characteristic of the biological fight-or-flight response syndrome had kicked in. These classically include a pounding heart rate, increased blood pressure, reduction in salivation, shaking, tightening of muscles, sharpened sense of awareness, and dilation of the pupils.

Nonetheless, those on both sides during this historic encounter in 1642 tried to communicate across the divide—which in this instance was a watery one, and not a stretch of open ground or a crenellated castle wall—although you have to admit resorting back and forth to trumpet-blowing is an uncommon way to go about trying to get your intentions and needs across. I guess we could say that a wink is sometimes a toot on a trumpet. Or maybe not.

The important point, and the reason I have related the story of this first recorded encounter between Europeans and the Maori, is that it plainly *wasn't* biology—specifically, some sort of supposed human biological predisposition toward violence and mayhem—that got in the way of making new friends and renewing the stores of "refreshments" and drinking water on board the Heemskerck and the Zeehaan. No, biology wasn't to blame. Instead, this is undeniably a case of good old-fashioned cross-cultural misunderstanding. A trumpet call can be both more and less than a wink well given and received. Human communication is a complicated business, and sad to say, it is not rocket science to observe that it is all too easy to be misunderstood.

26

Friend or Facebook?

Principle 2: People like to be connected.

I THINK SOME people, at least those of a certain age, do not know quite what to make of Facebook and other social networking services on the Internet. While I was writing these words, it was reported in the news that Facebook.com alone had more than one billion users. This service was launched early in 2004, so the growth of this modern company has been phenomenal.

Part of the success of this venture is apparently the simple fact that users must register to have access to this service, and once they have completed the process, they are more than just users of this site. Unlike most Web sites, Facebook is not merely a source of information, images, videos, recipes, and so forth. Facebook is interactive. Its users "exist" on the site as known and recognizable individuals. Their personalities, likes, dislikes, adventures, silly Halloween parties, and public hopes and aspirations "live" there and are accessible to others who have been permitted to see such information as "friends" or potential would-be friends for the asking. Messages can be exchanged, comments offered, likes and dislikes signaled and fittingly recorded (although there is famously no "dislike" button to click on a Facebook wall). In addition, users can form common-interest online groups, organize real-time activities as different as school outings to Walt Disney World Resort and revolutionary protests in public squares in faraway places, and the list goes on.

In short, to use jargon introduced earlier (Chapter 22), Facebook and similar services can be used to build social capital. Or to use again that Maori word, Facebook has *mana*—it can be a *potent* way of making, maintaining, and cultivating our relationships with others for reasons diverse and sundry.

Facebook, therefore, is almost like having a real social life, except that it really isn't. It is too easy using Facebook, for example, to send a birthday greeting to friends identified by the service as having a birthday in the coming week. Perhaps even more to the point, Facebook just notified me that a friend is about to have a birthday, and did I want to send her birthday greetings? She died more than a year ago. Also I just can't help feeling that hugs delivered via the Internet not only lack the physical contact that is, after all, a defining element of a really good hug, but it is also almost impossibly hard to "read" whether virtual hugs given this way have been rendered with real feeling or are just a halfhearted and semi-automatic gesture handed out with lightning speed along digital subscriber lines and lots of fiber-optic cable.[1]

On the other hand, I am equally convinced that people who are skeptical about the value of social networking services may be missing one of the evolutionary lessons that can be learned from the enormous popularity of this modern way of staying connected with other people. What Facebook and similar services tell us in ways that simply cannot be ignored is that a lot of people not only like to be connected with other people, but also actively seek out other people to be connected with. And what strikes me as particularly relevant is that individuals can do so in the comparative safety and mostly risk-free virtual social environment of the Internet.

You don't have to be Sherlock Holmes, in short, to see that Facebook is a bona fide clue to the real character of human nature. But if most people really do like having friends, then why are we sometimes reluctant to reach out and make friends with strangers?

Just as I concluded in the previous chapter, we cannot blame biology or evolution for this reticence. Yes, sometimes fear of the unknown may be part of the reason. But to put it simply, we have to *learn* to be afraid of strangers. This is *not* an inherent part of our biological heritage as human beings despite what Charles Darwin and other evolutionists have often told us.

AS NOTED PREVIOUSLY (Chapter 14), *The Descent of Man* (1871) is Charles Darwin's most complete statement on the subject of ourselves. Though it takes him a long time to get to the point, the Wizard of Down House eventually tells us: "The social instincts lead an animal to take pleasure in the society of its fellows, to feel a certain amount of sympathy with them, and to perform various services for them." This is a good start, however delayed, yet sadly he then qualifies these seemingly conventional observations. "But these feelings and services are by no means extended to all the individuals of the same species, only to those of the same association."[2]

If you are like me, it may take a moment to see what he was getting at here when he wrote these words. Darwin was evidently of the belief that people somehow naturally *come in associations* instead of just *living* in them. Nevertheless you would think, given Darwin's evolutionary point of view, that it would have seemed altogether obvious to him that there is nothing inherent about "associations" that would keep people who are in them from also caring about people outside them. And for sure, Darwin himself did hold views fully in keeping with what we have called the friendship hypothesis.

Here, for example, is a statement in *The Descent of Man* that sounds right at home with this hypothesis. "The feeling of pleasure from society is probably an extension of the parental or filial affections, since the social instinct seems to be developed by the young remaining for a long time with their parents; and this extension may be attributed in part to habit, but chiefly to natural selection." Darwin then even goes on to suggest: "With respect to the origin of the parental and filial affections, which apparently lie at the base of the social instincts, we know not the steps by which they have been gained; but we may infer that it has been to a large extent through natural selection."[3] So far, so good.

It is dismaying, therefore, to discover in his writings that he held racist views that were absolutely typical of the era in which he lived, especially when it came to those he labeled as savages. "It is no argument against savage man being a social animal, that the tribes inhabiting adjacent districts are almost always at war with each other; for the social instincts never extend to all the individuals of the same species."[4]

Given such a conventional outlook, it may be hardly surprising that Darwin would further assert: "Most savages are utterly indifferent to the sufferings of strangers, or even delight in witnessing them."[5] Or that he would conclude that savages are strongly prone to group extermination. "With highly civilised nations continued progress depends in a subordinate degree on natural selection; for such nations do not supplant and exterminate one another as do savage tribes."[6]

As an American I find the phrase "depends in a subordinate degree on natural selection" to be a fine example of what many Americans might label as British reserve and indirectness, but luckily for clarity, if not Darwin's standing in my own eyes, he then elaborates on what he is getting at: "Extinction follows chiefly from the competition of tribe with tribe, and race with race.... and when of two adjoining tribes one becomes less numerous and less powerful than the other, the contest is soon settled by war, slaughter, cannibalism, slavery, and absorption."[7]

Why would even someone as knowledgeable as Charles Darwin hold astonishingly dismissive claims about people he thought of as savages?

I SOMETIMES GIVE a lecture called "Three Modes of Thought." Darwin's commonsensical way of thinking about human associations—by which he evidently means human groups, communities, tribes, and so on—exemplifies one of these three modes, by far the most common one. This way of seeing the world is called *typological thinking*.

This mode of thought takes it as self-evident that things in this world of ours come in *types* or *kinds*—or *tribes*—and treats the words we use to talk about things as if they were empty containers into which we put things once we have grasped correctly the proper "labeling" or "meaning" of these verbal containers. The logic runs something like this: if *words = things*, then any given noun is a container for a certain kind or type of thing.

Take, for instance, the claim that there are about 6,900 different languages in use today on planet Earth. The linguist George Lakoff and his colleague Mark Johnson have observed: "Our experiences with physical objects (especially our own bodies) provide the basis for an extraordinarily wide variety of ontological metaphors, that is, ways of viewing events, activities, emotions, ideas, etc., as entities and substances."[8] Although there must be an easier way to put into words what they are trying to say, a few examples may suffice. Consider the following conventional statements about language and languages.

Languages seen as objects
My German is rusty.
Russian frightens me.
I find Spanish easy to grasp.
These languages have been in contact for a long time.

Languages as substances
Her French is fluent.
German is hard.
I find his accent impenetrable.
What he had to say was very dense.

Languages as containers
Can you put that into words?
Would you please put that into plain English?

Did you get anything out of what she said?
Can that be translated into English?

Languages as places
How do you say that in French?
She can't get very far in Polish.
Oh, I can find my way around Norwegian easily enough.
In the middle of the conversation, the old man slipped into Yiddish.

These examples all show how truly conventional it is for us to talk about language and languages as if they were substances, things, places, or containers.

Lakoff and Johnson have suggested that metaphorical statements like these are commonly seen by most of us as self-evident descriptions of the way things really are because such expressions, such figures of speech, seem so utterly natural or normal. That words and languages are *not* objects, substances, containers, or places on earth but instead learned behavioral repertoires of signs, symbols, vocalizations, and mental actions may seem irrelevant and unimportant. It may even strike many of us as simply pedantic to insist that talking or thinking this way about language does not prove that "they" are things that have edges, or boundaries, or that languages can "contain" people inside them who are distinct and identifiable as such simply because they speak differently. Yet a statement like "Isn't she French?" is much more problematic than you might think. So too is calling someone a savage.[9]

WHAT IS THE second mode of thought that I include in my lecture? This way of seeing the world is called *fractal geometry*—a label that refers to a fairly new branch of mathematics pioneered in recent years chiefly by Benoit B. Mandelbrot, the Polish-French-American (so much for the notion that language or citizenship can be used to label people unambiguously!) who died in 2010 at the age of 85.[10] The technical details of this kind of geometry need not delay us, but the bottom line is worth noting. Mandelbrot showed us how some of the most outwardly complex and indescribable shapes or forms can be broken down successfully into smaller versions of the same basic overall shape—regardless of their size, these mini-versions of the same shape are said to be all "self-similar." In turn, these mini-versions can then be broken down into yet smaller mini-mini-versions of the same shape, and still again, these mini-mini-versions can be broken into yet even smaller versions that then can be further broken down into... well, you get the picture.

FIGURE 16 A Sierpinski triangle. (*Source*: http://upload.wikimedia.org/wikipedia/
commons/b/b7/SierpinskiTriangle.PNG).

A classic example of what a fractal figure looks like is what you get when
you divide a big triangle first into four smaller triangles by placing dots at the
midpoint of each side, and then connecting these dots with lines (Figure 16).
Once you repeat this same dot-and-line maneuver over and over for every
smaller triangle you get, the number of triangles grows because each time you
are creating ever smaller triangles within triangles within triangles. In the
world of fractal geometry this is called a Sierpinski triangle. Something to
remember for your next dinner party.

However, the most interesting fractal shapes are not those that are as regularly wrought as triangles within triangles. It could be said that the whole
point of fractal geometry is that this is the geometry of the bizarre, irregu-
lar, and seemingly complex. For example, this geometry is great for dealing with things like clouds or the coastlines of real places—say, Maine or
Ireland. Fractal geometry can also be used to create hauntingly beautiful art
(Figure 17). Strictly speaking, in fact, fractal geometry is not really designed
for use in our man-made world of nice, neat, regular shapes and objects such
as triangles, squares, chessboards, or stud-walls made out of well-seasoned
two-by-fours.

FIGURE 17 An imaginary fractal galaxy. (*Source*: http://commons.wikimedia.org/wiki/ File:GalaxyOfGalaxies.jpg).

If we take fractal geometry to heart, the implication is clear. We need to think twice, maybe even thrice, before blithely assuming that an "association" (to use Darwin's term) as big as the city of Chicago is necessarily all that different in its ways from a place of association that is a great deal smaller—say, the size of Peoria, Illinois, or a village on the Sepik coast. Similarly, when it comes to social life, how true is it that families, neighborhoods, villages, towns, cities, nations, or the world are as different from one another as we may believe?

THE THIRD MODE of thought, the one that I think best shows what is wrongheaded about Darwin's acceptance of our commonsense way of thinking about human associations, communities, groups, or tribes as boxes or containers into which people can be put is also a relatively new mathematical way of thinking about things, or rather about relationships.

Modern social network analysis (SNA) is both a body of theory and a set of relatively new computer-aided techniques used in the analysis and study of relational information about contacts, ties, or connections linking individuals or groups with one another. Examples of such relational data would be information on who regularly attends the same social events, civic meetings, church gatherings, and so on; how much crude oil is being shipped between Iraq and the United States; and how scientists working in different fields of research collaborate with one another when writing professional papers.[11]

Although again there is no need to go into detail, SNA is a rigorous and analytically exacting way of studying and reporting on how people live and work in groups of all sorts and sizes—some as informal as breakfast clubs and hip-hop groups, others as influential and globally consequential as the World Court, the United Nations, and multinational corporations.

Mark Newman, who is one of the leaders in this new field of applied mathematics, has explained that a network is a set of items usually called *vertices* or *nodes* together with the connections between them, called *edges* or *ties*.[12] In the social sciences, a primary focus of network research is on how individuals (call them "nodes") interact with one another to maintain enduring associations (call them "edges"), and on the social, economic, and practical consequences of alternative network arrangements.

Visual mapping is commonly used in SNA research to show the patterning of network relationships. Figure 18 depicts three alternative ways of mapping a simple network made up of the same seven nodes. In (a), these nodes have been placed at equal distances in a circular pattern. As simple as this social network mapping is, it is clear that each node in this network (from now on, let's substitute the word "individual" or "person" since we are talking

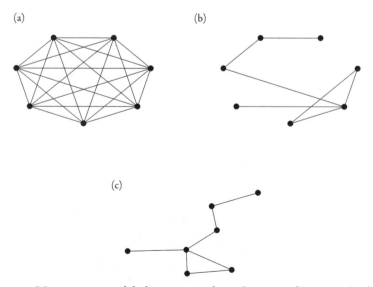

FIGURE 18 Mapping a network linking seven nodes in three ways. (*Source*: author.)

about social network analysis, not just network analysis in a generic sense) is linked directly with all of the others.

However, in many real-life situations, it is likely that each of the nodes/ individuals represented will be directly linked with only some of the others in such a network, not with all of them. This more realistic fact of life is mapped in (b), where only connections equal to, or greater than, a certain "tie strength" are shown. For example, the lines drawn may indicate which individuals work together with one another every day of the work week, not just occasionally or a couple of times a month. In (b) it is now easy to see that the connections between these seven individuals are structured for this or some other reason, or reasons—an observation that may well be worth further research.

Note that the placement of the individuals mapped in (b) is in itself uninformative. These seven people are shown in exactly the same locations where they were originally put in (a)—that is, in a purely arbitrary circle. Therefore, the length of the lines connecting these people with one another is similarly arbitrary and uninformative. How long these lines are tells us nothing about who is "more strongly connected with," "closer to," or "more similar to" whom.

Fortunately, SNA experts have devised a number of ways of mapping social relationships that incorporate such useful additional information. These specialist techniques include metric- and nonmetric multidimensional scaling, principal components analysis, spring-embedding, and other mapping strategies.[13] The mapping of the seven people in our imaginary network shown in (c) was drawn using the SNA method called spring-embedding. Given this mapping, it is much easier to observe that three of the individuals in this network evidently work together as a team of some sort, but only one of these three has much to do with the other four in the social network being shown. Possibly this individual is the team leader for this small trio of colleagues.

I HAVE DESCRIBED these three modes of thought to introduce a central idea. If you look at the world from the perspective of SNA, what Darwin called "associations"—and most of us today would probably call groups, communities, ethnic groups, tribes, or nations, and the like—do not look at all like boxes or containers of some other sort that we can put people into and then properly label as such. Instead of thinking of human associations as invisible boxes or containers, SNA shows us that our lives are defined instead by the kinds of *relationships* we have with other people. You are free to call them *edges* if you would prefer, but however labeled, there is no way to get around the reality that most of us like having relationships—for example, friendships—with other people.

This lesson was underscored vividly in the late 1960s by a famous, if somewhat flawed, social experiment done by Stanley Milgram, a social psychologist. He demonstrated that people living in America's heartland could get a letter hand-delivered to an address near Boston, Massachusetts, by asking that it be handed on from person to person with the understanding that each person temporarily receiving the letter had to pass it on to someone he or she knew on a first-name basis. Milgram's finding: it took an average of six steps, six direct personal connections, to get the letter delivered—a result that gave rise to the now familiar saying that everybody on earth is linked to everyone else by only "six degrees of separation."[14]

You may be saying that this is all very nice and good to hear, but what about my reluctance to strike up conversations with strangers? What does my timidity, bashfulness, or simple cowardice have to do with social network analysis? More than you may realize.

27

What Was the Garden of Eden Like?

Principle 3: Ask a friend to be your go-between.

IT WAS NOT until 1769 that other Europeans known to history reached New
Zealand in Abel Tasman's footsteps, or rather his wake—although having put
this far-off corner of the world on the global map, it seems rather unlikely that
absolutely nobody else from Europe got there during all the years between
1642 and 1769.[1] This time the foreigners were Lieutenant James Cook and the
crew of *His Majesty's Bark Endeavour*. For the most part, these new strangers
fared far better than Tasman had, although not without some blood being
shed over the course of the six months of their stay in New Zealand waters
during the latter part of 1769 and the first months of the following year. Cook
and his company, however, were aided in their encounters with local people
by having with them a remarkable Tahitian navigator named Tupaia who
was able to communicate successfully with his Maori cousins (both Tahitian
and Maori are closely related Polynesian languages—some would call them
merely dialects of one another).[2]

As every sailor in a foreign port looking for companionship for an hour
or a night supposedly knows, linguistic competence is not a prerequisite for
making friends with strangers. Furthermore, two people being able to understand one another verbally is no guarantee they will be able to understand one
another intellectually or emotionally. This is, after all, what is at the root of a
great deal of daily miscommunication and misunderstanding. Either failing
can lead to anger, hurt, and sometimes bloodshed. In short, the Leslie effect
can be real and sometimes frightening. Here is one of my favorite examples.

THE YEAR WAS 1969, exactly two centuries after Cook had arrived for the first time in New Zealand. The place was a small harbor in the Solomon Islands, an elongated archipelago in the southwestern Pacific north northwest of New Zealand that was once notorious among foreigners for headhunters, cannibals, and treachery. Although this particular harbor had never seen a cruise ship or a travel agent, it was the kind of picture-perfect tropical retreat that tourists dream about. Gently rolling waves sweeping over black-sand beaches, gracefully swaying palm trees, spectacular blue water.

Out in the middle of the bay where my local friend and I had just stopped paddling our small outrigger canoe, the sun was brutally hot. I was wondering why we had halted our journey so far from land in any direction. I wanted to reach the shade of the palm trees on the coral sand island at the mouth of the harbor that both of us then called home. Beneath us, a sea snake rippled its silent way through sea water that was almost unbelievably clear. Not far off, birds were swooping down to take small fish leaping frantically out of the water to escape pursuit by bigger fish.

My companion, the leader of a prominent family on our island home, and also the harbor's elected representative to the local government council, had an uncommonly deep, rich, commanding voice. He said nothing at all for a long moment or two. Then he spoke slowly and with what seemed like unusual caution. "John, do you know what the people are saying about you?" he asked, naming the village on the far side of the harbor we had just finished visiting so I could do a brief archaeological survey around there.

"No," I replied, matching his caution, "what *are* they saying?"

"They say they see you talking to someone they cannot see. And they saw you find that old stone ax on the path running out from the village. That ax must have belonged to one of their ancestors. They say they have walked that way every day of their lives, and yet they never saw it lying there. They asked me to tell them how you knew where to find it. They say the reason must be that the person you are talking to who they cannot see must have told you it was there."

"Oh. Are they saying anything else?"

He lowered his voice and with even greater care responded: "They are saying this proves you must be a devil or a spirit. This is why they gave you food to eat and a coconut to drink."

There are times in every life when you sense you have reached a fork in the road where a careless word or deed could forever change the character of the rest of your days. For a brief fraction of a second, I wondered what would happen if I acknowledged that the villagers were entirely right. No, of course

I was not a demon. Good heavens! But yes, they had cleverly deduced that I was one of their long-departed relatives.

Fortunately, good sense got the better of me. I laughed, and said: "You know how I am. I'm always talking to myself. And you know I am an archaeologist. I am trained to find things that people long ago threw away."

With what seemed a real, if momentary, sigh of relief, my friend then laughed, too. He indicated this was exactly what he had told the people in the village when they voiced their concerns about me. He assured me he did not think I was a demon, or an ancestor spirit!

There was a pause in our conversation while we both savored the situation. We then put our paddles in the water once more, and proceeded on our way to the island. We had not gone far, however, before my friend, who was seated behind me in the narrow canoe, asked if I would answer one more question for him. It was something he had always wondered about. He had read about it in the Bible. He asked: "What was the Garden of Eden like?"

On the rare occasions when I tell this true story, I always worry that those hearing it may dismiss what happened back then in the middle of that beautiful harbor in the Solomon Islands as a funny anecdote about the strength of jungle superstitions. Yet reflect a moment. The people in that village had every right to be suspicious of my character and motives. I was a stranger who had, believe it or not, come all the way from America intent on doing something truly bizarre, if not crazy. I was collecting the trash their ancestors had thrown away long, long ago, and I was claiming that I could learn from such rubbish about what had happened there in the past. I was definitely talking to someone they could not see (or so it seemed). I did indeed find a stone ax on that path through the trees that they took every day to go down to the beach. I can well imagine that almost anybody confronting a strange person like me for the first time might arrive at similar suspicions, similar fears.

As far as I can see, all it took to turn what I saw as a normal work day into what they saw as a potentially dangerous situation was just one more logical ingredient—the premise that apparitions are real and can retrieve lost possessions, or are able to communicate in some hidden way with strangely behaving Americans who can do the job for them. Granted, you don't believe in ghosts, or at any rate, not ghosts at noon in an otherwise serene tropical setting. But is it fair to dismiss their questions, concerns, and fears as superficial and parochial?

This was in 1969, not 1869. I have no idea whether a hundred years earlier, or even 50 years earlier, I would have been treated with the same caution. My hunch is that I probably would have, provided both they and I had approached my unannounced arrival in a reasoned way, which is how I did it in 1969—with a mutual friend leading the way.

WHAT HAPPENED TO me at that village was a far cry from the popular stereotype of the Pacific Islander as a wild savage driven by the cannibal's lust for human flesh. A graphic instance of that horrific old stereotype was proffered in 1926 by Father Bruno Hagspiel, an American member of the Society of the Divine Word, while relating a voyage he had taken along the Sepik coast of northern New Guinea some years earlier:

> Mentally the natives of New Guinea have the capacity of white children of about the age of twelve years. They have no alphabet or written signs of any kind, and throughout a thousand years they have progressed but little. The reason for this seems clear. Before the white man came, they were divided into tribes or villages which were constantly at war with one another. The native when captured, eked out the food supply of the conquering tribe. Many a weak tribe has entirely disappeared through acting as a casual larder to satisfy the meat hunger of one stronger. The thought of such happenings kept every native close to his own village.[3]

It would be a decided understatement to suggest that Father Hagspiel was badly misinformed.

You might think that this old stereotype of the bloodthirsty and cannibalistic savage would have been laid to rest long ago, but as we have seen, this hasn't been the case. Remarkably, too, this way of thinking about other people is not just alive and well in popular culture. For instance, Edward O. Wilson at Harvard was not just speaking for himself when he wrote recently that "tribalism" is one of the basic flaws of human nature. Wilson shares the opinion others have as well that modern groups "are psychologically equivalent to the tribes of ancient history and prehistory."[4] And for those holding this view of ourselves, our inner sense of "tribalism" may go well beyond just having an earnest desire to bond with others sharing our interests, hopes, likes, or hatreds. As we have previously discussed, Wilson wants us to accept that "our bloody nature, it can now be argued in the context of modern biology, is ingrained because group-versus-group was a principal driving force that made us what we are."[5]

However misguided this claim may be (by now you know what I think of this idea), it is only fair to acknowledge, as the anthropologist Fredrik Barth once remarked, that practically all social science reasoning rests on the premise that discrete groups of people live on planet Earth that can be variously labeled as *tribes, ethnic groups, populations, societies,* or *cultures.*[6] Indeed, as the sociologist Rogers Brubaker has observed: "Few social science concepts would seem as basic, even indispensable, as that of group."[7] In short, in keeping with the distinctions made in Chapter 26, much of thinking in the social sciences has been *typological.*

It is worth asking, therefore, why this time-honored typological way of talking about human diversity still seems so natural, so self-evident, so obviously true despite the reality that nowadays so many of us are participating firsthand in the delights of social networking far and wide via Facebook, Twitter, or Snapchat. Here is my guess. It is a fairly safe bet that people living in other places will not be just like you or me. After all, as discussed in Chapter 15, isolation-by-distance and spatial auto-correlation aren't just statistical abstractions. Therefore, if there is a reason or a need—however good or bad—to draw a line between "us" and "them," something can always be found or imagined to justify doing so. Hence it does not call for a huge leap of faith to conclude also that human beings really do live in separate tribal-like groups or societies.

It is not hard to find anthropological support for this observation. Half a century ago the anthropologist James Watson reported that people he knew well in the Eastern Highlands of New Guinea were skilled at pointing out to him how they differed from people in neighboring communities, even though most of these small communities had experienced radical episodes of revision in their membership:

> Most groups are formed in a highly fluid sociopolitical field, intermittently marked by relocations, realignments, and the patriation of alien immigrants who have been expelled by hostile neighbors from their own lands elsewhere. Restless or disgruntled insiders split off to form new groups; refugee outsiders are recruited from time to time to reinforce the ranks of those remaining. To the literal-minded genealogist, the long-term kinship and continuity of each such group seem confused, even compromised.[8]

Despite the social instability of their communities, Watson found that people where he was working had no difficulty at all in drawing lines:

> I came to a paradoxical conclusion: no matter how numerous, small, near, and nearly identical the polities of the Eastern Highlands may

be, no matter how permeable their boundaries or how checkered the history of their membership, they will consider themselves and will be thought to be distinct ethnic units.[9]

It is likely, therefore, that dividing the world into "us" and "them" may be a common human trait, although this does not mean doing so is part of human nature. In any case, history unquestionably shows us that many people have not been reluctant to do so. All the more reason, therefore, to ask a mutual friend to be your go-between.

28

The Strength of Weak Ties?

Principle 4: New friends are new pathways.

ACCORDING TO GOOGLE Scholar, Mark Granovetter's classic 1973 paper "The strength of weak ties" had been cited almost 29,000 times when I last looked at the beginning of August 2014. This means that on average it has been cited professionally almost twice a day for the last 40 years. This statistical information makes me quite jealous since absolutely nothing I have written and published can hold a candle to this astonishing achievement. Moreover, this success is well-deserved, and I am not just saying this to be nice.

In this paper, Granovetter, a professor at Stanford University, uses social network analysis to examine how the strength of our ties with others can have an effect on our social mobility, the diffusion of ideas, the political organization of society, and on a more general level, the cohesion of society writ large.[1] He defines *tie strength* in a fairly intuitive way as the amount of time as well as the emotional intensity and intimacy (in a confiding sense, rather than a sexual one, although I don't think he rules out the latter) devoted to our relationships, as well as the mutual benefits characterizing our dealings with other people. In addition, he notes that there is evidence showing that the stronger the connection between two people, the more likely they are to be similar to one another in a number of ways.

One consequence of having strong ties with someone is that you are also likely to have strong ties with that person's friends, and if it is true that people who are tied strongly with one another socially and emotionally are also likely to be similar to one another, groups of friends are likely to form social groups, or cliques, marked by—let's be polite about this—a high degree of redundancy (my word, not Granovetter's), although some more strident social critics might be less kind and say instead that cliques of friends are often at risk of becoming dull, boringly predictable, closed-minded, and so forth.

And consider for a moment what the "so forth" in this regard can mean. Failure to have social ties with others beyond our own clique and comfort zone can, however unintentionally, lead to ignorance, disdain, and even the dehumanization of others whom we don't personally know anything at all about beyond perhaps hearsay and the prejudicial statements made by those we know. From a human point of view, such avoidable failings all fall in my opinion under the rubric "irresponsible." Stronger words could also be used, for what we are talking about can lead to appalling consequences, including genocide.

Fortunately, however, although we may be given to spending most of our time, energy, and discretionary income on only a small number of people with whom we feel we are closely linked by shared kinship, hobbies, political views, and the like, most of us do not limit our activities only to such a distinguishable and perhaps distinguished few. Most people also have weaker ties with other individuals, and fortunately these weaker ties can serve as bridges of a sort between cliques, or communities, of people. Importantly, these weaker links, these bridges, can also serve as pathways along which new information, innovations, material things, and even people, too, can "flow" from clique to clique, group to group, place to place.[2]

Although perhaps counterintuitive, therefore, Granovetter's analysis leads to the provocative idea that these "weak ties" are extremely important because they are more likely to link people in different groups together better than strong ties do since the latter tend to be inward looking and constraining. Hence what is key to our engagement with and integration into larger social realms beyond the confines of our immediate families and intimate social groups are our *weaker* ties with others elsewhere and farther afield. In short, however marginal to our daily lives, being able to say hello to strangers and initiate new relationships with them—with or without the assistance of go-betweens—can be absolutely vital to our success as individuals and perhaps our success as a species, as well.

THIS LAST THOUGHT can be brought home by going back once again to where I began the intellectual journey you and I have been taking together in this book—not to the Pufendorf Institute for Advanced Study, but rather to the great island of New Guinea. James A. Michener opens *Tales of the South Pacific*, his Pulitzer Prize–winning collection of short stories about World War II, with these simple words: "I wish I could tell you about the South

Pacific. The way it actually was. The endless ocean. The infinite specks of coral we call islands." So movingly did he talk about the war and its human stories that for many of us it is impossible to think about coconut palms and island people without also thinking about Bali-ha'i, Nurse Nellie Forbush from Little Rock, First Lt. Joe Cable, Emile De Becque, and Bloody Mary and her daughter, the beautiful Liat.[3]

Michener was writing mostly about the Coral Sea and the Melanesian islands of the southwestern Pacific, not New Guinea. Nonetheless, several generations of anthropologists have come away from doing field work in New Guinea and elsewhere in this part of the Pacific with something less dramatic but in many respects more important to say. Far from being a savage realm of isolation and bloodshed, people in this part of the world are astonishingly linked with one another by far-reaching social networks.

Unfortunately, and presumably because they have been mostly blind to friendship as a civil and evolutionary force, anthropologists and others writing about these islanders have generally written about their social networks linking people and families in different hamlets and villages as a primitive, or grassroots, kind of economic activity. As a consequence, these ties have invariably been labeled in the writings of anthropologists and others as "trade partnerships" or "partnership exchange," and the published descriptions of such alliances are often as bloodless and lifeless as the words in the phrase "far-reaching social networks."[4] But perhaps scholars can be excused, since they are usually not trying to write like James Michener.

Or perhaps they should not be too easily forgiven. The anthropologist Epeli Hau'ofa (1939–2009) was born in Papua New Guinea. His parents were Tongan missionaries working there. At a symposium on the future of anthropology in Melanesia held in Canberra, Australia, in January 1975, Hau'ofa spoke passionately both as someone being trained then professionally to be an anthropologist and also as a Pacific Islander. He was finding it difficult to balance these two identities, one professional, the other personal.[5]

In New Guinea, for instance, some well-educated people had been telling him that they regarded anthropologists with distaste. "As a former tutor in the University of Papua New Guinea and as someone to whom islanders talk with little self-conscious politeness or deference, I have been struck by the claims by people that 'anthropologists do not really understand us,' 'do not present a complete or fair picture of us,' and as Tongans say, "they do not know how we feel.'"

Part of the problem, he said, was simply miscommunication about the aims of anthropology as a social science. Islanders expect anthropologists to be more like novelists and social historians and less like scientists given to using incomprehensible social science jargon.

Speaking as an anthropologist, Hauʻofa tried to put his finger on the problem: "They cooperate with us thinking that we are going to tell their stories taking their points of view into consideration." And then they get disappointed by what anthropologists finally say about them.

But Hauʻofa did not see the issue as simply one about miscommunication and the use of social science jargon. He also felt that in some of their writings, anthropologists were distorting the truth, particularly about the dark-skinned islanders of Melanesia. "Somehow or other we have projected onto Melanesian leaders the caricature of the quintessential Western capitalist: grasping, manipulative, calculating, and without a stitch of morality."

Lest it be charged that he was grossly exaggerating, he was willing to name at least one anthropologist whom he saw as being guilty of such distortion. In his opinion, the eminent American anthropologist Marshall Sahlins was writing about Melanesians in such a disparaging way that he seemed to be saying Melanesian leaders are motivated purely by selfishness and have no genuine interest in the welfare of their people. Hauʻofa not only felt this is not true, but worse, that such a characterization was deplorable—clever, thoughtless, and insulting.

Unfortunately, however, Hauʻofa also did not see what Sahlins had been saying about Melanesians as unusual:

> This may be an extreme example but it is indicative of the fact that after decades of anthropological field research in Melanesia we have come up only with pictures of people who fight, compete, trade, pay bride-prices, engage in rituals, invent cargo cults, copulate and sorcerise each other. There is hardly anything in our literature to indicate whether these people have any such sentiments as love, kindness, consideration, altruism and so on. We cannot tell from our ethnographic writings whether they have a sense of humour.[6]

These are strong words. However, I definitely think not all anthropologists are guilty of neglecting to portray Melanesians—using Hauʻofa's words—"as rounded human beings who love as well as hate, who laugh joyously as well as quarrel, who are peaceful as well as warlike, and who are generous and kindly as well as mean and calculating." Consider the following example, which I think shows us also that the weak links of what is today called "tourism" are not just a manifestation and side benefit of the growth of capitalism, industrialization, globalization, and the establishment of nation-states.

IN 1935, THE Australian anthropologist Ian Hogbin reported in the journal *Oceania* on what he saw as trading expeditions between the Schouten Islands and coastal communities on the New Guinea mainland.[7] The Schoutens are a chain of six small volcanic islands spread out over 56 miles (90 km) of ocean in an east–west chain roughly 30 miles (48 km) off New Guinea's northeastern coast. Hogbin had lived the previous year on Wogeo (modern Vokeo), the westernmost island. He tells us not only about how these islanders were accustomed to traveling back and forth between them visiting their friends, but also how every few years they sailed to the New Guinea mainland "for the purpose of carrying on trade."

You initially get the impression from what Hogbin tells us that those taking these infrequent mainland trips have fairly down-to-earth aims in mind. The friends they have in different places on the coast whom they visit there can supply them with things not made on Wogeo. For instance, clay cooking pots can be had from friends at Kep on the mainland whose resident potters are locally famed experts in this art and craft; similarly, beautiful handwoven baskets made of grasses collected from the swamps at the mouth of the Sepik River can be obtained as gifts from friends at other coastal villages there. And elsewhere along the coastline, he relates, they can similarly count on being given all sorts of specialty items, such as shell scrapers, spoons made out of cassowary bone, and tobacco, as well as shell bracelets and other kinds of fancy goods for personal adornment, including bird of paradise feathers, and hair ornaments decorated with dogs' teeth and cowrie shells. In return, Hogbin tells us, Wogeo Islanders reciprocate with gifts of their own specialty items, such as fishing nets and edible nuts, including delicious *galip* nuts (*Canarium indicum*).

Hogbin's inventory, however, of all the differing things Wogeo people get and give while they are traveling on one of these long-distance voyaging expeditions does not end with just this listing of these types of material things that can be gotten and given. Here is Hogbin's accounting of some of the more surprising items that may also be involved:

> Canoes are occasionally bartered away, and on a couple of occasions villages on the mainland have "bought" Wogeo dances. I understand that amongst themselves the mainlanders trade regularly in dances. Magic too is sometimes exchanged for material goods. Wogeo love

magic is said to be better than that from any other place, while the islanders themselves have obtained a good many spells to cause diseases from elsewhere.[8]

Hogbin's understanding is correct. My friend Jim Roscoe, who has worked for many years in this part of New Guinea, reports that people here "engage in an import and export of ritual and artistic culture that reaches intensities almost unparalleled in the nonindustrial world."[9] In May 1932, for example, the New Zealand anthropologist Reo Fortune—he was in New Guinea then with his wife, the famous Margaret Mead (their marriage ended in 1935)— witnessed the purchase of a dance complex called "Shenei" at an inland village on the north coast that included the right to make, use, and if so desired later also sell to others the masks, attire, and body ornaments associated with this prestigious dance. This purchase, which took place over a period of three days, was arranged with the help of the purchasers' local friends (specifically, people whom the purchasers call *buanyim*, "road friends"—a local word that Mead alternately translates in her own reports as "trade friends" or "gift friends").[10]

In light of all this evident buying and selling, should we conclude that this is a grass-roots kind of commerce? The purchase of the dance complex observed by Fortune certainly did have the earmarks of an out-and-out purchase. Although she did not witness this purchase, Mead was later willing to write that people locally obtained things like net bags, wooden plates, shell rings, and clay pots by "haggling," "vending," "bartering," and the like. She dismissed the fact that those involved spoke about their acquisitions in terms of affection, friendship, and gratitude. She evidently believed this was just a ruse to cover up the actual business being done under the guise of civility and friendship.

However, I think it is important to take note of three things about how Hogbin describes what he witnessed. First, transactions between friends were certainly not impersonal. They had little in common with buying a tall iced coffee at your local Starbucks. Second, what was being given and gotten was not always useful, or even necessary, in any practical, material sense. Third, when offering friends in different places new dances, spells, myths, magic, stories, chants, and other forms of esoteric knowledge, the transfers had to be accomplished face-to-face while the visitors were still around, and before they had sailed off on down the coast to see what their friends in other places were up to—and see what they might have that could be packed up and taken home as solid proof of the success of the voyage and appropriateness of the time spent away from home and family duties.

In short, labeling the exchange of things, however useful or impractical, as "trade" or "exchange," and labeling the people involved as "trading partners" or "trade friends" underplays the fact that the giving-and-getting of things can have little to do with commerce and economics, or supply and demand. Instead, giving and receiving can be a nuanced and meaningful way of marking social ties and enduring friendships.[11] Or as I like to say when I am wearing my museum curator's hat, material things like clay pots and dance masks—as well as nonmaterial things like spells and dances—can be a very effective way for people to mark and mediate human relationships. Case in point: who in our own corner of the globe would dream of showing up at a friend's party without a bottle of wine, a fine cheese, a bouquet of flowers, or box of chocolates—accompanied by a handshake or a kiss—to hand to the host or hostess upon arrival?

This observation, which applies equally well to the Aitape area where Welsch and I have worked, holds true elsewhere in New Guinea. In 1933–1934, Camilla Wedgwood lived on Manam Island, which is 7 miles (11 km) off the New Guinea mainland near the mouth of the Sepik River, and 87 miles (140 km) east of Wogeo. Here is what she wrote about Manam "trade" and "trading partners" (locally called *tawa*):

> It would be a mistake, however, to regard these "trading expeditions" as being merely of economic value or importance. Often a man will join such an expedition only for the pleasure of the trip and of seeing his *tawa*, and often boys of fourteen or more will be taken with their fathers, or even sent alone with fellow villagers, in order that they may meet their fathers' *tawa* and their sons, who will be their own *tawa*. Nor are women and small girls debarred from going to visit their friends and parents' friends. In particular, it seems to give a man pleasure to take an eight or nine year old daughter with him, and to deck her out for the occasion with a wealth of dogs' teeth.... These trading expeditions, then, though they are important from an economic standpoint, also fulfill an important social function, since through the system of *tawa* the natives of Manam are able to make and preserve important social contacts with "foreign" and potentially hostile communities, thus preventing that isolation which so easily leads to cultural stagnation and thence to degeneration.[12]

PLEASE DON'T GET me wrong. It is certain that people in some regions of New Guinea have been engaged in activities that we would be fully justified in labeling as business, not just as expressions of friendship. The archaeologist Jim Allen, for instance, has estimated that at the turn of the 20th century there were literally hundreds of Motu potters in the Port Moresby area on the south coast of Papua New Guinea who were making something on the order of 30,000 to 35,000 pots annually, a level of production he sees as possibly unrivaled elsewhere in New Guinea.[13] They were in the pottery-making business so that they could obtain edible sago starch through exchange from people on the mainland as far away as the Purari River delta hundreds of miles to the west. And they made a lot of pots because they needed to, since food locally was in short supply.[14]

Therefore, I think the lesson to be drawn from these several ethnographic examples is fairly straightforward. It is not always easy to fathom the motives of other people. Put succinctly, they can do similar things for different reasons, and different things for similar reasons. But just because people live in exotic far-off places does not have to mean it is impossible to put ourselves at least mentally in their shoes.

As a case in point, Ian Hogbin further reported in 1935 that when Wogeo Islanders sailed off to visit people in other places, they knew that once they got to where they were headed, they would be staying with old friends of the family. They did not need to make a motel or hotel reservation, or call ahead for a tent site or RV hookup at a campground near their destination (although, come to think of it, the large Schouten Island voyaging canoes used on these long-distance trips could be likened to modern camper vans). Nonetheless, I think the word "tourism" shouldn't be avoided when talking about what these islanders were up to back when Hogbin was visiting with them. Here, for instance, is something else Hogbin tells us that I think supports this likelihood:

> One may be quite sure that an expedition provides topics of conversation for several months. The natives love new places,... and as the topography and, to a certain extent, the flora and fauna of the mainland are different from that of the islands all sorts of strange things are seen. Many Wogeo myths refer to places on the mainland, and the older men always make a point of showing these to those who are making the trip for the first time. Expeditions are also popular because, with one or two other institutions, such as the festival accompanying the presentation of food by one village to another, they are thought to have a direct influence on the peace and harmony of the community.[15]

I should add that Hogbin also says that once ashore, the women traveling on one of these expeditions "usually give a hand with the cooking," and some of the men may help their hosts with fishing or garden work. Yet nothing was actually expected of visitors from overseas, and "many people just sit about and so have a complete holiday." Furthermore, other commentators have more recently reported that sexual adventurism might also be part of the appeal of getting away from home for a while.[16] The more things change, the more they remain the same?

If all this doesn't convince you that there has been an element of tourism about Wogeo canoe voyaging (or for that matter, an element of tourism in what Rob Welsch and I witnessed on the Sepik coast many years later), here is what Hogbin reports about what happens at home at the conclusion of these overseas voyages to mainland New Guinea:

> The canoes are hauled up, and a dance takes place ... before the various crews depart for their own villages. Towards evening the ornaments are publicly displayed in a long line and those who have been given large quantities acquire prestige.... While the ornaments are being displayed those who have remained behind are at liberty to help themselves. This is regarded as a return for looking after the village and tending the gardens. They take only what everyone considers to be a fair share, for if they laid themselves open to the charge of greed their reputations would suffer considerably.... Relatives may beg for a pot or two or a basket, which is always given because a person knows that later on he may want to ask a favour himself.[17]

AT THE RISK of spoiling the mood and playing into the hands of critics who insist, somewhat like the late Professor Hau'ofa, that social scientists have no inner sense of joy or humor, I think it is important to take note of the fact that these infrequent overseas voyages away from the hustle and bustle—the strong ties—of daily life on the Schouten Islands can be seen as fine examples of how influential such classically "weak ties" can be in the social life of individuals, families, and local communities. Mark Granovetter has described the unexpected interplay he has identified between strong and weak ties as a paradox. Perhaps, but however described, by keeping people open to new opportunities, relationships, and novel ideas, weak ties such as these between the mainland and these very small islands may be instrumental to the successful—and enjoyable—conduct of life.

By now, however, you may be thinking "Got it! But so what? What do overseas canoe voyages between here and there in far off New Guinea have to do with me? Especially since the only voyages I ever take are by computer, not canoe?" Or asked another way: canoe-voyaging aside, how "strong" or "weak" are the distance-defying ties facilitated these days by the Internet and modern social media?

I think the honest answer would have to be that at present nobody knows for sure whether being so broadly, easily, and perhaps frequently "connected" only virtually via the Internet is as effective and fulfilling as actually being able to sit down and talk with other people, say, over a cup of tea and a raisin scone with or without butter or a low-fat heart-healthy substitute spread.

Here, however, is my own reading of the tea leaves. Evolution has equipped us to be social in intimate and often largely subconscious face-to-face ways. It is not a foregone conclusion, therefore, that Facebook, Twitter, or Snapchat are the equal to what millions of years of evolution have done for us in more down-to-earth and humdrum ways.

Case in point, one recent study of young adults at the University of Michigan looked at how Facebook usage influences our sense of well-being. The results obtained suggest that the more college kids use Facebook, the *worse* they are likely to feel. Conversely, direct social contact with others, face-to-face or by telephone, leads them to feel *better* over time. (Unfortunately, this study did not evaluate whether Skype and other webcam-plus-voice social media have a similarly negative impact on an individual's perceived sense of well-being.)

Given what is now known about human evolution, these research results do not seem at all surprising. As the researchers at Michigan summed up their findings:

> The human need for social connection is well established, as are the benefits that people derive from such connections. On the surface, Facebook provides an invaluable resource for fulfilling such needs by allowing people to instantly connect. Rather than enhancing well-being, as frequent interactions with supportive "offline" social networks powerfully do, the current findings demonstrate that interacting with Facebook may predict the opposite result for young adults—it may undermine it.[18]

29

Meet Me on the Marae?

Principle 5: Where there's a will, there's a way.

IF YOU HAVE seen one of the stage or movie versions, or better still have read the book, you know that in Charles Dickens' 1843 classic tale *A Christmas Carol*, Ebenezer Scrooge—a tight-fisted, squeezing, wrenching, grasping, scraping, clutching, covetous, old sinner—is confronted by the ghosts of Christmas Past, Present, and Yet to Come in the course of his reclamation as a human being worthy of the label. Toward the end of the time he spends with the rapidly aging Ghost of Christmas Present (I wonder if Dickens intended this designation to be a play on words?), Scrooge notices something strange about the giant apparition before him. He soon learns that they are not alone.

> "Forgive me if I am not justified in what I ask," said Scrooge, looking intently at the Spirit's robe, "but I see something strange, and not belonging to yourself, protruding from your skirts. Is it a foot or a claw?"
>
> "It might be a claw, for the flesh there is upon it," was the Spirit's sorrowful reply. "Look here."
>
> From the foldings of its robe, it brought two children; wretched, abject, frightful, hideous, miserable. They knelt down at its feet, and clung upon the outside of its garment.
>
> "Oh, Man! look here. Look, look, down here!" exclaimed the Ghost.

Scrooge sees there a boy and girl. Dickens describes them as meager, ragged, scowling, and wolfish; yet prostrate, too, in their humility. "Where angels might have sat enthroned, devils lurked, and glared out menacing. No change, no degradation, no perversion of humanity, in any grade, through all the mysteries of wonderful creation, has monsters half so horrible and dread."

> Scrooge started back, appalled. Having them shown to him in this way, he tried to say they were fine children, but the words choked themselves, rather than be parties to a lie of such enormous magnitude.
>   "Spirit! are they yours?" Scrooge could say no more.
>   "They are Man's," said the Spirit, looking down upon them. "And they cling to me, appealing from their fathers. This boy is Ignorance. This girl is Want. Beware them both, and all of their degree, but most of all beware this boy, for on his brow I see that written which is Doom, unless the writing be erased. Deny it!" cried the Spirit, stretching out its hand towards the city. "Slander those who tell it ye! Admit it for your factious purposes, and make it worse. And bide the end!"
>   "Have they no refuge or resource?" cried Scrooge.
>   "Are there no prisons?" said the Spirit, turning on him for the last time with his own words. "Are there no workhouses?"
>   The bell struck twelve.[1]

This climactic moment in the story, just in case you hadn't gotten the author's point earlier in the tale, is Dickens' allusion to the consequences of being greedy, selfish, and self-centered.

I might be tempted to suggest that Scrooge is Dickens' surrogate for that Enlightenment misanthrope Thomas Hobbes, but sadly a decade after writing *A Christmas Carol*, he penned a scathing satire on the idea of the noble savage that surpassed in the vehemence of its rhetoric anything Hobbes had written about how solitary, poor, nasty, brutish, and short our lives had once been back when we were all living in a state of nature. "My position is," Dickens told his readers, "that if we have anything to learn from the Noble Savage, it is what to avoid. His virtues are a fable; his happiness is a delusion; his nobility, nonsense."

To back up this astonishingly dismissive set of opinions, he even trotted out the usual stereotype of the savage so dear to many in a place like Victorian England. "All the noble savage's wars with his fellow-savages (and he takes no pleasure in anything else) are wars of extermination—which is the best thing I know of him, and the most comfortable to my mind when I look at him. He

has no moral feelings of any kind, sort, or description; and his 'mission' may
be summed up as simply diabolical."[2]

These are hard words to read, but if I were to fault Dickens only for what
he foresees as the possible fate of our species in *A Christmas Carol*, it would
be to add the thought that there was surely a third child hiding somewhere
within the folds of the Spirit's ample robe. This youngster was just as wretched,
abject, frightful, hideous, and miserable as the two presented by the Spirit to
Scrooge for his enlightenment—in my own mind's eye he is the fraternal twin
of the child called Ignorance. This child, however, is named Fear.

Fear and anxiety are certainly part of human nature despite the fact that
there is little that is uniquely human about fear as a response to strange, threatening, or in other ways disturbing situations or things. A social networking
giant like Facebook may now be able to boast that it has linked more than one
billion friends with one another, but the jury is still out on how far making
friends with strangers in the relative safety and security of this service easily
spills over into the real world of Want, Ignorance, and Fear.

One of the principal implications of the friendship hypothesis is that
human beings have evolved the cognitive and emotional skills needed to take
the measure of most people, however strange they may appear to be on first
encounter. What natural selection has not fully equipped us to do, however,
is judge the motivations and intents of many people all at once—say, when
they all suddenly show up on your doorstep unannounced, or when they have
arrived unexpectedly on the outskirts of town. What to do then can be genuinely frightening and risky.

What should anyone do in such potentially threatening situations? I would
like to believe there are a number of good ways to handle this kind of human
encounter, but here I would like to suggest one strategy in particular. This way
of overcoming fear and uncertainty won't work if you are in a hallway or come
upon a band of strangers in an alley late at night. But it can work, and often
brilliantly so—judging by my own experiences—if they have instead arrived
at the edge of town, metaphorically or in fact. It is a way to welcome strangers
en masse invented, as far as I can tell, by the Maori of New Zealand. It's also a
way I believe we all should learn about and seriously consider using. I call this
way of saying hello to strangers "hosting *marae* encounters."

IN 1905 GEORGE Dorsey, the chief Curator of Anthropology at the newly
established Field Columbian Museum (now the Field Museum), was traveling through Europe purchasing things to enrich the collections of this fledgling scientific institution in the New World.[3] On July 22, Dorsey wrote to the

Museum's Director, F. J. V. Skiff, asking permission to purchase a long list of things from the firm of J. F. G. Umlauff of Hamburg, Germany's foremost dealer in natural history specimens and cultural objects.

Item no. 14 on Dorsey's list read as follows: "New Zealand house... 20,000 [German] marks" (about $4,760, a goodly sum in 1905 when the average new home cost $3,000). As he explained to Skiff: "This is the only complete Maori house in existence outside of New Zealand." Umlauff himself had purchased this house a few years earlier, Dorsey reported, from an Englishman who had purportedly owned it for many years. This ornately carved wooden building had been pronounced by an authority at the Berlin Museum to be one of the most interesting museum-worthy specimens ever offered for sale in Europe.

Dr. Dorsey attached a description of the house, together with a boxed set of mounted photographs showing all its carved wooden panels, a catalog now stored in the Rare Book Room at the Field Museum. His recommendation to Skiff was unmistakable. "I should consider that we were extremely fortunate in being able to secure such a unique habitation at a price not much in advance of the cost of transportation from New Zealand to America."

In a letter to George Dorsey dated July 8, 1905—two weeks before Dorsey had sat down to write Skiff—J. F. G. Umlauff had already made it clear that he was under the impression that Dorsey had received, or would soon have, Skiff's permission to take this magnificent building back to Chicago. "Besides these collections [listed earlier in the same letter to Dorsey] you bought still a Maori-house as photographed and described for the sum of $ 5000.– with the condition, that you can cancel this purchase till the 22nd. inst.[ance], by telegraphing the word 'no.'" Dorsey did not receive this letter in time to telegraph back yea or nay.

Umlauff wrote again on the 24th. "Enclosed I beg to hand you my letter of the 8th inst.[ance] with the confirmation of your order, which I had addressed to Southampton. But as the ship had already sailed, it did not reach you, and was returned to me, but it came in my possession only the 22nd. inst." Since Dorsey had not said the magic word "no" by the 22nd, "you bought from me a Maori-house as photographed and described for the sum of $ 5000.–. The house will be packed and made ready for shipment with the other goods." Thus the fate of this remarkable Pacific Islands artifact was sealed by chance more than human choice.

WHILE THIS HOUSE reached America safely, it was not exhibited in Chicago for another 20 years because of lack of space in the Field Museum's original building on the south side of the city (the building that now houses Chicago's Museum of Science and Industry). In 1925, after the Field Museum had moved a few miles north to its current location on the shore of Lake Michigan near the heart of the city, its many pieces were taken from storage by Curator Ralph Linton and erected more or less exactly as Umlauff had tried to reconstruct them in Hamburg at the turn of the 20th century. The Museum's annual report for that year boasts that "it is the only Maori building extant that has a completely carved front, and its decorations show Maori art at its best."

In 1986 the Field Museum was the fourth, and last, American venue for a traveling exhibition on Maori art from New Zealand collections. More than 100 Maori elders, dignitaries, artists, and others came to Chicago to open this beautiful exhibition with full Maori formality. At the Museum's request, two elders from Tokomaru Bay, the Maori community in New Zealand where the house (we are now certain) had been built in 1881, were part of this foreign delegation. For the first time since the Museum had purchased this structure in 1905, it was possible for us to meet directly with people from there to talk

FIGURE 19 Ruatepupuke II, a Maori *wharenui* (meeting house), The Field Museum, Chicago; originally built at Tokomaru Bay, Aotearoa/New Zealand, 1881. (*Photograph*: author.)

about their house and its future—in particular, about whether it should be repatriated back to New Zealand.

Several weeks after the Chicago opening of this traveling exhibition, I led a group of 18 Chicagoans to Tokomaru Bay to continue the dialogue between Chicago and the Maori on their own turf. These conversations led to a pivotal resolution. The community at Tokomaru decided that rather than asking for it to be repatriated to New Zealand this house should remain in Chicago so that they—working side by side with the staff at the Field Museum—could restore it as a living outpost of Maori art and culture in the New World.

By the early 1990s, we had dismantled the Museum's old 1925 restoration of the house, cleaned and stabilized all its wooden pieces, and rebuilt it in a special gallery on the Upper Galleries floor of the Museum. New woven reed panels (called *tukutuku*) for the house were made at Tokomaru Bay and then shipped to Chicago. The house was formally opened again to the public by a delegation of 15 people from Tokomaru Bay on March 9, 1993 (Figure 19).

As one consequence of the Field Museum's close collaboration with Tokomaru Bay, we now know for sure that this house in Chicago was built there in 1881 to honor *Ruatepupuke*, a legendary figure who is said to have brought the art of woodcarving to the Maori people from the underwater house of the sea god, Tangaroa. The ridgepole of the building is his spine; the rafters are his ribs, and the wide boards along the roof at the front are Ruatepupuke's arms outstretched to welcome visitors.

GETTING PEOPLE TO sit down and talk with one another is not easy. This is especially true if the people who ought to be talking to one another are not on speaking terms—sworn political or religious enemies, say, or people who see themselves as too different in the color of their skins, their cultural backgrounds, their social experiences, or their wealth and educational achievements. All too often building bridges instead of walls gets put off until something terrible happens. By then, the people caught up in the midst of a crisis may be the very ones who should have been talking to one another all along. Yet by then, they may see themselves as so deeply at odds with one another that asking them to sit down and talk together may seem entirely out of the question.

Does this have to mean that when human conflicts get this bad, all hope is lost? Definitely not. It is possible to create a place where people of all walks of life can talk with one another and be heard—even people who have not been on speaking terms for years. Working with the Maori people of Tokomaru Bay introduced me to how they have been doing this for countless generations.

The Maori have a word for the kind of place I am talking about: *Temarae-nuiateaotumatauenga*. This long, seemingly unpronounceable word may be written out for easier reading as *Te-marae-nui-atea-o-Tumatauenga*. Either way, this word means "the great open field of Tū of the angry face." Tū is the ancient Maori god of war. "Angry face" refers to the fearsome Maori custom of challenging your enemy before battle (or nowadays, say, before a rugby match) by grimacing menacingly while rapidly thrusting your tongue in and out.

What is important, however, is how this lengthy word begins: *Te marae*.

A *marae* in New Zealand is a large open courtyard in front of a community meeting house (that is, a *wharenui* such as Ruatepupuke II) where two groups of people formally meet and greet one another. If a *hui* (formal meeting) does not take place on a marae, other locations indoors or out are temporarily set aside and used for the same purpose.

Although practices and conventions vary from community to community, the purpose of a marae encounter remains the same. Before getting down to business, be it social, political, or whatever, the hosts (who are called *tangata whenua*, "people of the land") must first welcome their visitors (who are called *manuhiri* or *manuwhiri*) to learn the objectives and credentials of those who have arrived from afar. In earlier times, these opening formal rituals of encounter (today, collectively called a *pohiri* or *powhiri*) on a marae were a tense and spiritually challenging way of finding out whether strangers had arrived with honorable or deceitful intentions in their hearts. Today, every

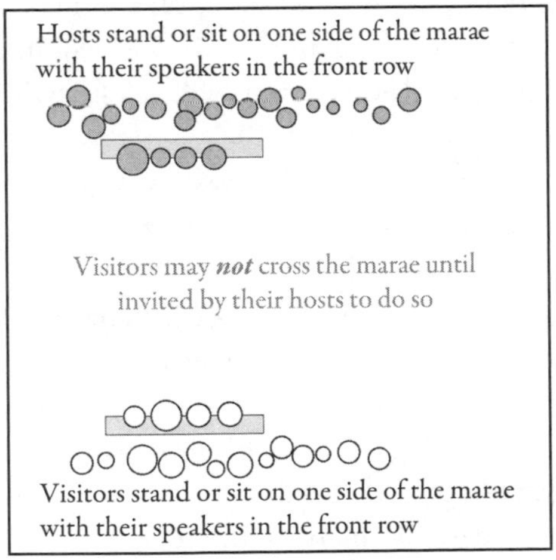

FIGURE 20 Plan of a marae encounter. (*Source*: author.)

pohiri on a marae remains an emotionally charged and extraordinarily power-ful event deeply felt by hosts and visitors alike.

When two communities meet one another on a marae, they are standing—figuratively speaking—on Tumatauenga's battlefield. However, instead of encountering one another with raised voices and weapons of war, each side brings to the meeting words, music, and song to express pride in the history and accomplishments of their community, and recognition of the similar standing and accomplishments of those facing them on the other side of the open field.

Marae encounters are grounded in basic Maori values. Many of these val-ues are shared by people everywhere on earth, not just in New Zealand: accep-tance of our human role as stewards of the earth; reverence for those who lived before us to whom we are all indebted; respect and love for family and community; and openness to others, even strangers. These basic human val-ues are key to creating successful opportunities for open discussion *kanohi ki te kanohi*, as the Maori say, "face to face."

WHAT HAPPENS DURING the formal welcoming (*pohiri*) of strangers on a marae takes place between two groups, or communities, of people (Figure 20). Although speeches are given by individuals who stand up to do so on behalf of everyone in their community, nobody introduces each speaker (they do this themselves), and care is taken to balance the number of speeches so that each community is equally represented. In some parts of New Zealand, those who stand up to talk take turns. First a speaker on the host's side will address the crowd, then a speaker on the visitors' side—back and forth, speaker fol-lowing speaker, ending finally with a speaker on the side of the hosting com-munity, people of the land where the marae is located. In other parts of the country, all of the designated host speakers will talk first; then the speakers for the visitors will do the same.

You can see, therefore, the two major reasons marae encounters are so dif-ferent from what most of us think of as town hall meetings, church services, or presidential debates. First, the individuals who stand up to speak are not just speaking for themselves. They are speaking on behalf of everyone else on their side of the marae. Second, regardless of whether the speeches are pre-sented back-and-forth across the marae, or are first given all on one side, and then on the other, the guiding principle or rule remains the same. Unlike dur-ing most public gatherings held outside New Zealand, just who is "on stage" at any one moment and who is "in the audience" changes by design during the course of a marae encounter. Said another way, first one side is "the audience" and the other side is "the actors." But then these roles are reversed. Those in the audience become the actors. Those who were formerly the actors become the audience.

We can see here the wisdom and strength of this formally structured way of encountering others, not just actual strangers but also people who haven't visited for a while and so need to be brought up to snuff on what's been happening locally since they were around last. This way of holding public gatherings favors not only *talking* to other people, but also *listening* to what other people have to say. Yet more to the point, even when people in the two communities meeting one another across the marae cannot fully understand the actual words being said on the other side because they are in another language (local speakers in New Zealand generally speak to their visitors in Maori, for example), nevertheless everybody has ample opportunity to "take the measure" of those "over there" in all the nonverbal ways that we humans have been gifted with by evolution that equip most of us to look beyond the words we hear to sense their real intent and measure their actual sincerity.

YOU DO NOT need to be, or even pretend to be, a New Zealand Maori to host marae encounters elsewhere on earth, even in your own backyard. I would like to propose to you one very good reason to do so.

The British psychologist John Bowlby (1907–1990) helped pioneer the study of attachment psychology. Bowlby reasoned that when we are with people we trust and feel attached to, our fear of strangers is lessened and we are able to be more tolerant of them and of their possibly bizarre or strangely unfamiliar ways of behaving.[4]

In keeping with this inference, Mario Mikulincer at the Interdisciplinary Center at Herzliya, Israel, and Phillip Shaver at the University of California, Davis, have shown experimentally that how hostile people are to those they judge to be in contending or warring social groups (for example, Israeli Jews and Israeli Arabs) is influenced by how secure they themselves feel. The research work they have done suggests that people who are secure, or can be induced to feel more secure in a particular context, are better able to tolerate intergroup diversity, are more given to maintaining broadly humane values, and are more likely to regard others compassionately.

In light of their findings, they have concluded that when families, communities, schools, religious institutions, and cultural media actively try to help individuals feel more secure, people are "better able to create a kinder and more tolerant, harmonious, and peaceful society."[5] In a word, they can move beyond just being politically correct to becoming emotionally connected.

Hosting a marae encounter (Appendix) in your own backyard or town hall on behalf of your family, community, school, religious institution, or civic group will not solve the world's problems. Yet it does not seem foolish to think that reaching out to others in this friendly, admittedly unusual but formal manner would be a step in the right direction.

30

Being in a Family Way?

Principle 6: A relationship is what you make of it.

AMONG THE QUESTIONS that human beings have been asking themselves for longer than anyone dare guess, a few stand out for many of us as supremely challenging. *Why are we here? Does God exist? Is there life after death?* Regrettably perhaps, these three fall squarely in the realm of theology, cosmology, theoretical physics, and philosophy.[1] However, a fourth question of comparable antiquity and significance is more directly approachable, although similarly thought-provoking: *What does it mean to be human?*

Unlike the first three, this question does fall in the realm of science, or at any rate, so I have argued here from start to finish. My goal, however, has not simply been to enlighten or entertain. Although elementary, the principles I draw (briefly summarized in Table 2) from what is currently known about human nature are principles that can be used in daily life, not just contemplated for their own sake or for their possible intellectual appeal. Furthermore, as I said back in Chapter 3, if we take the friendship hypothesis to heart, we may be able to tinker more successfully with our evolutionary heritage in social rather than biological ways to achieve greater control over the future of our species. After all, as Yogi Berra said, if you don't know where you're going, you might not get there.

I would now like to leave you with two final observations about friends and human nature to underscore why our talent for friendship should be both celebrated and cultivated.

Table 2

Six Principles	Explanation	What to Watch Out For
1. It is easy to be misunderstood.	Cognitive niche construction, and our inability to read the minds of others directly and unambiguously	The "Leslie effect"
2. People like to be connected.	Biological evolution and social learning	"Strong links" can easily favor social isolation, ignorance, and narrow-minded uniformity
3. Ask a friend to be your go-between.	Building your social networks while dealing safely with fear and uncertainty	Fools rush in where angels fear to tread
4. New friends are new pathways.	Building your social capital by adding new "links" to your existing social networks	Needlessly avoiding people who are different from you
5. Where there's a will, there's a way.	Creating social situations that strengthen and extend your social networks	Categorically dividing other people into *us* vs. *them*
6. A relationship is what you make of it.	Cognitive niche construction	Believing that cast-iron human relationships are always biological rather than social

THE FIRST IS about hate. Despite popular wisdom to the contrary, I think we have to accept that hate is not an emotion but rather a kind of learned social relationship—although it is true enough that being hateful taps into underlying basal emotions such as fear, rage, and possibly also at times lust. Hence the opposite of love is not hate, not if we take the former to mean our evolved predisposition to seek out others, be close to them physically, and if Coan and Beckes are correct, make them part of ourselves mentally if not physically.

Furthermore, from an evolutionary point of view I think we also need to accept that hate can be a waste of time, effort, and metabolic energy. Instead of helping us survive and reproduce, hate can too easily isolate us from others and set up social barriers where there is no real need for them. In short, hate makes little evolutionary sense. (However, if you believe in group selection—tribe against tribe as envisioned, say, by Edward O. Wilson as described in Chapter 15—you may choose to disagree with me on this point, but know ahead of time that I will stand my ground peacefully but firmly.)

There is another reason, too, for not accepting the conventional wisdom that hate must be seen as one of our built-in emotions. Embracing this assumption encourages us to see human emotions as either positive or negative. Yet from an evolutionist's perspective, a genuinely primal emotion such as fear is not negative but positive since it is not inherently irrational to be afraid of things and situations that look uncertain, risky, or downright dangerous. Therefore, instead of seeing love as something positive [+], and hate as its opposite as something negative [–] on a scale from the one to the other with a neutral point [0] somewhere between these two emotional extremes, we need another way of thinking about hate and its allied human responses, such as revenge and humiliation.

It should come as no surprise to you that the logic I favor is the relational, or binary, logic of social network analysis (SNA). Specifically, when dealing with human relationships, what is key is whether first and foremost there either is (call it 1) or there isn't (call it 0) a relationship (*link, tie, connection,* etc., in the language of SNA) of some kind between two people (*nodes, edges*), and second whether it is useful to note as well how weak [0.0] or strong [+1.0] the link happens to be when there is one (the strength of our social ties with others can be expressed in SNA as numerical values ranging between weak and strong; e.g., 0.00, +0.25, +0.65, etc.). Needless to say, it may also be important to take note of the dimensions or characteristics of the relationships involved—what they are about, and why they exist—but how many of these details need to be taken into account is not a foregone conclusion. And in this regard, it is a wise thing to remember that one of the basic rules of science is never make an explanation for something more complicated than it needs to be.

NOW MY SECOND and final observation. It is also about how your brain (your Lou, Laurence, and Leslie) and your emotional life (your social being) are entwined, for better and sometimes for worse. My example is a personal one. Consider the human relationship called *adoption.*

Many people in North America see adoption as an unfortunate way of becoming a family. It is commonly said that the ties binding an adoptive family together are weaker than "natural" ties of blood. Many will tell you also that adoption is difficult and risky—especially so when a child does not "match" the parents in appearance and background. Furthermore, some see adoption as a rather sinister practice—particularly in the case of adoptions across ethnic, racial, and national lines—since this route to what has been called "alternative parenthood" allegedly "severs" a child from his or her "real" family, ethnic roots, and cultural heritage—in a word, from the child's "true" identity as a human being.[2] This is not a pretty picture at all.

Anthropologists know firsthand, however, that what seems challenging in one place on earth may not be seen as such in another. In this regard, Pacific Island societies are famous in the anthropological literature for seeing adoption as a loving and generous undertaking benefiting the whole of society, not just the individuals involved. And one of the things that I have learned both as an anthropologist and as the parent of a child "not born to me" is that "blood ties" and genetic relatedness in the arena of social life are only as meaningful as we care to make them be.

My son Gabriel is living proof of how the heart listens to what the head tells it about human relationships. When I was in Paraguay in 1991 adopting Gabriel—he was 13 months old when I arrived down there to do so—I found myself often struggling to come up with some way to talk about other people who would also become emotionally committed to him without using words that would label him in needless ways as "an adopted child." I was uncomfortable with using words such as *godfather* or *godmother* because I saw these terms as too uncertain in their meaning and intent. As an anthropologist I was searching for words that would resonate with what the Samoans call a child's *aiga*—the "family" in the broader sense of all those supporting a child's nurturance and well-being. But try as I did, I could not come up with the right words.

Adopting my son took three months owing to delays and difficulties in the court system in Asunción handling adoption decrees. I was there well south of the border taking care of him for all that time. Finally the judge responsible for adoptions signed his decree, and we began getting ready to leave for Wisconsin via Miami and Chicago. I woke up in the middle of the night with a sudden realization (my Leslie had been at work even as I slept). We did not need to find the right words. There were lots of good words to use: father, mother, sister, brother, grandmother, great-grandmother, etc. No, we didn't need special *words*. But we did need a *process*, a way to build a family—an *aiga*—for him that would not be based on "blood" or "kinship" as understood by most Americans.

Once home, we legally adopted Gabriel again, this time in the State of Wisconsin. The final paperwork required to do this was straightforward: a single-page typed form. After our official visit to the local courthouse

REGISTRY OF ADOPTION

===

In the Matter of the Adoption of

PETITION FOR

ADOPTION

TO THE FAMILY OF GABRIEL STOWE TERRELL:

The petition of _____, a resident of the
_____ of _____, County of _____, State
of _____, respectively represents and shows to the Family,

1. That the petitioner desires to be adopted as a _____ of
Gabriel Stowe Terrell.

2. That the best interests of the petitioner will be promoted by such
adoption, and that the petitioner is suitable for adoption.

3. That the petitioner is of good moral character and reputable standing
in the community and of ability to properly maintain the relationship sought
by this adoption.

IT IS ORDERED AND ADJUDGED, that adoption be and is hereby granted, and
from and after the date hereof, said petitioner shall be deemed to all intents
and purposes a _____ of Gabriel Stowe Terrell.

Dated at _____, _____
this _____ day of _____, 19____

_____
Family member authorizing the adoption

_____
Family member authorizing the adoption

_____, being duly sworn, does depose and say
that he/she is the petitioner above named; that he/she has heard and read the
foregoing petition and knows the contents thereof, and that the same is true
to the best of his/her knowledge and belief.

_____
Signature of the petitioner

Subscribed and sworn to before me
this _____ day of _____, 19____

_____
Witness to the petition

FIGURE 21 Registry of adoption. (*Source*: author.)

to complete and sign the requisite form before the proper authorities,
I reworked the language on the Wisconsin adoption form to turn the adoption process around (Figure 21). My new form, as you can see here, states
that Gabriel and his family are the ones who are adopting someone else—
the "petitioner"—as a family member. And as part of our "legal" process,
the petitioner must declare the *kind of relationship* being sought with the
child involved.

Only a few people have been adopted into Gabriel's family in this way, only those seeking a genuinely nurturing "family" role in his life. Nonetheless, Gabriel now has four fathers, four mothers, a much older sister, a number of aunts and uncles, and even a great-grandmother.

At first we had absolutely no idea how people would handle being adopted in this fashion. While we have never tested the fact, these adoptions are not actually legal (at least I don't think so). But we have always treated them as if they were. And what has proved to be especially moving about them is how seriously and emotionally every person who has been adopted has explained *why* she or he was requesting the particular kind of relationship with Gabriel that must be specified on our family form. The explanations given have always been sincere, emotional, and often remarkably detailed.

My reason for telling you about these family adoptions is uncomplicated. There is no question whatsoever that the people who have been adopted into Gabriel's family see themselves as family members. This is not a pretense or a sham. Regardless of the actual legality of our process, these adoptions are about as real as anything can possibly be from a human point of view. What has astonished me is that my son also feels the same way. These people *are* his family in every meaningful sense of the word.

This simple fact was brought home to me one evening when he was still young enough to not mind being tucked in and given a kiss before going to sleep. Out of the blue he looked up at me and said "If you die, then...." He proceeded to name, one after another, every single person we had adopted as family. He named absolutely nobody who had not been adopted, regardless how well he knew them.

So it seems obvious at least to me that in his head and in his heart he knew he had a family, an extended one that would be there for him regardless. All because of a semi-legal form, a fitting way of using this single sheet of paper, and the willingness on the part of everyone concerned to see themselves "as family" without in any way leaning on our conventional notions of "blood" or "biological kinship."

Hence here's my final observation. I have already suggested that the *strength of the social bonds we have with others is not a product of evolution* but rather of what we make of the relationships we form—of how our brains have learned to think about other people as colleagues, friends, companions, and loved ones. As a way of saying good-bye let me now suggest also that the remarkable thing about human nature is that *what we think can be just as real as what we feel*. We have evolution to thank for this. And also Lou, Laurence, and Leslie. So as they say in some parts of the United States, don't make yourself a stranger.

How to Host a Marae Encounter

BUILDING NEW BRIDGES,
NOT NEW WALLS
A HANDBOOK FOR HOSTING
MARAE ENCOUNTERS
Version 4.0—February 20, 2011

A Note about this Handbook

This handbook was written originally as a guide for community groups and teachers using the *marae atea* of Ruatepupuke II at the Field Museum in Chicago, IL, U.S.A.

In its present form, however, this handbook is intended for use by people anywhere outside New Zealand who may wish to hold a marae encounter.

Although based on Maori concepts and principles, this handbook is not intended as a guide to Maori thought, practice, or values, and should not be interpreted as such.

This handbook was conceived and written by John Edward Terrell, PhD, Regenstein Curator of Pacific Anthropology at The Field Museum, with the assistance of Caitlin Andrew, Jeremy Bleeke, Elizabeth Durham, Sara Hamdan, Surya Kundu, and Sage Morgan-Hubbard, 2009 and 2010 Regenstein Pacific Interns at the Museum.

Though this handbook may be freely reproduced and modified, it is to be understood that anyone using or adapting this guide agrees to acknowledge the source and collaborative authorship.

Contents

1. Should You Do This?

Getting people to sit down and talk with one another is not easy. This is particularly true if the people who ought to be talking with one another aren't even on speaking terms—sworn political or religious enemies, say, or people who see themselves as too different in the color of their skins, their cultural backgrounds, their social experiences, or their wealth and educational achievements.

All too often building bridges instead of walls gets put off until something terrible happens. By then, the people caught up in the midst of a crisis may be the very ones who should have been talking to one another all along. Yet by then, they may see themselves as so deeply at odds with one another that asking them to sit down and talk together may seem entirely out of the question.

Does this have to mean that when human conflicts get this bad, all hope is lost? Definitely not. In this handbook you will find step-by-step instructions on how to create both places and opportunities for people of all walks of life to talk with one another and be heard—even people who have not been on speaking terms for years, possibly for generations.

In this handbook, these special places are called *marae atea*. These are two ancient Polynesian words that together mean "open area" or "courtyard." And the opportunities that you will learn how to create for people to talk with and learn from one another are called *marae encounters*.

Building New Bridges, Not New Walls

On April 7, 2009, during his first foreign trip as President of the United States, Barack Obama held a question-and-answer session with college students at the Tophane Cultural Center in Istanbul, Turkey. During the town hall style meeting, he told them how much he was counting on young people to help shape a more peaceful and prosperous future.

He realized, he said, that there had been political tensions and disagreements between Turkey and the United States in recent years. At times, people on both sides had lost the sense that both nations have shared interests and values, and that they can have a partnership that serves their common hopes and common dreams.

So he had come to Turkey to reaffirm the importance of the partnership between Turkey and the United States. "I believe we can have a dialogue that's open, honest, vibrant, and grounded in respect," he told the students. "We can't afford to talk past one another, to focus only on our differences, or to let the walls of mistrust go up around us. Instead we have to listen carefully to each other. We have to focus on places where we can find common ground and respect each other's views, even when we disagree."

Creating the Right Place, the Right Opportunity

There is something ambiguous and wonderful about the word *place*. The Tophane Cultural Center in Istanbul where Mr. Obama was meeting with students in April 2009 was not just a good place to talk with them about the future. It was also a good opportunity to do so.

As Obama explained: "Simple exchanges can break down walls between us, for when people come together and speak to one another and share a common experience, then their common humanity is revealed. We are reminded that we're joined together by our pursuit of a life that's productive and purposeful, and when that happens mistrust begins to fade and our smaller differences no longer overshadow the things that we share. And that's where progress begins."

This handbook describes an innovative way—and yet, as you will see in the next section, also an ancient way—of strengthening human relationships grounded on mutual interest and respect, a new (but old) way of creating places and opportunities for people to listen to one another, and thereby find common ground and respect for one another's views, even if at times they may also discover that on some things they must agree to disagree.

In a nutshell, hosting a marae encounter asks people to:

1. Take a good long look at themselves as a community (even if they haven't previously thought of themselves as being one).
2. Figure out together what being a community means to them.
3. Explain themselves as a community to another group of people.
4. Raise issues, concerns, or other topics they would like to discuss with these people...
5. who are similarly preparing to do the very same thing in return
6. at the place selected to be the marae for the encounter, and at the agreed on time,
7. all followed by a meal together, and then lots of good talk—sometimes serious, sometimes humorous, but always open and down-to-earth.

The World Is What You Make of It

"The world will be what you make of it," President Obama told those students in Turkey that early afternoon. "You can choose to make new bridges instead of new walls."

We could not agree more with the promise and optimism of this simple observation. Most important, you do not have to be President of the United States to build the bridges described in this handbook.

2. *Standing on the battlefield of* Tumatauenga

The Maori people of New Zealand in the South Pacific have a word for it: *Temaraenuiateaotumatauenga.*

This long, seemingly unpronounceable word can be written out for easier reading as *Te-marae-nui-atea-o-Tumatauenga.* Either way, this word means "The great open field of Tū of the angry face."

Tū is the ancient Maori god of war. "Angry face" refers to the fearsome Maori custom of challenging your enemy before battle (or these days, before a rugby match) by grimacing menacingly while rapidly thrusting your tongue in and out.

What is important, however, is how this lengthy word begins: *Te marae.*

Te Marae, the Place

A marae in New Zealand is a large, open courtyard in front of a community meeting house (or *wharenui*) where two groups of people formally meet and greet one another.

If a *hui* (formal meeting) does not take place on a marae, other locations indoors or out are temporarily set aside and used for the same purpose.

Although practices and conventions vary from community to community in Aotearoa (the Maori name for New Zealand), the purpose of a marae encounter remains the same. Before getting down to business, be it social, political, or whatever, the hosts (who are called *tangata whenua*, "people of the land") must first welcome their visitors (who are called *manuhiri* or *manuwhiri*) to learn the objectives and credentials of those who have arrived from afar.

In ancient times, these opening formal rituals of encounter (today, collectively called a *pohiri* or *powhiri*) on a marae were a tense and spiritually challenging way of finding out whether strangers had arrived with honorable or deceitful intentions in their hearts.

Today, every *pohiri* on a marae remains an emotionally charged and extraordinarily powerful event deeply felt by hosts and visitors alike.

Te Marae, the Opportunity

A marae encounter in New Zealand is a unique blend of talk, ceremony, performance, and hospitality.

When two communities meet one another on a marae, they are standing—figuratively speaking—on Tumatauenga's battlefield. However, instead of encountering one another with raised voices and weapons of war, each side brings to the meeting words, music, and song to express pride in the history and accomplishments of their community, and recognition of the similar standing and accomplishments of those facing them on the other side of the open field.

Marae encounters are grounded in basic Maori values. Many of these values are shared by people everywhere, not just in New Zealand: acceptance of our role as stewards of the earth; reverence for those who lived before us to whom we are all indebted; respect and love for family and community; and openness to others, even strangers.

These basic human values are key to creating successful opportunities for open discussion *kanohi ki te kanohi*, as the Maori say, "face to face."

3. Getting started

Marae encounters are a proven way of letting other people learn about what you believe in, what you hope to accomplish in life, and how you and others with whom you live, work, or collaborate are trying to answer the age-old questions "who am I?" and "why am I here?"

Hosting marae encounters with other people can turn strangers into friends, and change the dynamics of "us against them" into "them and us."

Hosting marae encounters can also be a positive, constructive, and engaging way of helping you and others cultivate and share a strong—maybe even a definitional—sense of community.

The Big Difference

There are many ways for people to meet with one another—such as formal debates, town hall meetings, and church services—and talk about interests and concerns of importance. But note that all of these types of gatherings have one basic thing in common. There is always someone directing what happens. There is always somebody in charge.

Marae encounters are different.

In sharp contrast, what happens during the formal welcoming (*pohiri*) of strangers on a marae takes place between two groups, or communities, of people. Although speeches are given by individuals who stand up to do so on behalf of everyone in their community, nobody introduces each speaker (they do this themselves), and care is taken to balance the number of speeches so that each community is equally represented.

In some parts of New Zealand, those who stand up to talk take turns (*tau utuutu*). First a speaker on the host's side will address the crowd; then a speaker on the visitors' side—back and forth, speaker following speaker, ending finally with a speaker on the side of the hosting community—the "people of the land" where the marae is located. In other parts of the country, all of the designated host speakers will talk first; then the speakers for the visitors will do the same (*paeke*).

You can see, therefore, the two major reasons marae encounters are so different from what most of us think of as town hall meetings, church services, or presidential debates.

First, the individuals who stand up to speak are not just speaking for themselves. They are speaking on behalf of everyone else on their side of the *marae atea*, the open courtyard or assembly ground.

Second, regardless whether the speeches are presented back-and-forth across the marae, or are first given all on one side, and then on the other, the guiding principle or rule remains the same. Unlike during most public gatherings held outside New Zealand, just who it is who is "on stage" at any one moment, and who is "in the audience," changes by design during the course of a marae encounter. Said differently, first one side is "the audience" and the other side is "the actors." But then these roles are reversed. Those in the audience become the actors. Those who were formerly the actors become the audience.

You can see here what is the wisdom and strength—the pivotal strength—of every marae encounter. This way of holding public gatherings favors not only *talking* to other people, but also *listening* to what other people have to say.

Decisions, Decisions

Marae encounters are held in New Zealand for many different reasons—for example, to welcome visitors, mediate conflicts, honor the dead, or hold public talks on any number of topics.

Outside New Zealand, if you also want to hold a marae encounter where you live or work, there are two things you must decide before you begin planning for such an event.

- *Why?* The reasons for holding a marae encounter do not have to be earth shattering or somber. Nevertheless, you can't expect people to participate if you don't make it clear to them what the encounter will be about.
- *Who?* Although often it may be obvious to you who you would like to see show up for an encounter you are planning, the question "who?" is not always an easy one to answer. The hard part may not be deciding who you want to see sitting or standing on the other side of the marae, but instead who you want to have on your own side of Tumatauenga's battlefield. Most of us belong to many different communities. Which of the ones you belong to is the right one for the encounter you have in mind? This may not be an easy question to answer.

The Key to Success

The most important thing to remember is that marae encounters are not simply about people meeting people, or only about people talking to people. They are first and foremost about one community greeting and meeting with another community.

4. Before the encounter

Any large, open, and relatively quiet area can be a great place to hold a marae encounter. A private lawn or at a public park will do, but so will a school gymnasium, hotel ballroom, or any other large indoor space. Particularly appropriate would be a place that has special significance or meaning to your community or group, such as a community center, church, synagogue, mosque, or other similarly established gathering place.

The Reason for the Encounter

We have learned to live and prosper all over this planet of ours. Yet today we are brushing elbows with our neighbors as never before. It is hardly surprising, therefore, that the same issues keep cropping up. Who has a right to live where? Who really owns the earth's resources? What are the proper social and religious values and public laws for maintaining peace, resolving conflicts, and making life worth living?

Given the way the world is now and has long been, it is also not surprising that building walls between people has seemingly been a human preoccupation. Consider some of history's famous examples. The walled cities of Troy and Jericho. The Great Wall of China. Hadrian's Wall, built by the Romans in northern England in the 2nd century A.D. The hated wall dividing Berlin built after World War II.

Building walls may not work in the long run as a social strategy, but clearly we humans are predisposed to believe that walls work. But what kinds of bridges rather than walls can be built instead?

There is no doubt that marae encounters can be an effective way of helping people resolve conflicts.

However, hosting an encounter with another group or community does not need to be done solely to solve difficulties that are keeping people at odds with one another. The pivotal strength of every marae encounter is that this way of holding community or group meetings favors not only *talking* with other people, but also *listening* to what others have to say.

Therefore, if you would like your group or community to host an encounter, don't overlook that hosting such an event can be fun, enjoyable, and a fine way of getting to know what other groups and communities are thinking, trying to do, and see as important.

Although holding marae encounters to help resolve social problems, political differences, or ethnic conflicts makes sense, this form of human engagement can also be a great way to learn directly from people whom you might otherwise rarely, or possibly never, encounter.

Regardless of the reason for holding a marae encounter, what really lies at the heart of every successful meeting of this sort is the honesty, openness, and willingness of all participants to share their lives, experiences, and concerns with others.

Here are only a few of the many good reasons for hosting a marae encounter:

Welcoming visitors. Any time you are being visited by people from outside your community, school, place of work or worship, consider greeting them as a group on their arrival by honoring them in this unusual way—with a marae encounter, a welcome that they will never forget.

Handling quarrels and disagreements. Hosting an encounter can be an astonishingly successful way of getting people who are strongly "taking sides" to sit down and talk directly with one another.

Learning from others. Holding a marae encounter can also be a good way of encouraging people of different faiths, political parties, social points of view, and life experiences to listen and learn from one another.

Sharing common interests. Inviting people to an encounter can be a great way of reaching out to other groups and communities having similar interests or concerns.

Who Should Participate?

The group or community organizing a marae encounter has the responsibility of inviting another group or community to the proposed meeting. Given how unconventional marae encounters are outside New Zealand, it may be necessary to explain in some detail to those being invited what is to happen and what will be expected of them.

Selecting the Speakers

Among the Maori, the art of formally speaking (*whaikorero*) on a marae is a highly cultivated and much celebrated form of expression, a true art form. The prestige (*mana*) of a community and its marae may be closely tied to the oratorical renown of its speakers.

How you go about picking people to speak for you on a marae outside New Zealand is largely up to you and your group or community. Yet keep in mind four basic points:

1. The prominence of a gathering anywhere on earth is often weighed by the number of people who get to stand up and speak. It is always a good idea for the invited group or community to ask ahead of time how many speakers their hosts plan to have on their side of the marae during the welcoming ceremonies, so that a like number of visitors can come prepared to speak in reply when their time comes.

2. Those speaking for each community should come prepared to do their best. It is a good idea to ask all speakers to practice beforehand. It is not just the number but also the skill of the speakers that makes for a rousing and successful encounter.

3. Speakers should never read their speeches from a prepared script or set of notes. A good speech during a marae encounter is judged not just by the words chosen, but also by the polish, feeling, and skill of the person delivering them.

4. Speeches on a marae should not be delivered from behind a podium. Each speaker simply stands up and addresses those on the other side face-to-face across the open field or area separating the visitors from the hosts.

Preparing the Speeches

The speeches given on a marae on behalf of the two groups or communities meeting there do not need to be lengthy or elaborate. However, it is important they be sincere and heartfelt. It is also important that they capture the spirit of the day, and that they are presented in as genial and skillful a way as possible.

In New Zealand, speeches on a marae are not impromptu, impulsive, or haphazard. Although the form and content may vary based on the community, the elements of a successful speech are often both familiar and predictable. While the skillfulness and conviction of these speeches are considered a measure of the importance and sincerity of the gathering, poor speeches and poor speakers weaken the quality, resonance, and gravity (all of which in the Maori language are encompassed by the word *mana*) of the entire occasion.

We are reluctant to spell out too fully what we see as some of the ideal ingredients of a good speech on a marae outside New Zealand. With the understanding, therefore, that these remarks are offered only as general guidelines, here are some elements you might want to consider including.

Even if everybody on both sides of the marae already knows for sure what the meeting is to be all about, speakers for the hosts should make their remarks chiefly ones of welcome, delight at seeing the visitors, and so forth. Pleasing words do not have to be insincere. Showing that you are aware of how accomplished are your visitors is always a good way to demonstrate respect and gratitude.

On the other side of the marae, it is appropriate for speakers on behalf of the visitors to begin by similarly acknowledging the accomplishments and prestige of both the place where the gathering is taking place and of those who are there to welcome them as hosts.

It is usually the duty of the speakers for the visitors to elaborate on where they have come from and why they have made the journey to be with their hosts on the marae atea.

Supporting Your Speakers

In New Zealand, it is conventional to follow each speech on a marae made during a formal welcome with a *waiata*, a chant or song, performed by the speaker's own group or community. This communal gesture confirms that the speaker who has just finished talking has spoken not just as an individual but for everyone in the speaker's community.

It is strongly recommended that marae encounters outside New Zealand adopt the same practice. It must be emphasized, however, that these entertaining moments should not become entirely separate public performances by those participating, and those stepping forward to join with their speaker should be careful not to move farther out on the marae than where he or she is standing. Instead, they should position themselves beside or behind him or her. The aim, after all, is to show support for the speaker by reaffirming the worth, sincerity, and substance of what has just been said.

Such a finishing touch, or garnish, to a fine speech can be both fun and a wonderful way to uphold the mana of both the speaker and of all those on his or her side of the marae.

5. Meeting on the marae

In New Zealand, a marae is not just a place where people meet. A marae is also a family gathering place—a *turangawaewae*, a word literally meaning "standing place" (*tūranga*) for "feet" (*waewae*), and commonly translated into English as "a place to stand." However described, a New Zealand marae is a place for *tangata whenua* (hosts) and *manuhiri* (visitors) to honor and take part in Maori ways of being with others.

STEP 1. Assembly

Although visitors may arrive at the place set aside for the encounter individually, or in small groups—as families, for instance—all visitors should gather together prior to the encounter somewhere near but away from the marae.

As they arrive, those in the visiting group or community may greet one another quietly. However, it is critical to the success of the encounter that nobody among the visitors makes the cardinal mistake of greeting anyone over on the host's side of the marae. Furthermore, visitors should never walk on to the area being used as the *marae atea* before being formally invited to do so by the hosts (see **Step 2**).

It is normal, and indeed quite appropriate, for all those who arrive as visitors to feel apprehensive. Who knows what the hosts want to say to them? How really welcome are they? Will those speaking on behalf of the visitors truly rise to the occasion? Or will their words spoken on the marae fall flat? Feeling tense, even worried, is also only to be expected if the encounter about to take place has been organized in hopes of resolving old disputes, misunderstandings, or rivalries.

STEP 2. Call to the Marae

It is the right of the host group or community to determine when visitors should be called to approach the marae atea. Usually this step is taken after it is clear that all the visitors have arrived, and everyone is waiting quietly in anticipation.

Keep in mind that this is a community occasion. Visitors should not move on to their designated side of the marae in single file, nor as couples or families only. The time has come to show to one and all that you are there together as a single group or community. And please, no stragglers. Remember, too, that there should be no talking, smoking, or giggling. The movement of the visitors to the marae should be done in a respectful and dignified manner.

The call (*karanga*) to the visitors initiating a marae encounter in New Zealand is always done by a woman (who is called the *kai karanga*). The call itself is typically a short, unearthly incantation, a ritual poem comprising set phrases such as "come forward, visitors from afar, welcome, welcome." These calls are ethereal and awe-inspiring. In response, a woman among the visitors (she is the *kai whakautu*) will return the host call in an equally ethereal and moving fashion generally using similarly traditional words and phrasing.

It goes without saying that outside New Zealand this powerful, emotionally charged moment at the beginning of an encounter does not need to be done in Maori, but whatever call you use should be more than just a hand signal, or an everyday greeting such as "y'all come!" These calls are the first words spoken between the hosts and the visitors, and they are intended to awaken the emotions.

Step 3. Advance

In New Zealand, different communities follow different conventions regarding how visitors should approach the marae when called to do so. Some ask that all of the visiting men be out in front, with women and children behind. In such instances, the speakers for the visitors and other important individuals may lead the procession. In other areas, community leaders will be out in front and immediately behind them will be women

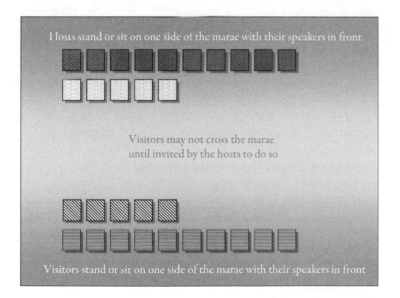

and children, with the rest of the men walking beside and behind (the reason: to protect women and children as they enter Tumatauenga's battlefield). Alternatively, it may be women and children who lead the way, with the speakers and other important persons walking beside them. However the visitors decide to move on to the marae, it is important that they do so slowly and with dignity. As a group, the visitors move to their side of the marae and silently take up position there.

STEP 4. Moment of Remembrance

Before anyone takes his or her seat, all of the visitors should reassemble as a group on the threshold of the marae atea, and then bow their heads for a few moments of remembrance for those who are no longer alive. The hosts should do the same. In New Zealand, it is entirely fitting at this time in an encounter for the living (*hunga ora*) to cry aloud and shed tears for the dead (*hunga mate*). Those taking part in an encounter outside Aotearoa should feel free to do the same.

This step in an encounter gives everyone time to reflect together on how and why they are all able to be there—and how others can no longer do so.

STEP 5. Formal Exchange of Speeches

In New Zealand, orations given on a marae during a formal welcome usually follow a fairly set pattern, although they will often include, for example, humorous asides and other less predictable elements.

Normally, although not invariably, the speakers for both the hosts and visitors will be men, not women. When his time comes, each speaker rises from his chair or bench to claim the stage, or rather the marae, while announcing his intention to do so with a set phrase such as *tihei mauri ora* (which roughly translates as "I breathe, it is life!"), strides on to the marae, and begins to address those on the opposite side.

Each oration concludes with a song (*waiata*) or dance (*haka*) during which the speaker is joined and supported by members of his group, as described in the previous section. Then he finishes his oration with a few last words.

In some parts of New Zealand, the speeches on a marae shift back and forth between the two communities meeting on Tumatauenga's battlefield. Normally a speaker on the hosts' side will stand up and talk first, then one on the visitors' side, until all of the orators on both sides have spoken. When following this convention (*tau utuutu*), however, the last speaker is always a speaker on the hosts' side.

Alternatively, all of the speakers on the hosts' side may speak first; then those for the visitors (a marae protocol in New Zealand called *paeke*). When this protocol is being followed, the last person to speak usually will still be someone on the hosts' side of the marae to assure that the responsibility and authority (*mana*) for the occasion remain on the shoulders of the hosts. Otherwise it might seem as if the visitors had taken over the encounter and stolen all the glory.

We suggest that outside New Zealand it is appropriate for the hosts of a forthcoming encounter to tell their visitors-to-be in advance how many people they should have ready to stand up and speak on their behalf.

In addition, what the speakers on both sides will talk about should be discussed and agreed upon in advance within each participating group or community.

As a final note, welcoming speeches on a marae are not direct debates. During welcoming ceremonies, it is appropriate to present what you want to talk about later in the day, but marae welcomes are not the same thing as college or courtroom debates during which points raised on one side are to be argued for or against by speakers on the other side of the marae. That can wait until everyone is sitting down afterwards (*see* the next division of this handbook).

Don't forget that each speech will require a communal show of support by others on the same side of the marae after the speaker has concluded his or her remarks. It is not necessary for everyone on the speaker's side to stand up and join in. But if nobody does so, it would be hard to avoid giving everybody the impression that the speaker had by then lost the support even of his or her own people.

Rest assured, it's not just the skill of the performers that counts; it's the spirit in which they join their speaker in song, poetic words, or dance.

STEP 6. Presentation of a Gift

After the final speaker on the visitors' side of the marae is finished and has been supported in an appropriate fashion by those in his or her community, he moves toward the center of the marae atea and places an envelope containing a *koha* (gift) on the ground. In New Zealand in earlier times, the koha would have normally been a gift of food. Today, it is generally a monetary contribution to help defray the expenses of the *hui* (gathering). The speaker returns to the visitors' side, and the koha is then picked up by someone from the hosts' side.

We strongly recommend that this step be included in marae encounters outside New Zealand, even if the koha is merely a token gift—something, say, readily identifiable as coming from the visiting community that will later serve as a warm reminder of the visitors and the encounter held with them.

STEP 7. Crossing the Marae

After the presentation of the koha, the two communities have arrived at the moment in an encounter where everybody may at last greet one another as friends, even as "one family."

At this time, the leader of the host community should formally invite all of the visitors to cross the marae for the first time, so that all the hosts may say hello to all the visitors. This is the final step that completes the transformation of strangers (*manuhiri*) into family members (*tangata whenua*) for the duration of their stay with the hosts.

6. Sitting down together
Sharing Food Together

All encounters should include a communal meal of some sort following the formal welcome on the marae. There are no specific guidelines for the type of food that should be offered. It can range anywhere from tea, coffee, milk, and cookies to more elaborate meals. The food should be provided by the host community, which is something the visiting community may want to keep in mind when deciding the nature of their *koha*.

An Honest Exchange of Views

Following the meal, everyone makes their way back to the marae. At this point, there is no predetermined seating; seats are often arranged in a circle, which reflects the new relationship created between the two communities and the sense of equality between all individuals participating.

All those wishing to do so are given the opportunity to say a few words about themselves, their community, or the encounter. There are no rules or limits about what can be said other than the usual rules of civility and good humor. Everyone should have the right to speak without interruption or interference

Saying Good-bye

Speeches of farewell at the end of an encounter are as important as those of welcome at the beginning. Since the visitors, not the hosts, are the ones who are about to depart for home, it is appropriate for the visitors to take the lead in saying good-bye. Since everyone is now, figuratively speaking, on the same side of the marae, these farewells should be informal and heartfelt.

And don't forget that it is never wrong to include a song or two.

Notes

CHAPTER 1

1. Pinker, Steven (2002). *The Blank Slate: The Modern Denial of Human Nature.* New York: Penguin Books.
2. Ingold, Tim (2006). Against human nature. In *Evolutionary Epistemology, Language and Culture: A Non-Adaptationist, Systems Theoretical Approach*, edited by Nathalie Gontier, Jean Paul Van Bendegem, and Diederik Aerts, pp. 259–81. Dordrecht, the Netherlands: Springer Science+Business Media.
3. Fuentes, Agustín, Jonathan Marks, Tim Ingold, Robert Sussman, Patrick V. Kirch, Elizabeth M. Brumfiel, Rayna Rapp, Faye Ginsburg, Laura Nader, and Conrad P. Kottak (2010). On nature and the human. *American Anthropologist* 112: 512–21.
4. Sussman in Fuentes et al. (2010), p. 514.
5. Wilson, Edward O. (1978). *On Human Nature.* Cambridge, MA: Harvard University Press, p. 99.
6. Pinker (2002), pp. 315–16.
7. Wilson, Edward O. (2012). *The Social Conquest of the Earth.* New York: Liveright (a division of W. W. Norton), p. 62.
8. Pinker, Steven (2011). *The Better Angels of Our Nature: Why Violence Has Declined.* New York: Viking, p. 1.
9. Sussman in Fuentes et al. (2010), p. 515.
   Sussman, Robert W. (2013). Why the legend of the killer ape never dies: The enduring power of cultural beliefs to distort our view of human nature. In *War, Peace, and Human Nature: The Convergence of Evolutionary and Cultural Views*, edited by Douglas P. Fry, pp. 97–111. New York: Oxford University Press.
10. Kahneman, Daniel, and Amos Tversky (1973). On the psychology of prediction. *Psychological Review* 80: 237–51, p. 237.
11. Kahneman, Daniel (2011). *Thinking: Fast and Slow.* New York: Farrar, Straus and Giroux.

CHAPTER 2

 1. Saastamoinen, Kari (2010). Pufendorf on natural equality, human dignity, and self-esteem. *Journal of the History of Ideas* 71: 39–62.
 2. Cavallar, Georg (2008). Vitoria, Grotius, Pufendorf, Wolff and Vattel: Accomplices of European colonialism and exploitation or true cosmopolitans? *Journal of the History of International Law Revue d'Histoire du Droit International* 10: 181–209.
    Miller, Nicholas P. (2008). The dawn of the age of toleration: Samuel Pufendorf and the road not taken. *Journal of Church and State* 50: 255–75.
 3. Waldron, Jeremy (1987). Theoretical foundations of liberalism. *The Philosophical Quarterly* 37: 127–50.
 4. Shanley, Mary Lyndon (1979). Marriage contract and social contract in seventeenth century English political thought. *Western Political Quarterly* 32: 79–91.
 5. Waswo, Richard (1996). The formation of natural law to justify colonialism, 1539–1689. *New Literary History* 27: 743–59.
 6. Phillipson, Coleman (1912). Samuel Pufendorf. *Journal of the Society of Comparative Legislation*, new series 12: 233–65.
    Strack, Thomas (1996). Philosophical anthropology on the eve of biological determinism: Immanuel Kant and Georg Forster on the moral qualities and biological characteristics of the human race. *Central European History* 29: 285–308.
 7. Pufendorf, Samuel von (1682). On the Natural State of Men. In *De Officio Hominis et Civis Juxta Legem Naturalem Libri Duo* (On the Duty of Man and Citizen According to Natural Law, Book 2), translated by Frank Gardner Moore. Reprinted 1964. New York and London: Oceana Publications. John Wildy & Sons, chapter 1, paragraph 7.
 8. Phillipson (1912).
 9. Pufendorf (1682), book 2, chapter 1, paragraph 8.
10. Rousseau, Jean-Jacques (1754). A Discourse on a Subject Proposed by the Academy of Dijon: What Is the Origin of Inequality among Men, and Is It Authorised by Natural Law? Translated by G. D. H. Cole. Constitution Society (2005), http://www.constitution.org/jjr/ineq_03.htm.
11. However, the philosopher John Locke may have seen the "state of nature" as not just a logical fiction, but an historical reality; see: Batz, William G. (1974). The historical anthropology of John Locke. *Journal of the History of Ideas* 35: 663–70.
12. Hindess, Barry (2007). Locke's state of nature. *History of the Human Sciences* 20: 1–20.
13. Pufendorf (1682), book 2, chapter 1, paragraph 9.

CHAPTER 3

 1. Pirsig, Robert M. (1974). *Zen and the Art of Motorcycle Maintenance: An Inquiry into Values.* New York: Bantam Books, p. 34.

2. Smail, Daniel L. (2008). *On Deep History and the Brain*. Berkeley: University of California Press, pp. 3–4.

3. Chapter 2, note 11: Hindess (2007).

4. Mack, Eric, and Gerald F. Gaus (2004). Classical Liberalism and Libertarianism: The Liberty tradition, pp. 115–30. In *Handbook of Political Theory*, Gerald F. Gaus and Chandran Kukathas, eds. London: SAGE, p. 116.

5. Sahlins, Marshall (2007). Hierarchy, equality, and the sublimation of anarchy: The Western illusion of human nature. *Tanner Lectures on Human Values* 27: 81–120.

CHAPTER 4

1. Dallenbach, Karl M. (1955). Phrenology versus psychoanalysis. *American Journal of Psychology* 68: 511–25.

   Parssinen, T. M. (1974). Popular science and society: The phrenology movement in early Victorian Britain. *Journal of Social History* 8: 1–20.

2. Butcher, James N. (2010). Personality assessment from the nineteenth to the early twenty-first century: Past achievements and contemporary challenges. *Annual Review of Clinical Psychology* 6: 1–20.

3. Carhart-Harris, R. L., and K. J. Friston (2010). The default-mode, ego-functions and free-energy: A neurobiological account of Freudian ideas. *Brain* 133: 1265–283.

4. Dietrich, Arne (2007). Who's afraid of a cognitive neuroscience of creativity? *Methods* 42: 22–27.

   Raichle, Marcus (2009). A brief history of human brain mapping. *Trends in Neurosciences* 32: 118–26.

   Sawyer, Keith (2011). The cognitive neuroscience of creativity: A critical review. *Creativity Research Journal* 23: 137–54.

5. Fiedler, Klaus (2011). Voodoo correlations are everywhere—not only in neuroscience. *Perspectives on Psychological Science* 6: 163–71.

   Hanson, Stephen José, and Martin Bunz, eds. (2010). *Foundational Issues in Human Brain Mapping*. Cambridge, MA: MIT Press.

   Mandler, George (2011). From association to organization. *Current Directions in Psychological Science* 20: 232–35.

6. Ramachandran, Vilayanur S. (2011). *The Tell-Tale Brain: A Neuroscientist's Quest for What Makes Us Human*. New York: W. W. Norton.

7. Yarkoni, Tal, Russell A. Poldrack, David C. Van Essen, and Tor D. Wager (2010). Cognitive neuroscience 2.0: Building a cumulative science of human brain function. *Trends in Cognitive Sciences* 14: 489–96.

   Buhle, Jason T., Jennifer A. Silvers, Tor D. Wager, Richard Lopez, Chukwudi Onyemekwu, Hedy Kober, Jochen Weber, and Kevin N. Ochsner (2013). Cognitive reappraisal of emotion: A meta-analysis of human neuroimaging studies. *Cerebral Cortex* doi:10.1093/cercor/bht154.

8. Colombo, Mateo (2013). Moving forward (and beyond) the modularity debate: A network perspective. *Philosophy of Science* 80: 356–77.

   Buller, David J., and Valerie Gray Hardcastle (2000). Evolutionary psychology, meet developmental neurobiology: Against promiscuous modularity. *Brain and Mind* 1: 307–25.

9. Sawyer (2011), pp. 147, 149.

10. Steinberg, Laurence (2005). Cognitive and affective development in adolescence. *Trends in Cognitive Sciences* 9: 69–74.

    Westermann, Gert, Sylvain Sirois, Thomas R. Shultz, and Denis Mareschal (2006). Modeling developmental cognitive neuroscience. *Trends in Cognitive Sciences* 10: 227–32.

    Kitayama, Shinobu, and Ayse K. Uskul (2011). Culture, mind, and the brain: Current evidence and future directions. *Annual Review of Psychology* 62: 419–49.

    Bardon, Jon (2012). Unlocking the brain. *Nature* 487: 24–26.

    Chiao, Joan Y., and Mary Helen Immordino-Yang (2013). Modularity and the cultural mind: Contributions of cultural neuroscience to cognitive theory. *Perspectives on Psychological Science* 8: 56–61.

11. Bullmore, Ed, and Olaf Sporns (2012). The economy of brain network organization. *Nature Reviews: Neuroscience* 13: 336–49.

12. Miller, George A. (1956). The magical number seven, plus or minus two: Some limits on our capacity for processing information. *Psychological Review* 63: 81–97, p. 91.

13. Today these alternative names are often used by psychologists to refer to different although closely related dimensions of how the brain works. "Working memory" refers to how information that we are attending to is being organized and processed; "short term" memory simply means the capacity to hold a certain amount of information in mind for a brief period, i.e., for a few seconds.

    Baddeley, Alan (2003). Working memory: Looking back and looking forward. *Nature Reviews: Neuroscience* 4: 829–39.

    Cowan, Nelson (2010). The magical mystery four: How is working memory capacity limited, and why? *Current Directions in Psychological Science* 19: 51–57.

    Nee, Derek Evan, Joshua W. Brown, Mary K. Askren, Marc G. Berman, Emre Demiralp, Adam Krawitz, and John Jonides (2013). A meta-analysis of executive components of working memory. *Cerebral Cortex* 23: 264–82.

    Cowan, Nelson (2013). Short-term and working memory in childhood. In *Wiley Handbook on the Development of Children's Memory*, Patricia J. Bauer and Robyn Fivush, eds., pp. 202 –39. Hoboken, NJ: Wiley-Blackwell.

14. Miller (1956), p. 91.

    Linhares, Alexandre, Daniel M. Chada, and Christian N. Aranha (2011). The emergence of Miller's magic number on a sparse distributed memory. *PLoS ONE* 6(1): e15592.

Mathy, Fabien, and Jacob Feldman (2012). What's magic about magic numbers? Chunking and data compression in short-term memory. *Cognition* 122: 346–62.

15. Nieuwenhuis, Sander, and Tobias H. Donner (2011). The visual attention network untangled. *Nature Neuroscience* 14: 542–43.

    Zanto, Theodore P., Michael T. Rubens, Arul Thangavel, and Adam Gazzaley (2011). Causal role of the prefrontal cortex in top-down modulation of visual processing and working memory. *Nature Neuroscience* 14: 656–61.

16. Chapter 1, note 11: Kahneman (2011).

    Kahneman, Daniel, and Shane Frederick (2005). A model of heuristic judgment. In *The Cambridge Handbook of Thinking and Reasoning*, Keith J. Holyoak and Robert G. Morrison, eds., pp. 267–93. Cambridge: Cambridge University Press.

17. Evans, Jonathan St. B. T. (2008). Dual-processing accounts of reasoning, judgment, and social cognition. *Annual Review of Psychology* 59: 255–78, p. 270.

18. Chapter 1, note 11: Kahneman (2011).

    Evans, Jonathan St. B. T. (2010). Intuition and reasoning: A dual-process perspective. *Psychological Inquiry* 21: 313–26.

19. Kahneman, Daniel (2003). A perspective on judgment and choice: Mapping bounded rationality. *American Psychologist* 58: 697–720.

    Samuels, Richard (2006). The magical number two, plus or minus: Dual process theory as a theory of cognitive kinds. In *Two Minds: Dual Process Theories of Reasoning and Rationality*, Jonathan St. B. T. Evans and K. Frankish, eds., pp. 129–46. Oxford: Oxford University Press.

20. Bulfinch, Thomas (1882). *The Age of Fable: Or Beauties of Mythology*. Boston: S. W. Tilton & Company, p. 17.

21. Trope, Yaacov, and Nira Liberman (2010). Construal-level theory of psychological distance. *Psychological Review* 117: 440–63.

    Allen, Andrew P., and Kevin E. Thomas (2011). A dual process account of creative thinking. *Creativity Research Journal* 23: 109–18.

22. Chapter 1, note 11: Kahneman (2011), p. 29, also p. 13.

23. Buckner, Randy L., Jessica R. Andrews-Hanna, and Daniel L. Schacter (2008). The brain's default network: Anatomy, function, and relevance to disease. *Annals of the New York Academy of Sciences* 1124: 1–38.

24. Schooler, Jonathan W., Jonathan Smallwood, Kalina Christoff, Todd C. Handy, Erik D. Reichle, and Michael A. Sayette (2011). Meta-awareness, perceptual decoupling and the wandering mind. *Trends in Cognitive Sciences* 15: 319–26.

25. Gruberger, Michal, Eti Ben-Simon, Yechiel Levkovitz, Abraham Zangen, and Talma Hendler (2011). Towards a neuroscience of mind-wandering. *Frontiers in Human Neuroscience* 5, article 56.

    Sawyer (2011), p. 146; Schooler et al. (2011).

    Corballis, Michael C. (2012). Mind wandering: Remembering the past and imagining the future share similarities. *American Scientist* 100: 210–17.

Schacter, Daniel L., Donna Rose Addis, Demis Hassabis, Victoria C. Martin, R. Nathan Spreng, and Karl K. Szpunar (2012). The future of memory: Remembering, imagining, and the brain. *Neuron* 76: 677–94.

Fox, Kieran C. R., Savannah Nijeboer, Elizaveta Solomonova, G. William Domhoff, and Kalina Christoff (2013). Dreaming as mind wandering: Evidence from functional neuroimaging and first-person content reports. *Frontiers in Human Neuroscience* 7, article 412.

Mooneyham, Benjamin W., and Jonathan W. Schooler (2013). The costs and benefits of mind-wandering: A review. *Canadian Journal of Experimental Psychology* 67: 11–18.

26. Morin, Alain (2006). Levels of consciousness and self-awareness: A comparison and integration of various neurocognitive views. *Consciousness and Cognition* 15: 358–71.

Kouider, Sid, Vincent de Gardelle, Jérôme Sackur, and Emmanuel Dupoux (2010). How rich is consciousness? The partial awareness hypothesis. *Trends in Cognitive Sciences* 14: 301–307.

27. Buckner, Randy L., and Daniel C. Carroll (2007). Self-projection and the brain. *Trends in Cognitive Sciences* 11: 49–57.

Gilbert, Daniel T., and Timothy D. Wilson (2009). Why the brain talks to itself: Sources of error in emotional prediction. *Philosophical Transactions of the Royal Society B: Biological Sciences* 364: 1335–341.

Trope, Yaacov, and Nira Liberman (2010). Construal-level theory of psychological distance. *Psychological Review* 117: 440–63.

Richardson, Alan (2011). Defaulting to fiction: Neuroscience rediscovers the Romantic imagination. *Poetics Today* 32: 663–92.

28. Sawyer, Keith (2011), p. 146.

Lieberman, Matthew D. (2013). *Social: Why Our Brains Are Wired to Connect*. New York: Crown, p. 301.

If I understand his argument correctly, the psychologist Matthew D. Lieberman suspects that when at rest what he calls our *mentalizing system*— which "reliably comes on whenever we have downtime, and is even on while we dream"—could be rehearsing and reconsolidating various kinds of social information that may improve our social skills. This may be so, but I doubt that Leslie restricts our inner thoughts only to matters pertaining to social pleasures and pains.

29. Baird, Benjamin, Jonathan Smallwood, Michael D. Mrazek, Julia W. Y. Kam, Michael S. Franklin, and Jonathan W. Schooler (2012). Inspired by distraction: Mind wandering facilitates creative incubation. *Psychological Science* 23: 1117–122.

30. If "Leslie thinking" is a better name than "mind wandering" for what the brain is doing when we are not devoting Laurence's resources to attending to what is

happening around us, then it is possible that what has been called the neurological "default network" may be where much of Leslie thinking is being done. See:

Andrews-Hanna, Jessica R. (2012). The brain's default network and its adaptive role in internal mentation. *Neuroscientist* 18: 251–70.

Andrews-Hanna, Jessica R., Jay S. Reidler, Christine Huang, and Randy L. Buckner (2010). Evidence for the default network's role in spontaneous cognition. *Journal of Neurophysiology* 104: 322–35.

Andrews-Hanna, Jessica R., Jonathan Smallwood, and R. Nathan Spreng (2014). The default network and self-generated thought: component processes, dynamic control, and clinical relevance. *Annals of the New York Academy of Sciences* 1316: 29–52.

Gilbert, Sam J., Iroise Dumontheil, Jon S. Simons, Chris D. Frith, and Paul W. Burgess (2007). Comment on "Wandering minds: The default network and stimulus-independent thought." *Science* 317: 43b.

Mason, Malia F., Michael I. Norton, John D. Van Horn, Daniel M. Wegner, Scott T. Grafton, and C. Neil Macrae (2007). Wandering minds: The default network and stimulus-independent thought. *Science* 315: 393–95.

Wilson, Thomas J., David A. Reinhard, Erin C. Westgate, Daniel T. Gilbert, Nicole Ellerbeck, Cheryl Hahn, Casey L. Brown, Adi Shaked (2014). Just think: The challenges of the disengaged mind. *Science* 345: 75–77.

31. Odling-Smee, F. John, Kevin N. Laland, and Marcus W. Feldman (2003). *Niche Construction*. Princeton, NJ: Princeton University Press.

32. Killingsworth, Matthew A., and Daniel T. Gilbert (2010). A wandering mind is an unhappy mind. *Science* 330: 932.

33. Graphic examples would be social and intellectual "revitalization movements" such as "cargo cults" in the southwestern Pacific; the "ghost dance" in post-Columbian native North America history; the American Civil Rights Movement in the 20th century; Post-Modernism in later 20th century European and American art, architecture, literature, and the social sciences; and the "Tea Party" movement in current American politics. For a specific example, see: Halper, Stefan (2011) President Obama at mid-term. *International Affairs* 87: 1–11. For background, see: Wallace, Anthony F. C. (1956). Revitalization movements. *American Anthropologist* 58: 264–81.

34. This observation has been made before: Peters, John Durham (1989). John Locke, the individual, and the origin of communication. *Quarterly Journal of Speech* 75: 387–99.

Locke, John. *An Essay Concerning Human Understanding*, 4th edition. London: Printed for Awnsham and John Churchil, and Samuel Manship, 1700. London, p. 235:

Man, though he have great variety of thoughts, and such from which others as well as himself might receive profit and delight; yet they are all within his own breast, invisible and hidden from others, nor can of themselves be made to appear. The comfort and advantage of society not being to be had without communication of thoughts, it was necessary that man should find out some external sensible signs, whereof those invisible ideas, which his thoughts are made up of, might be made known to others. For this purpose nothing was so fit, either for plenty or quickness, as those articulate sounds, which with so much ease and variety he found himself able to make. Thus we may conceive how WORDS, which were by nature so well adapted to that purpose, came to be made use of by men as the signs of their ideas; not by any natural connection that there is between particular articulate sounds and certain ideas, for then there would be but one language amongst all men; but by a voluntary imposition, whereby such a word is made arbitrarily the mark of such an idea. The use, then, of words, is to be sensible marks of ideas; and the ideas they stand for are their proper and immediate signification.

(text transcription: http://www.gutenberg.org/cache/epub/10616/pg10616.html)

CHAPTER 5

1. Davies, Hugh L., Jocelyn M. Davies, Russell C. B. Perembo, and Wilfred Y. Lus (2003). The Aitape 1998 tsunami: Reconstructing the event from interviews and field mapping. *Pure and Applied Geophysics* 160: 1895–922.
2. http://earthquake.usgs.gov/earthquakes/
3. Terrell, John Edward, and Esther M. Schechter, eds. (2011). Archaeological Investigations on the Sepik Coast of Papua New Guinea. *Fieldiana: Anthropology* 42: 1.
4. Tappin, David R., Philip Watts, and Stéphan T. Grilli (2008). The Papua New Guinea tsunami of 17 July 1998: Anatomy of a catastrophic event. *Natural Hazards and Earth System Science* 8: 243–66.
5. Welsch, Robert (January–February 1999). Papua New Guinea begins rebuilding after tidal wave disaster. *In the Field*, p. 7.
6. Rilling, James K., David A. Gutman, Thorsten R. Zeh, Giuseppe Pagnoni, Gregory S. Berns, and Clinton D. Kilts (2002). A neural basis for social cooperation. *Neuron* 35: 395–405.

   Nowak, Martin A. (2006). Five rules for the evolution of cooperation. *Science* 314: 1560–563.

   Rand, David G., and Martin A. Nowak (2013). Human cooperation. *Trends in Cognitive Sciences* 17: 413–25.
7. Warneken, Felix, Karoline Lohse, Alicia P. Melis, and Michael Tomasello (2011). Young children share the spoils after collaboration. *Psychological Science* 22: 267–73.
8. Alexander, Marcus, and Fotini Christia (2011). Context modularity of human altruism. *Science* 334, 1392–394, p. 1392.

   Hrdy, Sarah Blaffer (2009). *Mothers and Others: The Evolutionary Origins of Mutual Understanding*. Cambridge, MA: Harvard University Press.
9. Silk, Joan B. (2003). Cooperation without counting: The puzzle of friendship. In *Genetic and Cultural Evolution of Cooperation*, P. Hammerstein, ed., pp. 37–54. Cambridge, MA: MIT Press, p. 37.
10. Henrich, Joseph, and Natalie Henrich (2006). Culture, evolution and the puzzle of human cooperation. *Cognitive Systems Research* 7: 220–45.

11. http://www.daily%20star.co.uk/news/latest-news/27%2001%2090/Cannibal-isle-for-Prince-Charles

CHAPTER 6

1. Chapter 5, note 10: Henrich and Henrich (2006).

    Bunnell, Tim, Sallie Yea, Linda Peake, Tracey Skelton, and Monica Smith (2012). Geographies of friendships. *Progress in Human Geography* 36: 490–507.

2. *Country Health Information Profiles: Papua New Guinea.* World Health Organization, Western Pacific Region. http://www.wpro.who.int/countries/png/25PNGpro2011_finaldraft.pdf

3. Hobbes, Thomas (1651). *Leviathan, or the Matter, Forme, & Power of a Common-Wealth Ecclesiasticall and Civill.* Reprint edition, 1909. Oxford: Clarendon Press, p. 96.

4. Chapter 2, note 6: Phillipson (1912); Chapter 2, note 5: Waswo (1996).

5. Ellingson, Ter (2001). *The Myth of the Noble Savage.* Berkeley: University of California Press.

6. Chapter 2, note 9: Rousseau (1754), part 1.

7. Höpfl, H. L. (1978). From savage to Scotsman: Conjectural history in the Scottish Enlightenment. *Journal of British Studies* 17: 19–40.

    Armitage, David (2004). John Locke, Carolina, and the "Two Treatises of Government." *Political Theory* 32: 602–27.

8. Ellingson (2001), p. 162.

9. Chapter 2, note 3: Waldron (1987).

10. We can add to this list also experts on water transport by the gall bladder and the biogeography of birds in the southwest Pacific: Diamond, Jared M. (2011). *The World Until Yesterday: What Can We Learn from Traditional Societies?* New York: Viking.

CHAPTER 7

1. Welsch, Robert L. (1998). *An American Anthropologist in Melanesia. A. B. Lewis and the Joseph N. Field South Pacific Expedition 1909–1913*, 2 vols. Honolulu: University of Hawai'i Press.

2. Putnam, F. W. (1893). Ethnology, anthropology, archaeology. In *The World's Columbian Exposition, Chicago, 1893*, Trumbull White and William Igleheart, eds., pp. 415–35. Boston: John K. Hastings, p. 415.

3. Welsch (1998), pp. 561–65.

4. Welsch, Robert L., and John Edward Terrell (1991). Continuity and change in economic relations along the Aitape coast of Papua New Guinea, 1909–1990. *Pacific Studies* 14(4): 113–28.

CHAPTER 8

1. Welsch, Robert L., and John Edward Terrell (1998). Material culture, social fields, and social boundaries on the Sepik coast of New Guinea. In *The Archaeology of Social Boundaries*, Miriam T. Stark, ed., pp. 50–77. Washington, DC: Smithsonian Institution Press.

CHAPTER 9

1. MacIntyre, Martha (1983). Warfare and the changing context of "kune" on Tubetube. *Journal of Pacific History* 18: 11–34.
2. Firth, Stewart (1983). *New Guinea under the Germans*. Port Moresby: WEB Books, p. 4.
3. Firth (1983), p. 93.
4. Terrell, John Edward, and Esther M. Schechter (2007). Deciphering the Lapita code: The Aitape ceramic sequence and late survival of the "Lapita face." *Cambridge Archaeological Journal* 17: 59–85.

    Terrell, John Edward, and Esther M. Schechter (2009). The meaning and importance of the Lapita face motif. *Archaeology in Oceania* 44: 45–55.
5. Golitko, Mark (2011). Provenience investigations of ceramic and obsidian samples using laser ablation inductively coupled plasma mass spectrometry and portable X-ray fluorescence. In *Exploring Prehistory on the Sepik Coast of Papua New Guinea*, John Edward Terrell and Esther M. Schechter, eds., pp. 251–87. *Fieldiana: Anthropology* n.s. 42.

    Golitko, Mark, James Meierhoff, and John Edward Terrell (2011). Chemical characterization of sources of obsidian from the Sepik coast (PNG). *Archaeology in Oceania* 45: 120–29.

    Golitko, Mark, Mark Schauer, and John Edward Terrell (2012a). Identification of Fergusson Island obsidian on the Sepik coast of northern Papua New Guinea. *Archaeology in Oceania* 47: 151–56.

    Golitko, Mark, John V. Dudgeon, Hector Neff, and John Edward Terrell (2012b). Identification of post-depositional chemical alteration of ceramics from the north coast of Papua New Guinea (Sanduan Province) by time-of-flight–laser ablation–inductively coupled plasma–mass spectrometry (ToF-LA-ICP-MS). *Archaeometry* 54: 80–100.

    Golitko, Mark, and John Edward Terrell (2012). Mapping prehistoric social fields on the Sepik coast of Papua New Guinea: Ceramic compositional analysis using laser ablation-inductively coupled plasma-mass spectrometry. *Journal of Archaeological Science* 39: 3568–580.
6. Golitko et al. (2012a); Golitko et al. (2012b); Golitko and Terrell (2012).
7. Terrell, John Edward (2012). Wooden platters and bowls in the ethnographic collections. In *Exploring Prehistory on the Sepik Coast of Papua New*

Guinea, John Edward Terrell and Esther M. Schechter, eds., pp. 175–95. *Fieldiana*: *Anthropology* n.s. 42.

CHAPTER 10

1. Specht, Jim, Tim Denham, James Goff, and John Edward Terrell (2013). Deconstructing the Lapita cultural complex in the Bismarck Archipelago. *Journal of Archaeological Research* 22: 89–140.
2. Luna, Regina Woodrom (2013). Turtlephilia in the Pacific: An integrated comparative analysis from the perspectives of biological, cultural, and spiritual ecology in a particular case of biophilia. PhD dissertation, University of Hawai'i at Mānoa (http://www.seaturtle.org/PDF/ReginaWoodromLuna_2013_PhD.pdf), p. xxii.
3. Allen, Melinda S. (2007). Three millennia of human and sea turtle interactions in Remote Oceania. *Coral Reefs* 26: 959–970, p. 964.
4. Chapter 9, note 4: Terrell and Schechter (2007); Terrell and Schechter (2009).

CHAPTER 11

1. Christakis, Nicholas A., and James H. Fowler (2009). *Connected: The Surprising Power of Our Social Networks and How They Shape Our Lives*. New York: Little, Brown and Company.
2. Chapter 9, note 2: Firth (1986), p. 94.
3. Keeley, Lawrence H. (1996). *War Before Civilization: The Myth of the Peaceful Savage*. New York: Oxford University Press.

    Haas, Jonathan, and Matthew Piscitelli (2013). The prehistory of warfare: Misled by ethnography. In *War, Peace, and Human Nature: The Convergence of Evolutionary and Cultural Views*, Douglas P. Fry, ed., pp. 168–90. New York: Oxford University Press.

CHAPTER 12

1. Strack, Thomas (1996). Philosophical anthropology on the eve of biological determinism: Immanuel Kant and Georg Forster on the moral qualities and biological characteristics of the human race. *Central European History* 29: 285–308.
2. Nisbet, Robert (1980). *History of the Idea of Progress*. New York: Basic Books, p. 229.
3. Kumar, Krishan (1997). Spencer, Herbert (1820–1903). In *The Dictionary of Anthropology*, Thomas Barfield, ed., pp. 443–44. Oxford: Blackwell.

    Francis, Mark (2007). *Herbert Spencer and the Invention of Modern Life*. Ithaca, NY: Cornell University Press.
4. Perrin, Robert G. (1976). Herbert Spencer's four theories of social evolution. *American Journal of Sociology* 81: 1339–359.

5. Spencer, Herbert (1857). Progress: Its law and cause. *Westminster Review* 67: 445–85, p. 446.

6. Spencer, Herbert (1893). *The Principles of Sociology*, Vol. 2. New York: D. Appleton and Company, p. 231.

7. Boas, Franz (1928). *Anthropology and Modern Life*. New York: W. W. Norton, pp. 67–68.

8. Wrangham, Richard W., and Luke Glowacki (2012). Intergroup aggression in chimpanzees and war in nomadic hunter-gatherers: Evaluating the chimpanzee model. *Human Nature* 23: 5–29. For additional commentary on the role of violence in human evolution and behavior, see:

   Fuentes, Agustín (2004). It's not all sex and violence: Integrated anthropology and the role of cooperation and social complexity in human evolution. *American Anthropologist* 106: 710–18.

   Fuentes, Agustín (2012). *Race, Monogamy, and Other Lies They Told You: Busting Myths about Human Nature*. Berkeley: University of California Press.

9. Chapter 3, note 2: Smail (2008).

10. Richard Waswo also credits Virgil's epic poem the *Aeneid*, the story of the foundation of the Roman Empire by the Trojans, for defining for Europeans "what constitutes civilization itself (settled agriculture and cities: tilling the earth, building walls and towers on it) as opposed to its opposite, savagery (dispersed nomadism: hunting and gathering in forests)." See: chapter 2, note 5: Waswo (1996), p. 743.

11. Price, T. Douglas, ed. (2000). *Europe's First Farmers*. Cambridge: Cambridge University Press, p. 1.

12. Marcus, Joyce (2008). The archaeological evidence for social evolution. *Annual Review of Anthropology* 37: 251–66.

13. Price, T. Douglas, and Ann B. Gebauer, eds. (1995). *Last Hunters, First Farmers: New Perspectives on the Prehistoric Transition to Agriculture*. Santa Fe: School of American Research Press.

14. Hanke, Lewis (1937). Pope Paul III and the American Indians. *Harvard Theological Review* 30: 65–102.

CHAPTER 13

1. Brown, H. Rap (1969). *Die Nigger Die!* Chicago: Lawrence Hill Books, p. 144.

2. Churchill, Winston S. (1925). Recent Expressions on World Peace. I. Shall We Commit Suicide? *The Historical Outlook* 16: 56–58.

3. Chapter 1, note 1: Pinker (2002), pp. 315–16.

4. Chapter 1, note 1: Pinker (2002), p. 329.

5. Kuhn, Thomas S. (1957). *The Copernican Revolution: Planetary Astronomy in the Development of Western Thought*. Cambridge, MA: Harvard University Press, p. 43–44.

6. Kuhn, Thomas S. (1977). *The Essential Tension: Selected Studies in Scientific Tradition and Change*. Chicago: University of Chicago Press, p. 323.

7. For example, the famed astronomer Tycho Brahe's late 16th century geoheliocentric proposal, which had the sun and moon going around the earth and the rest of the planets moving around the sun; see: Gingerich, Owen (2004). *The Book Nobody Read: Chasing the Revolutions of Nicolaus Copernicus*. New York: Penguin Books.

CHAPTER 14

1. Terrell, John Edward (1986). *Prehistory in the Pacific Islands: A Study of Variation in Language, Customs, and Human Biology*. Cambridge: Cambridge University Press, pp. 94–95.

2. Weiner, Jonathan (1995). *The Beak of the Finch: A Story of Evolution in Our Time*. New York: Vintage Books, Random House, p. 17.

3. Sulloway, Frank J. (1982). Darwin and his finches: The evolution of a legend. *Journal of the History of Biology* 15: 1–53, p. 8.

4. Sulloway (1982), p. 7.

5. Ruse, Michael (2003). *Darwin and Design: Does Evolution Have a Purpose?* Cambridge, MA: Harvard University Press, pp. 124–28.

6. Darwin, Charles (1839). *Journal of Researches into the Geology and Natural History of the Various Countries Visited by H.M.S. Beagle*, facsimile reprint of the 1st ed. New York: Hafner, 1952, p. 474.

7. Sulloway (1982), p. 9.

8. Even after he was told by people on the islands that there were plants and animals that are unique to each island in the Galapagos—and he started taking greater care to label where he had obtained his specimens in the archipelago—Darwin did not try to gather a complete series of specimens from each of the four islands he visited; see: Himmelfarb, Gertrude (1959). *Darwin and the Darwinian Revolution*. New York: Doubleday, pp. 115–16.

9. Darwin (1839), p. 474.

10. Sulloway (1982), p. 10.

    Sulloway, Frank J. (1984). Darwin and the Galapagos. *Biological Journal of the Linnean Society* 21: 29–59, pp. 47–50.

11. Sulloway (1982), p. 10.

12. Sulloway (1982), p. 22; Sulloway (1984), p. 45.

13. Driscoll, Carlos A., David W. Macdonald, and Stephen J. O'Brien (2009). From wild animals to domestic pets, an evolutionary view of domestication. *Proceedings of the National Academy of Sciences of the USA* 106, Suppl. 1: 9971–978.

14. Hare, Brian, and Michael Tomasello (2005b). Human-like social skills in dogs? *Trends in Cognitive Sciences* 9: 439–44.

15. Thalmann, Olaf, Beth Shapiro, P. Cui, Verena J. Schuenemann, Susanna K. Sawyer, D. L. Greenfield, et al. (2013). Complete mitochondrial genomes of ancient canids suggest a European origin of domestic dogs. *Science* 342: 871–74.

16. Wobber, Victoria, Brian Hare, Janice Koler-Matznick, Richard Wrangham, and Michael Tomasello (2009). Breed differences in domestic dogs' (*Canis familiaris*) comprehension of human communicative signals. *Interaction Studies* 10: 206–24.

17. Gácsi, Márta, Borbála Györi, Ádám Miklósi, Zsófia Virányi, Enikö Kubinyi, József Topál, and Vilmos Csányi (2005). Species-specific differences and similarities in the behavior of hand-raised dog and wolf pups in social situations with humans. *Developmental Psychobiology* 47: 111–22.

    Miklósi, Ádám, Enikö Kubinyi, József Topál, Márta Gácsi, Zsófia Virányi, and Vilmos Csányi (2003). A simple reason for a big difference: Wolves do not look back at humans, but dogs do. *Current Biology* 13: 763–66.

18. Hare and Tomasello (2005b), p. 443.

    Hare, Brian (2007). From nonhuman to human mind: What changed and why? *Current Directions in Psychological Science* 16: 60–64.

19. Boehm, Christopher (2008). Purposive social selection and the evolution of human altruism. *Cross-Cultural Research* 42: 319–52, at 346.

20. Hare and Tomasello (2005b), p. 443.

21. Knauft, Bruce M. (1987). Reconsidering violence in simple human societies: Homicide among the Gebusi of New Guinea. *Current Anthropology* 28: 457–500.

    Knauft, Bruce M. (2011). Violence reduction among the Gebusi of Papua New Guinea—and across humanity. In *Origins of Altruism and Cooperation*, R. W. Sussman and C. R. Cloninger, eds., pp. 203–25. Developments in Primatology: Progress and Prospects 36. New York: Springer Science+Business Media.

22. Knauft, Bruce M. (2011), p. 466.

23. Hare, Brian, and Michael Tomasello (2005a). The emotional reactivity hypothesis and cognitive evolution. Reply to Miklósi and Topál. *Trends in Cognitive Sciences* 9: 464–65.

24. Kaminski, Juliane (2008). The domestic dog: A forgotten star rising again. *Trends in Cognitive Sciences* 12: 211–12.

25. Simon, Herbert A. (1990). A mechanism for social selection and successful altruism. *Science* 250: 1665–668.

26. Darwin, Charles (1898). *The Descent of Man and Selection in Relation to Sex*, 2nd ed., revised and augmented. New York: D. Appleton and Company, p. 121.

CHAPTER 15

1. Barnes, Trevor J. (2008). Geography's underworld: The military–industrial complex, mathematical modelling and the quantitative revolution. *Geoforum* 39: 3–16.

2. Diamond, Jared M. (1978). Niche shifts and the rediscovery of interspecific competition: Why did field biologists so long overlook the widespread evidence for interspecific competition that had already impressed Darwin? *American Scientist* 66: 322–31.

   Schoener, Thomas W. (1982). The controversy over interspecific competition: Despite spirited criticism, competition continues to occupy a major domain in ecological thought. *American Scientist* 70: 586–95.

3. Simberloff, Daniel (1980). A succession of paradigms in ecology: Essentialism to materialism and probabilism. *Synthese* 43: 3–39.

   Barnes (2008).

   Brown, James H. (1999). The legacy of Robert Macarthur: From geographical ecology to macroecology. *Journal of Mammalogy* 80: 333–44.

   Sepkoski, David (2005). Stephen Jay Gould, Jack Sepkoski, and the "quantitative revolution" in American paleobiology. *Journal of the History of Biology* 38: 209–37.

   Sterner, Beckett, and Scott Lidgard (2014). The normative structure of mathematization in systematic biology. *Studies in History and Philosophy of Biological and Biomedical Sciences* 46: 44–54.

4. Hamilton, William D. (1964a). The genetical evolution of social behavior. I. *Journal of Theoretical Biology* 7: 1–16, p. 1.

5. Kohn, Marek (2004). *A Reason for Everything: Natural Selection and the British Imagination*. London: Faber and Faber.

6. MacKinnon, Katherine C., and Agustín Fuentes (2011). Primates, niche construction, and social complexity: The roles of social cooperation and altruism. In *Origins of Altruism and Cooperation*, R. W. Sussman and C. R. Cloninger, eds., pp. 121–43. New York: Springer.

7. Hamilton, William D. (1964a).

   Hamilton, William D. (1964b). The genetical evolution of social behavior. II. *Journal of Theoretical Biology* 7: 17–52.

8. In Hamilton's own words:

   As to the nature of inclusive fitness it may perhaps help to clarify the notion if we now give a slightly different verbal presentation. Inclusive fitness may be imagined as the personal fitness which an individual actually expresses in its production of adult offspring as it becomes after it has been first stripped and then augmented in a certain way. It is stripped of all components which can be considered as due to the individual's social environment, leaving the fitness which he would express if not exposed to any of the harms or benefits of that environment. This quantity is then augmented by certain fractions of the quantities of harm and benefit which the individual himself causes to the fitnesses of his neighbors. The fractions in question are simply the coefficients of relationship appropriate to the neighbors whom he affects: unity for clonal individuals, one-half for sibs, one-quarter for half-sibs, one-eighth for cousins,....and finally zero for all neighbors whose relationship can be considered negligibly small. (1964a: 8)

9. Park, Julian H. (2007). Persistent misunderstandings of inclusive fitness and kin selection: Their ubiquitous appearance in social psychology textbooks. *Evolutionary Psychology* 5: 860–73.

   Connor, Richard C. (2010). Cooperation beyond the dyad: On simple models and a complex society. *Philosophical Transactions of the Royal Society of London B: Biological Sciences* 365: 2687–697.

   West, Stuart A., Claire El Mouden, and Andy Gardner (2011). Sixteen common misconceptions about the evolution of cooperation in humans. *Evolution and Human Behavior* 32: 231–62.

10. Chapter 1, note 7: Wilson (2012), p. 274.

11. Wilson, David Sloan, and Edward O. Wilson (2007). Rethinking the theoretical foundation of sociobiology. *Quarterly Review of Biology* 82: 327–48.

12. Hamilton, William D. (1971). Selection of selfish and altruistic behavior in some extreme models. In *Man and Beast: Comparative Social Behavior*, J. F. Eisenberg and Wilton S. Dillon, eds., pp. 57–91. Washington, DC: Smithsonian Institution Press, pp. 80–81.

13. See: also Kohn (2004), pp. 272–74.

14. The list could be longer than the four I discuss here. At the top of the list some would add the seemingly bland question "What is an individual?" As Lynn Nyhart at the University of Wisconsin, Madison, and my colleague Scott Lidgard at the Field Museum in Chicago have written, in the 20 years prior to the publication of Darwins's *On the Origin of Species* in 1859 what they describe as "the problem of the individual" was one of the major issues of mid-19th century biology. "The perceived importance of this problem ebbed and expanded repeatedly over the next 150 years, and is once again at the forefront of biology." See: Nyhart, Lynn K. and Scott Lidgard (2011). Individuals at the center of biology: Rudolf Leuckart's *Polymorphismus der Individuen* and the ongoing narrative of parts and wholes. With an annotated translation. *Journal of the History of Biology* 44: 3734–43.

15. Grafen, Alan (2009). Formalizing Darwinism and inclusive fitness theory. *Philosophical Transactions of the Royal Society of London B: Biological Sciences* 364: 3135–141.

   West et al. (2011).

16. Allen, Benjamin, Martin A. Nowak, and Edward O. Wilson (2013). Limitations of inclusive fitness. *Proceedings of the National Academy of Sciences of the USA* PNAS Early Edition, 5 pp. http://www.pnas.org/cgi/doi/10.1073/pnas.1317588110

17. Hrdy, Sarah Blaffer (1999). *Mother Nature: Maternal Instincts and How They Shape the Human species*. New York: Ballantine Books, pp. 29–32.

18. Hamilton (1971), p. 83.

19. Liben-Nowell, David, Jasmine Novak, Ravi Kumar, Prabhakar Raghavan, and Andrew Tomkins (2005). Geographic routing in social networks. *Proceedings of the National Academy of Sciences of the USA* 102: 11623–1628.

Chapter 5, note 6: Nowak, Martin A. (2006).

Gastner, Michael T., and Mark E. J. Newman (2006). The spatial structure of networks. *European Physical Journal B : Condensed Matter and Complex Systems* 49: 247–52.

Rand, David G., and Martin A. Nowak (2013). Human cooperation. *Trends in Cognitive Sciences* 17: 413–25.

20. Hamilton himself described the tendency for individuals to be genetically similar due to isolation-by-distance thusly: "With many natural populations it must happen that an individual forms the center of an actual local concentration of his relatives which is due to a general inability or disinclination of the organisms to move far from their places of birth. In such a population, which we may provisionally term 'viscous,' the present form of selection may apply fairly accurately to genes which affect vagrancy" (1964a, p. 10).

21. Lehmann, Laurent, Virginie Ravigné, and Laurent Keller (2008). Population viscosity can promote the evolution of altruistic sterile helpers and eusociality. *Proceedings of the Royal Society of London B: Biological Sciences* 275: 1887–895.

Ohtsuki, Hisashi, Christoph Hauert, Erez Lieberman, and Martin A. Nowak (2006). A simple rule for the evolution of cooperation on graphs and social networks. *Nature* 441: 502–505.

Nowak. Martin A. (2012). Evolving cooperation. *Journal of Theoretical Biology* 299: 1–8.

Powers, Simon T., Jason Noble, Jordi Arranz, and Manuel de Pinedo (2011). Explaining cooperative groups via social niche construction. http://eprints.soton.ac.uk/272841/1/Bristolabstract%20(1)%20(1).pdf

Rousset, F., and S. Lion (2011). Much ado about nothing: Nowak et al.'s charge against inclusive fitness theory. *Journal of Evolutionary Biology* 24: 1386–392.

22. Hamilton (1971), p. 73.

23. Nowak (2006).

24. Weins, John A. (1977). On competition and variable environments: Populations may experience "ecological crunches" in variable climates, nullifying the assumptions of competition theory and limiting the usefulness of short-term studies of population patterns. *American Scientist* 65: 590–97.

25. Sussman, Robert. W., Paul A. Garber, and James M. Cheverud (2011). Reply to Lawler: Feeding competition, cooperation, and the causes of primate sociality. *American Journal of Primatology* 73: 91–95.

26. West et al. (2011).

27. Nowak, Martin A., Corina E. Tarnita, and Edward O. Wilson (2010). The evolution of eusociality. *Nature* 466: 1057–62.

28. They are not alone: Bowles, Samuel, and Herbert Gintis (2011). *A Cooperative Species: Human Reciprocity and Its Evolution*. Princeton, NJ: Princeton University Press.

CHAPTER 16

1. Chapter 15, note 18: Nowak (2006), p. 1560; Rand and Nowak (2013).
2. Mehdiabadi, Natasha J., Ulrich G. Mueller, Seán G. Brady, Anna G. Himler, and Ted R. Schultz (2012). Symbiont fidelity and the origin of species in fungus-growing ants. *Nature Communications* 3:840
3. Compton, Stephen G., Alexander D. Ball, Margaret E. Collinson, Peta Hayes, Alexandr P. Rasnitsyn, and Andrew J. Ross (2010). Ancient fig wasps indicate at least 34 Myr of stasis in their mutualism with fig trees. *Biology Letters* 6: 838–42.
4. Note: You may be relieved to hear, however, that the crunchy parts in figs are seeds, not wasps.
5. Sussman, Robert W., and Paul A. Garber (2007). Cooperation and competition in primate social interactions. In *Primates in Perspective*, Christina J. Campbell, Agustín Fuentes, Katherine C. MacKinnon, Melissa Panger, and Simon K. Bearder, eds., pp. 636–51. New York: Oxford University Press.

   Tomasello, Michael (2011). Human culture in evolutionary perspective. In *Advances in Culture and Psychology*, Vol. 1, Michele J. Gelfand, Chi-yue Chiu, and Ying-yi-Hong, eds., pp. 5–51. New York: Oxford University Press.
6. Silk, Joan B. (2002b). Using the f-word in primatology. *Behaviour* 139: 421–46, p. 423.

   Chapter 5, note 9: Silk (2003).
7. Clutton-Brock, T. H., S. J. Hodge, and T. P. Flower (2008). Group size and the suppression of subordinate reproduction in Kalahari meerkats. *Animal Behaviour* 76: 689–700.
8. Thornton, Alex and Katherine McAuliffe (2006). Teaching in wild meerkats. *Science* 313: 227–29.
9. Thornton, Alex, Jamie Samson, and Tim Clutton-Brock (2010). Multi-generational persistence of traditions in neighbouring meerkat groups. *Proceedings of the Royal Society* B: 3623–629.
10. Lusseau, David, Ben Wilson, Philip S. Hammond, Kate Grellier, John W. Durban, Kim M. Parsons, Tim R. Barton, and Paul M. Thompson (2006). Quantifying the influence of sociality on population structure in bottlenose dolphins. *Journal of Animal Ecology* 75: 14–24.

   Lusseau, David (2007). Evidence for social role in a dolphin social network. *Evolutionary Ecology* 21: 357–66.

   Lusseau, David, and Larissa Conradt (2009). The emergence of unshared consensus decisions in bottlenose dolphins. *Behavioral Ecology and Sociobiology* 63: 1067–77.

11. Bruck, Jason (2013). Decades-long social memory in bottlenose dolphins. *Proceedings of the Royal Society of London B: Biological Sciences* 280, doi: 10.1098/rspb.2013.1726.
12. http://news.nationalgeographic.com/news/2008/03/080312-AP-dolph-whal.html
13. Hart, Donna, and Robert W. Sussman (2005). *Man the Hunted: Primates, Predators, and Human Evolution.* Cambridge, MA: Westview Press.
14. Clutton-Brock, Tim (2009). Cooperation between non-kin in animal societies. *Nature* 462: 51–57.
15. Chapter 12, note 8: Fuentes (2004).
    Sterelny, Kim (2012). *The Evolved Apprentice: How Evolution Made Humans Unique.* Cambridge, MA: MIT Press.
16. Hart, Donna, and Robert W. Sussman (2005).
17. Stanford, Craig B. (1999). *The Hunting Apes: Meat Eating and the Origins of Human Behavior.* Princeton, NJ: Princeton University Press.
18. Chapter 14, note 19: Boehm (2008), p. 326.
19. Stanford (1999).
20. Sussman, Robert W., Paul A. Garber, and Jim M. Cheverud (2005). Importance of cooperation and affiliation in the evolution of primate sociality. *American Journal of Physical Anthropology* 128: 84–97.
    Sussman and Garber (2007).
21. Chapter 15, note 25: Sussman, Garber, and Cheverud (2011), pp. 91–92.
    Hart and Sussman (2005).
22. Some have argued for a much older date: Beaumont, Peter B. (2011). The edge: More on fire-making by about 1.7 million years ago at Wonderwerk Cave in South Africa. *Current Anthropology* 52: 585–95.
23. Jacob, François (1977). Evolution and tinkering. *Science* 196: 1161–166.

CHAPTER 17

1. Dunbar, Robin I. M., and Susanne Shultz (2007). Evolution in the social brain. *Science* 317: 1344–347.
2. Barrett, Louise, and Peter Henzi (2005). The social nature of primate cognition. *Proceedings of the Royal Society of London B: Biological Sciences* 272: 1865–875.
3. Powell, Joanne, Penelope A. Lewis, Neil Roberts, Marta García-Fiñana, and Robin I. M. Dunbar (2012). Orbital prefrontal cortex volume predicts social network size: An imaging study of individual differences in humans. *Proceedings of the Royal Society of London B: Biological Sciences* 279: 2157–162.
    van Schaik, Carel P., Karin Isler, and Judith M. Burkart (2012). Explaining brain size variation: From social to cultural brain. *Trends in Cognitive Sciences* 16: 277–84.

4. Panksepp, Jaak (2011). Cross-species affective neuroscience decoding of the primal affective experiences of humans and related animals. *PLoS ONE* 6(9): e21236.

5. Griffin, Donald R. (2001). *Animal Minds: Beyond Cognition to Consciousness.* Chicago: University of Chicago Press.

6. Chapter 4, note 24: Schooler et al. (2011).

7. de Waal, Frans B. M., and Pier Francesco Ferrari (2010). Towards a bottom-up perspective on animal and human cognition. *Trends in Cognitive Sciences* 14: 201–207.

8. Apperly, Ian A. (2012). What is "theory of mind"? Concepts, cognitive processes and individual differences. *Quarterly Journal of Experimental Psychology* 65: 825–39.

9. Gobbini, Maria Ida, Aaron C. Koralek, Ronald E. Bryan, Kimberly J. Montgomery, and James V. Haxby (2007). Two takes on the social brain: A comparison of theory of mind tasks. *Journal of Cognitive Neuroscience* 19: 1803–814.

10. Waytz, Adam, Kurt Gray, Nicholas Epley, and Daniel M. Wegner (2010). Causes and consequences of mind perception. *Trends in Cognitive Sciences* 14: 383–88.

11. Call, Josep, and Michael Tomasello (2008). Does the chimpanzee have a theory of mind? 30 years later. *Trends in Cognitive Sciences* 12: 187–92, at 191.

    Tomasello, Michael, Josep Call, and Brian Hare (2003). Chimpanzees understand psychological states—the question is which ones and to what extent. *Trends in Cognitive Sciences* 7: 153–56.

    Chapter 16, note 5: Tomasello (2011).

12. Chapter 14, note 18: Hare (2007).

13. Apperly, Ian A. (2012).

14. Apperly, Ian A., and Stephen A. Butterfill (2009). Do humans have two systems to track beliefs and belief-like states? *Psychological Review* 116: 953–70.

CHAPTER 18

1. Tomasello, Michael, Malinda Carpenter, Josep Call, Tanya Behne, and Henrike Moll (2005). Understanding and sharing intentions: The origins of cultural cognition. *Behavioral and Brain Sciences* 28: 675–735.

2. Chapter 16, note 5: Tomasello (2011), p. 6.

3. Tomasello, Michael, and Esther Herrmann (2010). Ape and human cognition: What's the difference? *Current Directions in Psychological Science* 19: 3–8.

4. Buller, David J. (2005). Evolutionary psychology: The emperor's new paradigm. *Trends in Cognitive Sciences* 9: 277–83.

    Buss, David M. (2009). The great struggles of life: Darwin and the emergence of evolutionary psychology. *American Psychologist* 64: 140–48.

Tooby, John, and Leda Cosmides (2005). The emergence of evolutionary psychology: What is at stake? In *The Handbook of Evolutionary Psychology*, David M. Buss, ed., pp. 5–67. Hoboken, NJ: John Wiley & Sons.

5. Chapter 16, note 15: Sterelny (2012), p. 13.
6. Rilling, James K. (2006). Human and nonhuman primate brains: Are they allometrically scaled versions of the same design? *Evolutionary Anthropology* 15: 65–77.
7. Roth, Gerhard, and Ursula Dicke (2005). Evolution of the brain and intelligence. *Trends in Cognitive Sciences* 9: 250–57.
8. Herrmann, Esther, Josep Call, María Victoria Hernández-Lloreda, Brian Hare, and Michael Tomasello (2007). Humans have evolved specialized skills of social cognition: The cultural intelligence hypothesis. *Science* 317: 1360–1366.
9. Leigh, Steven R. (2012). Brain size growth and life history in human evolution. *Evolutionary Biology* 39: 587–99.
   Schoenemann, P. Thomas (2006). Evolution of the size and functional areas of the human brain. *Annual Review of Anthropology* 35: 379–406.
10. Rilling, James K., and Thomas R. Insel (1999). The primate neocortex in comparative perspective using magnetic resonance imaging. *Journal of Human Evolution* 37: 191–223.
11. Barrett, Louise, Peter Henzi, and Drew Rendall (2007). Social brains, simple minds: Does social complexity really require cognitive complexity? *Philosophical Transactions of the Royal Society of London B: Biological Sciences* 362: 561–75.
    Dunbar, Robin I. M. (1992). Neocortex size as a constraint on group size in primates. *Journal of Human Evolution* 20: 469–93.
    Dunbar, Robin I. M. (1998). The social brain hypothesis. *Evolutionary Anthropology* 6: 178–90.
    Dunbar, Robin I. M. (2003). The social brain: Mind, language, and society in evolutionary perspective. *Annual Review of Anthropology* 32: 163–81.
    Dunbar, Robin I. M. (2009). The social brain hypothesis and its implications for social evolution. *Annals of Human Biology* 36: 562–72.
    Rilling, James K. (2008). Neuroscientific approaches and applications within anthropology. *Yearbook of Physical Anthropology* 51: 2–32.
    Chapter 17, note 3: van Schaik et al. (2012).
12. Chapter 17, note 1: Dunbar, and Schultz (2007).
13. van Schaik, Carel P., and Judith M. Burkart (2011). Social learning and evolution: The cultural intelligence hypothesis. *Philosophical Transactions of the Royal Society of London B: Biological Sciences* 366: 1008–16.
    Herrmann et al. (2007).
14. Chapter 16, note 5: Tomasello (2011).
    Moore, Richard (2013). Social learning and teaching in chimpanzees. *Biology and Philosophy* 28: 879–901.
15. Chapter 16, note 5: Tomasello (2011), pp. 5, 6.

16. Martin, Robert D. (2007). The evolution of human reproduction: A primatological perspective. *Yearbook of Physical Anthropology* 50: 59–84.

   Martin, Robert D. (2013). *How We Do It: The Evolution and Future of Human Reproduction*. New York: Basic Books.

17. Skoyles, John R., and Dorion Sagan (2002). *Up from Dragons: The Origins of Human Intelligence*. New York: McGraw-Hill.

CHAPTER 19

1. Schwartz, Stefanie (2003). Separation anxiety syndrome in dogs and cats. *Journal of the American Veterinary Medical Association* 222: 1526–532.

2. Chapter 24, note 28: Lieberman (2013), p. 226.

3. Hollan, Douglas (2012). Emerging issues in the cross-cultural study of empathy. *Emotion Review* 4: 70–78.

4. Decety, Jean (2011a). The neuroevolution of empathy. *Annals of the New York Academy of Sciences* 1231: 35–45.

5. Decety, Jean (2011b). Promises and challenges of the neurobiological approach to empathy. *Emotion Review* 3: 115–16.

   Engelen, Eva-Maria, and Birgitt Röttger-Rössler (2012). Current disciplinary and interdisciplinary debates on empathy. *Emotion Review* 4: 3–8.

   Walter, Henrik (2012). Social cognitive neuroscience of empathy: Concepts, circuits, and genes. *Emotion Review* 4: 9–17.

6. Chapter 15, note 6: MacKinnon and Fuertes (2011).

7. Chapter 15, note 16: Hrdy (1999).

8. Lingle, Susan, Sergio M. Pellis, and W. Finbarr Wilson (2005). Interspecific variation in antipredator behaviour leads to differential vulnerability of mule deer and white-tailed deer fawns early in life. *Journal of Animal Ecology* 74: 1140–149.

9. Haskell, Shawn P., Warren B. Ballard, Mark C. Wallace, Mary H. Humphrey, and David A. Butler (2010). Postpartum group cohesion of sympatric deer in Texas. *Journal of Wildlife Management* 74: 1686–692.

10. Lingle et al. (2005).

11. Amarello, Melissa (2012). Social snakes? Non-random association patterns detected in a population of Arizona black rattlesnakes (*Crotalus cerberus*). Unpublished M.S. thesis, Arizona State University.

12. Brown, William S., Marc Kéry, and James E. Hines (2007). Survival of timber rattlesnakes (*Crotalus horridus*) estimated by capture-recapture models in relation to age, sex, color morph, time, and birthplace. *Copeia* 2007: 656–71.

13. Amarello, Melissa, Jeffrey J. Smith, and John Slone (2011). Family values: Maternal care in rattlesnakes is more than mere attendance. Available from *Nature Proceedings* http://dx.doi.org/10.1038/npre.2011.6671.1

14. Soares, Marta C., Redouan Bshary, Leonida Fusani, Wolfgang Goymann, Michaela Hau, Katharina Hirschenhauser, and Rui F. Oliveira (2010). Hormonal

mechanisms of cooperative behaviour. *Philosophical Transactions of the Royal Society of London B: Biological Sciences* 365: 2737–750.

15. Rilling, James K., Ashley C. DeMarco, Patrick D. Hackett, Richmond Thompson, Beate Ditzen, Rajan Patel, and Giuseppe Pagnoni (2012). Effects of intranasal oxytocin and vasopressin on cooperative behavior and associated brain activity in men. *Psychoneuroendocrinology* 37: 447–461.

16. Kosfeld, Michael, Markus Heinrichs, Paul J. Zak, Urs Fischbacher, and Ernst Fehr (2005). Oxytocin increases trust in humans. *Nature* 435: 673–76.

  Heinrichs, Markus, Bernadette von Dawans, and Gregor Domes (2009). Oxytocin, vasopressin, and human social behavior. *Frontiers in Neuroendocrinology* 30: 548–57.

  Ross, Heather E., and Larry J. Young (2009). Oxytocin and the neural mechanisms regulating social cognition and affiliative behavior. *Frontiers in Neuroendocrinology* 30: 534–47.

17. Soares et al. (2010).

18. Bartz, Jennifer A., Jamil Zaki, Niall Bolger, and Kevin N. Ochsner (2011). Social effects of oxytocin in humans: Context and person matter. *Trends in Cognitive Sciences* 15: 301–309.

19. Coan, James (2011). The social regulation of emotion. In *Handbook of Social Neuroscience*, J. Decety and J. T. Cacioppo, eds., pp. 614–23. New York: Oxford University Press.

20. Chapter 15, note 16: Hrdy (1999), p. 167.

21. Hrdy, Sarah Blaffer (2002). The past, present, and future of the human family. *The Tanner Lectures on Human Values* 23: 57–110, p. 60.

22. Hrdy (2002), pp. 71, 97.

23. Hrdy (1999), p. 207; see also chapter 5, note 8: Hrdy (2009), p. 171.

24. Kaye, Kenneth (1982). *The Mental and Social Life of Babies. How Parents Create Persons*. Chicago: University of Chicago Press.

  Swain, James E., Jeffrey P. Lorberbaum, Samet Kose, and Lane Strathearn (2007). Brain basis of early parent–infant interactions: Psychology, physiology, and *in vivo* functional neuroimaging studies. *Journal of Child Psychology and Psychiatry* 48: 262–87.

25. Coan, James A. (2008). Toward a neuroscience of attachment. In *Handbook of Attachment: Theory, Research, and Clinical Implications*, 2nd ed., Jude Cassidy and Philip R. Shaver, eds., pp. 241–65. New York: Guilford Press.

  Beckes, Lane, and James A. Coan (2011). Social baseline theory: The role of social proximity in emotion and economy of action. *Social and Personality Psychology Compass* 5: 976–88.

Beckes, Lane, James A. Coan, and Karen Hasselmo (2012). Familiarity promotes the blurring of self and other in the neural representation of threat. *Social Cognitive and Affective Neuroscience*, doi:10.1093/scan/nss046.

Coan, James A., Lane Beckes, and Joseph P. Allen (2013). Childhood maternal support and social capital moderate the regulatory impact of social relationships in adulthood. *International Journal of Psychophysiology* 88: 224–31.

26. Beckes and Coan (2011), pp. 976–77.

CHAPTER 20

1. Bögels, Susan M., Susanne Knappe, and Lee Anna Clark (2013). Adult separation anxiety disorder in *DSM-5*. *Clinical Psychology Review* 33: 663–74.

2. Chapter 19, note 1: Schwartz (2003), p. 1526.

3. Solomon, Andrew (2012). *Far from the Tree: Parents, Children, and the Search for Identity*. New York: Scribner.

4. Cusi, Andrée M., Anthony Nazarov, Katherine Holshausen, Glenda M. MacQueen, and Margaret C. McKinnon (2012). Systematic review of the neural basis of social cognition in patients with mood disorders. *Journal of Psychiatry & Neuroscience* 37: 154–69.

5. Dodge, Kenneth A., Jennifer E. Lansford, Virginia Salzer Burks, John E. Bates, Gregory S. Pettit, Reid Fontaine, and Joseph M. Price (2003). Peer rejection and social information-processing factors in the development of aggressive behavior problems in children. *Child Development* 74: 374–93.

6. Bentacourt, Theresa S., Ivelina I. Borisova, Marie de la Soudière, and John Williamson (2011). Sierra Leone's child soldiers: War exposures and mental health problems by gender. *Journal of Adolescent Health* 49: 21–28.

7. See also: Roscoe, Paul (2007). Intelligence, coalitional killing, and the antecedents of war. *American Anthropologist* 109: 485–95.

8. Pelphrey, Kevin A., James P. Morris, Gregory McCarthy, and Kevin S. LaBar (2007). Perception of dynamic changes in facial affect and identity in autism. *Social Cognitive and Affective Neuroscience* 2: 140–49.

9. Chevallier, Coralie, Gregor Kohls, Vanessa Troiani, Edward S. Brodkin, and Robert T. Schultz (2012). The social motivation theory of autism. *Trends in Cognitive Sciences* 16: 231–39.

Laursen, Brett, William M. Bukowski, Kaisa Aunola, and Jari-Erik Nurmi (2007). Friendship moderates prospective associations between social isolation and adjustment problems in young children. *Child Development* 78: 1395–404.

10. Bauminger, Nirit, and Connie Kasari (2000). Loneliness and friendship in high-functioning children with autism. *Child Development* 71: 447–56.

11. White, Susan W., and Roxann Roberson-Nay (2009). Anxiety, social deficits, and loneliness in youth with autism spectrum disorders. *Journal of Autism and Developmental Disorders* 39: 1006–13.

12. Bauminger, Nirit, Cory Shulman, and Galit Agam (2003). Peer interaction and loneliness in high-functioning children with autism. *Journal of Autism and Developmental Disorders* 33: 489–507.

13. Cacioppo, John T., Louise C. Hawkley, Greg J. Norman, and Gary G. Berntson (2011). Social isolation. *Annals of the New York Academy of Sciences* 1231: 17–22.

14. Robison, John Elder (2008). *Look Me in the Eye: My Life with Asperger's*. New York: Three Rivers Press, p. 211.

CHAPTER 21

1. Odling-Smee, F. John, Kevin N. Laland, and Marcus W. Feldman (1996). Niche construction. *American Naturalist* 147: 641–48.

    Day, Rachel L., Kevin N. Laland, and John Odling-Smee (2003). Rethinking adaptation: The niche-construction perspective. *Perspectives in Biology and Medicine* 46: 80–95.

    Laland, Kevin N., and Michael J. O'Brien (2011). Cultural niche construction: An introduction. *Biological Theory* 6: 191–202.

2. Chapter 14, note 1: Terrell (1986), pp. 177–79.

3. Mehdiabadi, Natasha J., and Ted R. Schultz (2010). Natural history and phylogeny of the fungus-farming ants (Hymenoptera: Formicidae: Myrmicinae: Attini). *Myrmecological News* 13: 37–55.

4. Suen, Garret, Clotilde Teiling, Lewyn Li., Carson Holt, Ehab Abouheif, et al. (2011). The genome sequence of the leaf-cutter ant *Atta cephalotes* reveals insights into its obligate symbiotic lifestyle. *PLoS Genet* 7(2): e1002007. doi:10.1371/journal.pgen.1002007, p. 1.

5. Chapter 16, note 2: Mehdiabadi et al. (2012).

6. Odling-Smee, F. John, Kevin N. Laland, and Marcus W. Feldman (2003). *Niche Construction: The Neglected Process in Evolution*. Princeton, NJ: Princeton University Press.

7. Brown, Gillian R., Thomas E. Dickins, Rebecca Sear, and Kevin N. Laland (2011). Evolutionary accounts of human behavioural diversity. *Philosophical Transactions of the Royal Society of London B: Biological Sciences*, 366: 313–24.

8. Kaufman, Allison B., Allen E. Butt, James C. Kaufman, and Erin N. Colbert-White (2011). Towards a neurobiology of creativity in nonhuman animals. *Journal of Comparative Psychology* 125: 255–72.

9. Christoff, Kalina, Alan M. Gordon, Jonathan Smallwood, Rachelle Smith, and Jonathan W. Schooler (2009). Experience sampling during fMRI reveals default network and executive system contributions to mind wandering. *Proceedings of the National Academy of Sciences of the USA* 106: 8719–724.

10. Pinker, Steven (2010). The cognitive niche: Coevolution of intelligence, sociality, and language. *Proceedings of the National Academy of Sciences of the USA* 107, Suppl. 2: 8993–999.

Tooby, John, and Irven DeVore (1987). The reconstruction of hominid behavioral evolution through strategic modeling. In *The Evolution of Human Behavior: Primate Models*, Warren G. Kinzey, ed., pp. 183–237. Albany: SUNY Press.

Iriki, Atsushi, and Miki Taoka (2012). Triadic (ecological, neural, cognitive) niche construction: A scenario of human brain evolution extrapolating tool use and language from the control of reaching actions. *Philosophical Transactions of the Royal Society of London B: Biological Sciences* 367: 10–23.

11. For example: Boyd, Robert, Peter J. Richerson, and Joseph Henrich (2011). The cultural niche: Why social learning is essential for human adaptation. *Proceedings of the National Academy of Sciences of the USA* 108, Suppl. 2: 10918–925.

Creanza. Nicole, Laurel Fogarty, and Marcus W. Feldman (2012). Models of cultural niche construction with selection and assortative mating. *PLoS ONE* 7(8): e42744. doi:10.1371/journal.pone.0042744

Whiten, Andrew, and David Erdal (2012). The human socio-cognitive niche and its evolutionary origins. *Philosophical Transactions of the Royal Society of London B: Biological Sciences* 367: 2119–129.

Flynn, Emma G., Kevin N. Laland, Rachel L. Kendal, and Jeremy R. Kendal (2013). Developmental niche construction. *Developmental Science* 16: 296–313.

12. Leslie thinking may involve what has been called in neuroscience the "default network"; see: Spreng, R. Nathan, Jorge Sepulcre, Gary R. Turner, W. Dale Stevens, and Daniel L. Schacter (2012). Intrinsic architecture underlying the relations among the default, dorsal attention, and frontoparietal control networks of the human brain. *Journal of Cognitive Neuroscience* 25: 74–86.

13. Schlegel, Alexander, Peter J. Kohler, Sergey V. Fogelson, Prescott Alexander, Dedeepya Konuthula, and Peter Ulric Tse (2013). Network structure and dynamics of the mental workspace. *Proceedings of the National Academy of Sciences of the USA* 110: 16277–6282.

14. Amit, Elinor, and Joshua D. Greene (2012). You see, the ends don't justify the means: Visual imagery and moral judgment. *Psychological Science* 23: 861–68.

15. Bereiter, Carl (1994). Constructivism, socioculturalism, and Popper's world 3. *Educational Researcher* 23: 21–23.

Cobb, Paul (1994a). Where is the mind? Constructivist and sociocultural perspectives on mathematical development. *Educational Researcher* 23: 13–20.

Cobb, John (1994b). An exchange: Constructivism in mathematics and science education. *Educational Researcher* 23: 4.

Sfard, Anna (1998). On two metaphors for learning and the dangers of choosing just one. *Educational Researcher* 27: 4–13.

16. Frith, Chris D., and Uta Frith (2008). Implicit and explicit processes in social cognition. *Neuron* 60: 503–10.

Firth, Uta, and Chris Firth (2010). The social brain: Allowing humans to boldly go where no other species has been. *Philosophical Transactions of the Royal Society of London B: Biological Sciences* 365: 165–76.

Firth, Chris D., and Uta Firth (2012). Mechanisms of social cognition. *Annual Review of Psychology* 63: 287–313.

17. Odling-Smee et al. (1996), p. 646.
18. Day et al. (2003), p. 81.
19. Chapter 16, note 2: Mehdiabadi et al. (2012).
20. Smith, Eric Alden (2011). Endless forms: Human behavioural diversity and evolved universals. *Philosophical Transaction of the Royal Society of London B: Biological Sciences* 366: 325–32.
21. Hruschka, Daniel J. (2010). *Friendship: Development, Ecology, and Evolution of a Relationship.* Berkeley: University of California Press.

CHAPTER 22

1. Laland, Kevin N., John Odling-Smee, and Marcus W. Feldman (2000). Niche construction, biological evolution, and cultural change. *Behavioral and Brain Sciences* 23: 131–75.
2. Clark, Andy (2006). Language, embodiment, and the cognitive niche. *Trends in Cognitive Sciences* 10: 370–74.
3. Portes, Alejandro (1998). Social capital: Its origins and applications in modern sociology. *Annual Review of Sociology* 24: 1–24.
   Portes, Alejandro (2000). The two meanings of social capital. *Sociological Forum* 15: 1–12.
4. Coleman, James S. (1988). Social capital in the creation of human capital. *American Journal of Sociology* 94, Suppl.: S95–S120, p. S98.
5. Robinson, David, and Tuwhakairiora Williams (2001). Social capital and voluntary activity: Giving and sharing in Maori and non-Maori society. *Social Policy Journal of New Zealand* 17: 52–71.
6. Burt, Ronald S. (2000). The network structure of social capital. *Research in Organizational Behaviour* 22: 345–423.
7. Keesing, Roger M. (1984). Rethinking "mana." *Journal of Anthropological Research* 40: 137–56.

CHAPTER 23

1. Hodgen, Margaret T. (1964). *Early Anthropology in the Sixteenth and Seventeenth Centuries.* Philadelphia: University of Pennsylvania Press, p. 35.
2. Hodgen (1964), p. 387.
3. Panksepp, Jaak (1992). A critical role for "affective neuroscience" in resolving what is basic about basic emotions. *Psychological Review* 99: 554–60.
   Panksepp, Jaak, and Jules B. Panksepp (2000). The seven sins of evolutionary psychology. *Evolution and Cognition* 6: 108–31.

Panksepp, Jaak (2011). Cross-species affective neuroscience decoding of the primal affective experiences of humans and related animals. *PLoS ONE* 6(9): e21236. doi:10.1371/journal.pone.0021236.

4. Ekman, Paul (1999). Basic emotions. In *Handbook of Cognition and Emotion*, Tim Dalgleish, and Mick J. Power, eds., pp. 45–60. Chichester: John Wiley & Sons.

Damasio, Antonio, and Gil B. Carvalho (2013). The nature of feelings: Evolutionary and neurobiological origins. *Nature Reviews Neuroscience* 14: 143–52.

5. Panksepp (2011), p. 8.

6. Cannon, Walter B. (1915). *Bodily Changes in Pain, Hunger, Fear and Rage: An Account of Recent Research into the Function of Emotional Excitement.* New York: D. Appleton and Company, p. vii.

7. Berkowitz, Leonard (2012). A different view of anger: The cognitive-neoassociation conception of the relation of anger to aggression. *Aggressive Behavior* 38: 322–33.

8. Panksepp, Jaak (2003). At the interface of the affective, behavioral, and cognitive neurosciences: Decoding the emotional feelings of the brain. *Brain and Cognition* 52: 4–14, p. 10.

9. Gerber, Eleanor Ruth (1985). Rage and obligation: Samoa emotion in conflict. In *Person, Self, and Experience: Exploring Pacific Ethnopsychologies*, Geoffrey M. White and John Kirkpatrick, eds., pp. 121–67. Berkeley: University of California Press, p. 137.

10. Coan, James A. (2011). The social regulation of emotion. In *Handbook of Social Neuroscience*, Jean Decety and John T. Cacioppo, eds., pp. 614–23. New York: Oxford University Press.

11. Gerber (1985), p. 138.

12. Gerber (1985), p. 128.

13. Gerber (1985), p. 131.

14. Gerber (1985), p. 131.

CHAPTER 24

1. Chapter 12, note 8: Wrangham and Glowacki (2012).

2. Stanford, Craig B. (2001). *The Hunting Apes: Meat Eating and the Origins of Human Behavior.* Princeton, NJ: Princeton University Press.

3. Sussman, Robert W., and J. Marshack (2010). Are humans inherently killers? *Global Non-Killing Working Papers* 1: 7–28.

4. Varki, Ajit, and David L. Nelson (2007). Genomic comparisons of humans and chimpanzees. *Annual Review of Anthropology* 36: 191–209.

5. Woods, Vanessa, and Brian Hare (2011). Bonobo but not chimpanzee infants use socio-sexual contact with peers. *Primates* 52: 111–16.

6. Surbeck, Martin, and Gottfried Hohmann (2008). Primate hunting by bonobos at LuiKotale, Salonga National Park. *Current Biology* 18: R906–R907.

7. Woods and Hare (2011), p. 115.

8. de Waal, Frans B. M. (1995). Bonobo sex and society: The behavior of a close relative challenges assumptions about male supremacy in human evolution. *Scientific American* 272 (3): 82–88.
9. If this statement seems mysterious: the "Virginia" mentioned here is an allusion to a famous editorial about Santa Claus that was published in the New York daily paper *The Sun* on September 21, 1897.
10. Chapter 19, note 25: Beckes et al. (2012).
11. Chapter 21, note 15: Bereiter (1994); Cobb (1994a); Sfard (1998).

    Christakis, Nicholas A., and James H. Fowler (2009). *Connected: The Surprising Power of Our Social Networks and How They Shape Our Lives*. New York: Little, Brown and Company.
12. Froese, Tom, Hiroyuki Iizuka, and Takashi Ikegami (2014). Embodied social interaction constitutes social cognition in pairs of humans: A minimalist virtual reality experiment. *Scientific Reports* 4: 3672 doi: 10.1038/srep03672.
13. Rousseau, Jean-Jacques (1754). A Discourse on a subject proposed by the Academy of Dijon: What is the Origin of Inequality among Men, and is it authorised by Natural Law. Translated by G. D. H. Cole. Constitution Society (2005), http://www.saylor.org/site/wp-content/uploads/2011/07/Discourse-on-Inequality.pdf

CHAPTER 25

1. Geertz, Clifford (1973). *The Interpretation of Cultures*. New York: Basic Books.
2. Beaglehole, J. C. (1966). *The Exploration of the Pacific*. Stanford: Stanford University Press.
3. Salmond, Anne (1991). *Two Worlds. First Meetings between Maori and Europeans 1642–1772*. Auckland: Penguin Books.
4. http://gutenberg.net.au/ebooks06/0600571h.html#journal
5. Heeres, J. E., ed. (1898 [2006]). *Abel Janszoon Tasman's Journal*, Project Gutenberg of Australia, p. 151.
6. Ian Barber (2012). Gardens of Rongo: Applying cross-field anthropology to explain contact violence in New Zealand. *Current Anthropology* 53: 799–808.

CHAPTER 26

1. Kross, Ethan, Philippe Verduyn, Emre Demiralp, Jiyoung Park, David S. Lee, Natalie Lin, Holly Shablack, John Jonides, and Oscar Ybarra (2013). Facebook use predicts declines in subjective well-being in young adults. *PLoS ONE* 8(8): e69841. doi:10.1371/journal.pone.0069841.
2. Darwin, Charles (1874). *The Descent of Man, and Selection in Relation to Sex*, 2nd ed. London: John Murray, p. 98.
3. Darwin (1874), p. 105.
4. Darwin (1874), p. 108.

5. Darwin (1874), page 117.

6. Darwin (1874), p. 143.

7. Darwin (1874), p. 182.

8. http://www.ethnologue.com/ethno_docs/distribution.asp?by=area
   Lakoff, George, and Mark Johnson (1980). *Metaphors We Live By*. Chicago: University of Chicago Press, p. 25.

9. Terrell, John (2001). The uncommon sense of race, language, and culture. In *Archaeology, Language, and History: Essays on Culture and Ethnicity*. John Terrell, ed., pp. 11–30 Westport, Connecticut: Bergin and Garvey.

10. Mandelbrot, Benoit B. (1982). *The Fractal Geometry of Nature*. New York: W. H. Freeman and Company.

11. Borgatti, Stephen P., Ajay Mehra, Daniel J. Brass, and Giuseppe Labianca (2009). Network analysis in the social sciences. *Science* 323: 892–95.

12. Newman, Mark E. J. (2003). The structure and function of complex networks. *SIAM Review* 56: 167–256.

13. Hanneman, Robert A., and Mark Riddle (2005). *Introduction to Social Network Methods*. Riverside: University of California. http://faculty.ucr.edu/%7Ehanneman/.

14. Travers, Jeffrey, and Stanley Milgram (1969). An experimental study of the small world problem. *Sociometry* 32: 425–43.
    Chapter 15, note 18: Liben-Nowell et al. (2005).
    Baronchellii, Andrea, Ramon Ferrer-i-Cancho, Romualdo Pastor-Satorras, Nick Chater, and Morten H. Christiansen (2013). Networks in cognitive science. *Trends in Cognitive Sciences* 17: 348–60.

CHAPTER 27

1. Palmer, Jonathan, Chris Turney, Alan Hogg, Noel Hilliam, Matt Watson, Erik van Sebille, Winston Cowie, Richard Jones, and Fiona Petchey (2014). The discovery of New Zealand's oldest shipwreck—Possible evidence of further Dutch exploration of the South Pacific. *Journal of Archaeological Science* 42: 435–41.

2. Tupaia was from the island of Rai'atea in the leeward islands of the archipelago that Cook named the Society Islands (purportedly in honor of the Royal Society of London).

3. Hagspiel, Bruno (1926). *Along the Mission Trail III. In New Guinea*. Techny, IL: Mission Press, p. 72.

4. Chapter 1, note 7: Wilson (2012), p. 57.

5. Chapter 1, note 7: Wilson (2012), p. 62.

6. Barth, Fredrik (1969). Introduction. In *Ethnic Groups and Boundaries: The Social Organization of Culture Difference*, Frederik Barth, ed., pp. 9–38. Boston, MA: Little, Brown and Company.

7. Brubaker, Rogers (2004). *Ethnicity Without Groups*. Cambridge, MA: Harvard University Press, p. 7.

8. Watson, James B. (1990). Other people do other things: Lamarckian identities in Kainantu Subdistrict, Papua New Guinea. In *Cultural Identity and Ethnicity in the*

Pacific, Jocelyn Linnekin and Lin Poyer, eds., pp. 17–41 at 17. Honolulu: University of Hawai'i Press, p. 18.

9. Watson (1990), p. 18.

CHAPTER 28

1. Granovetter, Mark S. (1973). The strength of weak ties. *American Journal of Sociology* 78: 1360–380.

2. Granovetter, Mark (1983). The strength of weak ties: A network theory revisited. *Sociological Theory* 1: 201–33.

3. Michener, James A. (1947). *Tales of the South Pacific*. New York: Macmillan.

4. Harding, Thomas G. (1994). Precolonial New Guinea trade. *Ethnology* 33: 101–25.

5. Hau'ofa, Epeli (1975). Anthropology and Pacific Islanders. *Oceania* 45: 283–89.

6. Hau'ofa (1975), p. 286.

7. Hogbin, H. Ian (1935). Trading expeditions in northern New Guinea. *Oceania* 5: 375–407.

8. Hogbin (1935), pp. 376–77.

9. Roscoe, Paul B. (1989). The pig and the long yam: The expansion of a Sepik cultural complex. *Ethnology* 28: 219–31, p. 219.

10. Dobrin, Lise, and Ira Bashkow (2006). "Pigs for dance songs": Reo Fortune's empathetic ethnography of the Arapesh roads. In *Histories of Anthropology Annual*, Vol. 2, Regna Darnell and Frederic W. Gleach, eds., pp. 123–54. Lincoln: University of Nebraska Press.

11. Anderson, Astrid (2003). Landscapes of sociality: Paths, places and belonging in Wogeo Island, Papua New Guinea. In *Oceanic Socialities and Cultural Forms: Ethnographies of Experience*, Ingjerd Hoëm and Sidsel Roalkvam, eds., pp. 51–70. Oxford: Berghahn Books.

12. Wedgwood, Camilla H. (1934). Report on research in Manam Island, Mandated Territory of New Guinea. *Oceania* 4: 373–403, pp. 395–396.

13. Allen, Jim (1976). Fishing for wallabies: Trade as a mechanism for social interaction, integration and elaboration on the central Papuan coast. In *The Development of Social Systems*, Michael Rowlands and Jonathan Friedman, eds., pp. 419–55. London: Duckworth.

14. Groves, Murray (1960). Motu pottery. *Journal of the Polynesian Society* 69: 2–22.

15. Hogbin (1935), p. 404.

16. Meeker, Michael E., Kathleen Barlow, and David M. Lipset (1986). Culture, exchange, and gender: Lessons from the Murik. *Cultural Anthropology* 1: 6–73.

17. Hogbin (1935), pp. 403–404.

18. Chapter 26, note 1: Kross et al. (2013).

CHAPTER 29

1. http://www.gutenberg.org/ebooks/46
2. http://www.readbookonline.net/readOnLine/2529/
3. This account of the history of our Maori meeting house after its removal from New Zealand sometime at the end of the 19th century is adapted from my account published in Arapata Hakiwai and John Edward Terrell (1994). *Ruatepupuke: A Maori Meeting House*. Chicago: Field Museum.
4. For a critical overview of attachment theory today, see: Beckes, Lane, Hans IJzerman, and Mattie Tops (2014). Toward a radically embodied neuroscience of attachment and relationships? Available at SSRN 2429522.
5. Mikulincer, Mario, and Philip R. Shaver (2007). Boosting attachment security to promote mental health, prosocial values, and inter-group tolerance. *Psychological Inquiry* 18: 139–56.

   Mikulincer, Mario, and Phillip R. Shaver (2012). An attachment perspective on psychopathology. *World Psychiatry* 11: 11–15.

CHAPTER 30

1. Bloom, Deborah (2006). *Ghost Hunters: William James and the Search for Scientific Proof of Life after Death*. New York: Penguin Books.
2. Terrell, John Edward, and Judith Modell (1994). Anthropology and adoption. *American Anthropologist* 96: 155–61.

Index